AN AMBER GLOW

An Amber Glow

The Story of England's World Cup-Winning Football

Peter Allen

MAINSTREAM
PUBLISHING

EDINBURGH AND LONDON

First published in Great Britain in 2000 by

MAINSTREAM PUBLISHING COMPANY (EDINBURGH) LTD

7 Albany Street, Edinburgh EH1 3UG

ISBN 1 84018 354 3

A catalogue record for this book is available
from the British Library

Typeset in 10½ on 13½ pt Joanna MT
Printed and bound in Great Britain by
Creative Print and Design Wales

Contents

Acknowledgements

It would not be against the true spirit of *An Amber Glow* to say it was the result of Anglo-German co-operation. I would like to thank all the Bavarians with whom I experienced so many car chases in the spring of 1996, especially Helmut Haller. His gracious manner impressed me far more than a World Cup-winner's medal ever could. Despite the inevitable goalkeeper jokes, Hans Tilkowski and Thorsten Riedel added Teutonic guile to an otherwise chaotic adventure. A Berliner, Sarah Schaefer, taught me even more about the new Germany. Her unique insight into a great but deeply perplexing nation was hugely appreciated.

On our side, I would like to thank those ordinary Englishmen who, in the summer of 1966, were driven to extraordinary feats by the demands of history. This book honours all of Sir Alf Ramsey's Wingless Wonders. The image of them on the most glorious day of so many lives is a stirring example of England's true heritage. It should be displayed every morning at school assemblies before our subdued nation becomes any more like Sweden.

Friends who provided invaluable advice include Henry Blofeld, Patrick O'Flynne, Bill Edgar and Shekhar Bhatia, with whom I attended my first England away game (2–1 to Sweden). Thanks to Judy Diamond for her editing, and everybody at Mainstream Publishing. Also Luigi Bonomi and Amanda Preston, of literary agency Sheil Land Associates. Most of all I would like to thank Paul Allen, whose scholarly and inspiring devotion to high European culture has seldom been reflected in my twin interests of newspaper journalism and football.

The Times, leading article, 26 April 1996:

The ball with which England defeated West Germany in the World Cup final of 1966 has attained almost mystical significance in the minds of soccer folk. Its leather panels are being fought over today as though they were relics of saints. Three decades on, it is a symbol of English soccer's finest hour. The fans want it back.

By English tradition the ball should never have left home at all. The icon should have gone to Geoff Hurst who scored a hat-trick in the 4–2 victory at Wembley. But as the final whistle was blown, the ball was snatched by a German, Helmut Haller, who cites an unlikely-sounding continental tradition that the last player to kick the ball gets to keep it. The defeated West German defied the referee's instruction to hand it back, and the souvenir of England's triumph disappeared.

What happened over the ensuing years is a mystery. Now there are as many as 30 footballs in Germany purporting to be the true relic. The most likely claim is that of Jurgen Haller, son of the player who ran away with the ball, who says he rediscovered the trophy in a cellar near Munich. He has now reportedly hired bodyguards and kicked the ball into the back of a safe deposit box. A rival ball has surfaced in Düsseldorf; there is talk of dozens more across Germany; a mysterious reappearance of the true ball in Leamington Spa is predicted.

Cheque books are out as tabloid newspapers, agents and football historians wrangle over who owns the battered leather talisman. The reluctance of the Germans to return this symbol of their defeat reflects the Thirty Years War that has been fought over the result of the game. The Germans have never fully accepted that they were beaten at Wembley in 1966, claiming that Geoff Hurst's second goal did not cross the line. Over the years teams of scientists, geometricians and engineers have been employed to analyse film and computer simulations in attempts to discredit the goal, all to no avail. These scientific teams could well be employed over the next 30 years trying to establish the authenticity of assorted balls; dye and leather now face tests as stringent as those used on the Turin Shroud.

Blame is falling once more on the football authorities for ever having let the ball vanish. We recall that they did seem to have been somewhat careless in 1966. Only weeks before the World Cup competition began, the Jules Rimet trophy was stolen. It turned up a few days before the kick-off, discovered behind a bush by a dog called Pickles.

Unlike the trophy, the World Cup ball cannot be melted down and has no material value. But try telling that to those who are now trying to cash in on its history. It should surely be returned to the only man who has a real claim on it: Geoff Hurst. Why should the Germans still want to hang on to what is, after all, a permanent symbol of their defeat? They may have thought it was all over 30 years ago. But it will not be, until the true World Cup ball is safely back in England.

1 · Opening Strike

Pickled cabbage invariably appears no matter what you order in a German restaurant. It's designed to give you something to toy with politely as you face up to the demands of a Kaiser-sized sausage.

At the Villa d'Este in Neusass the waiters smear the concoction on every spare plate inch. It might look like a microbiological research project, but there is seldom any sign of culinary dissent. Most mealtimes you'll find around ten diners shovelling down the sauerkraut with the kind of non-committal efficiency with which modern Germans do everything. As fair-minded citizens of a forward-thinking democracy they don't want to involve themselves in unseemly complaints. They would rather keep a low profile and tip well.

The restaurant is just a few miles from Augsburg, where the unearthly genius Wolfgang Amadeus Mozart perfected his music on harpsichord and virginals. The composer's father, Leopold, was born in the city. Other legendary sons include Rudolph Diesel, whose contribution to those noisy engines favoured by long-distance lorry drivers and miserable Frenchmen needs no explanation. Willy Messerschmitt, with a surname unmatched as a cocktail-party ice-breaker, was also a local boy. So too was Hans Holbein, the artist who produced piggy-eyed portraits of some of our most famous historical characters, most notably Henry VIII.

When I arrived at the Villa d'Este for a working lunch it was to visit Augsburg's most famous footballing son, Helmut Haller. One of the greatest midfielders ever to play for West Germany, he started life as a short-back-and-sides apprentice at his home club before joining Bologna and then Juventus. In Italy he learnt to express himself with style and panache, partly through his new blond Teddy-boy quiff. He then returned to Germany for a final spell with BC Augsburg when he adopted a Henry Plantagenet bowl cut complete with long straggly bits at the back. It had a nice 1970s feel to it and suited his move into one of the only business ventures open to retired professionals at the time: a vaguely pretentious restaurant churning out very ordinary dishes at prices which reflected their close links to minor celebrity.

The best anecdote about Haller, however, was that he had stolen a football from the victorious England team after the World Cup final at Wembley

Stadium in 1966. Thirty years later I was one of the many British journalists who made their way to southern Germany to try and get the ball back.

I'd had trouble getting a table at the Villa d'Este. A stocky, bald compatriot had stopped me at the front door. He looked as though he had all the formal qualifications necessary to become a professional bouncer outside an English city-centre pub, namely a conviction for assault occasioning actual bodily harm. Five of his colleagues were already negotiating for the ball inside the restaurant and he did not want me joining them.

'Not for you,' he had warned, lowering his head in a manner which could easily have been interpreted as a gentle bow of acknowledgement. It actually meant he was preparing to ram me on the chin with his bony pate.

'There's spaghetti flying about all over the place in there,' he explained, overestimating the restaurant's ability to deliver its promise of 'the rich flavours of Italy intertwined with the fruits of Germany'. Those who under-stand the subtleties of aspirational Bavarian menus will know compulsory vegetable paste and giant rolls of fatty meat blackened at high temperatures is what was really on offer, perhaps with a side dish of fettuccine.

'You're better off turning back and going home ... Thanks for coming,' the bouncer added.

He was already offering mitigation for the possibility of an imminent act of extreme violence. His fists clenched. His brow clenched. His oddly-shaped nose appeared to clench too.

'But I'm a brother journalist,' I stuttered. The door guard's fraternal head began to hover inches below my unprotected nose.

Thankfully my photographer stepped in. Cameramen aren't just brought into this world to wreak havoc at celebrity gatherings, or to climb trees and other high-rise objects in order to gain the best vantage-point for taking their pictures. Although it's these chimp-like qualities which make them particularly endearing, their other day-to-day uses on overseas assignments are indispensable. They can do all kinds of practical things like wiring laptop computers to the stereo system of souped-up Skoda Turbos in Albania, or persuade a gun-wielding militiaman in the Yemen to spare the Westerners and take the camel. Their reassuring lack of sentimentality at scenes of unspeakable sadness all over the world is always massively reassuring. The inner strength of anybody who can calmly initiate a conversation about DIY or Formula One while recording evidence of slaughter and needless destruction in a desolate hell-hole can only be admired.

As the photographer lifted his camera to take a picture of the dining-room, the increasingly aggressive doorman flung himself at the lensman's black polo-neck. He would have gone for a head leap, but the photographer was more than six foot tall and wore an intimidating air force moustache. Soon the pair were rolling about in the Villa d'Este's lobby, shouting and making allusions to each other's likeness to sensitive parts of the human anatomy. Aware of their surroundings, they made some appropriate cultural references, including consistent use of a Germanic word beginning with C (that's another thing photographers are particularly good at).

I felt slightly concerned for my companion's health but recalled what a senior executive editor had once told me on the subject of attacks on photographers: 'That's what they're there for,' he had advised.

The inside of the restaurant was immaculate. Apart from Italian pepper grinders and a few Ukrainian waiters, the interior was a Germanic idyll of cleanliness and order. Regulars stared down at their steaming bowls with a quiet determination, their cheeks occasionally bulging as they executed their gastronomic duties to the beat of canned oompha music.

I made my way to a spare place, on a table next to a local TV producer. I knew instantly that he was German – not just because of his name (and how many non-Germans are called Klaus?) but because he had an oversized Kaiser moustache and a pair of those rimless glasses which all painfully intelligent Teutons seem to wear.

You could tell Klaus was a TV producer because there were eight members of two camera teams sitting round the table with him. Like TV people all over the world, they looked uncomfortably ambitious as they bellowed into mobile telephones, using the word 'package' all the time. It would not have surprised me if they had been talking to each other, despite sitting just inches apart.

The pickled cabbage arrived in an instant. I stuck my fork into it a few times, making sure it didn't get anywhere it could do any harm, like the inside of my mouth. The others at my table had been trying to underplay the importance of their starters for around 20 minutes. They did so in much the same way that astute European diplomats try to underplay the importance of things they don't like very much but which get in the way all the time, like French lorry drivers.

Soon the sauerkraut was to become impossible to ignore.

There were journalists from all over Britain and Germany in the restaurant. I recognised five adversaries from home sitting immediately opposite. To begin with they had followed the example of the indigenous dining population and suffered their meals with a dignified resolve. My appearance, however, prompted one to lose control. He did what all 'Brits abroad' end up doing after the initial high of their first draught of foreign lager has worn off: he started intimidating the locals.

The reporter swaggered towards the TV people. As optimistic members of a conciliatory federal republic, the Germans might well have mistaken his approach as friendly. Sadly, it was intended as an act of ill-meaning aggression. Before he reached his target, though, the British journalist managed to knock over a waiter carrying a large plate of sauerkraut.

The tray of food flew four feet in the air before sending a paste-like, salty shower cascading over the lofty broadcasters. Bizarrely, the waiter also sprang about two feet in the air, but he landed in a neat pile on the wooden floorboards. He did not hurt anybody as he writhed about in agony, clutching his ankle.

Interestingly, the cabbage stuck fast in blond hair and made those check sports jackets favoured by middle-aged German businessmen and TV producers look even more unsightly. As a segment exploded on his right chest pocket, it was left to Klaus to display just how calm modern Germans can remain in the face of immense provocation.

'Just ignore them. If we fuss, it encourages them,' he said sensibly, if not entirely correctly.

You do not need to fuss to encourage English journalists.

As Klaus tried to scratch the cabbage-coloured stain from his cabbage-coloured jacket, he carried on trying to act non-committal, as befitted an upstanding member of a federal republic. He told me how the unjustly wasted pickled cabbage was a particular favourite of former Bayern Munich footballer Gerd Muller. Just as gallows humour has always seen the English through hard times, modern Germans can be relied upon to come up with a pithy anecdote in times of crisis.

'Der Bomber' (as Muller was nicknamed) was a regular visitor to the Villa d'Este. The player's predatory instincts for scoring goals had helped his national side to numerous famous wins. He had scored in Germany's 1974 World Cup final win, and poached the extra-time goal which saw Germany beat England 3–2 in the quarter-finals of the 1970 competition. The chefs often joked that it was Muller's penchant for high-fibre pickled cabbage that gave him the energy to succeed on the field of play. It was an interesting thought, but Muller's choice of dish was actually irrelevant: he always ended up with pickled cabbage because he only ever went to German restaurants.

As Klaus chatted to me nervously, I noticed the unmistakable Haller sitting at a table with his grown-up son, Jurgen. The restaurateur's blond hair had faded to a silvery grey, and had been combed down ruthlessly to reflect the responsibilities of fatherhood and then middle age. His frame, always slightly portly thanks to the energising pasta diet he had adopted in Italy, had filled out a bit more but the impish face of old remained unchanged. Haller sipped a glass of whisky and stared around with the same theatrically quizzical look which had worked so well on Swiss referees when he was at the top of his game.

Haller's expression had become particularly pensive when we arrived at noon following a two-hour flight from Heathrow to Munich. We would have got there earlier if we'd gone by Lufthansa but the photographer insisted on catching the British Airways 7.45 flight, thereby allowing him to collect a few more executive club points and air miles. The points would one day earn him a platinum-coloured luggage tag, and the miles might one day win him a free weekend break in Tirana. He also wanted to take advantage of his right to sit in the BA club lounge and sip a tomato juice while talking about DIY and Formula One with high-flying sales reps. Photographers are like that.

A rival English team – comprising no fewer than four reporters and two photographers – had spent the entire morning trying to persuade Haller to hand back the 1966 World Cup ball so that they could return it to England in a blaze of glory.

They got to the Villa d'Este at 7 a.m., just when the first cabbage lorries were arriving. By lunchtime they had gone through the complete reporter's guide to trying to persuade somebody to tell/give you something with the minimum of fuss and preferably in time for next edition (unabridged version).

In the extremely imprecise language of such pragmatic negotiations they had talked to Haller about our 'footballing' royal family's desperation to get the ball back. Even the sovereign herself – from a family once called Saxe Coburg und Gotha, of course – thought of little else. The Queen ranked the theft, which she had witnessed at first hand, as a low point in her 44-year reign. It was down there with her children's divorces and James Callaghan.

The journalists tried to put pressure on Haller by reminding him of his duty as an honorary member of the Fraternity of Soccer Buddies, a little-known organisation originating in Arkansas after the USA'94 World Cup with high-powered contacts in Bobby Charlton's soccer schools. The negotiators had even offered unlikely intelligence about a diplomatic treaty which tied in the reformation of football cheats with greater moves towards European unity and a single currency, or something like that. It's always best to keep this kind of talk as vague as possible, especially when dealing with Germans.

The TV journalists had taken up their restaurant positions at around 11 a.m. It would be unfair to say they had turned up to produce a few spiteful reports about uncouth British hacks being rude and unpleasant to foreigners. They weren't interested in short, chauvinistic soundbites confirming all the hackneyed clichés about loutish Brits abroad. Nor were they bothered about filing brief reports about pugnacious Anglo-Saxons making fools of themselves in the name of an outdated nationalistic ideology. No, the Germans wanted to produce a two-hour documentary on the subject.

That was why there was more trouble in Neusass that day than its restrained, neutral population had experienced since the last anti-nuclear demonstration had passed through five years earlier. As the kind of place where the Alsatians carry their own pooper-scoopers, the sizeable provincial centre felt uncomfortable with discord of any kind. Locals like Klaus were proud of their environmentally sound waterways and half-timbered rural buildings. They were proud of their position among hectares of undulating pasture in the patchwork of former independent states which made up their prosperous, forward-thinking federation. And they were particularly proud of Richard Steiff who had created the first teddy bear in the nearby Schwabian Woods in 1902. He had been working in his Aunt Margarete's toy factory when he stuck a few spare furry bits together. The American corporate giant FAO Schwartz brought three thousand of the resulting dolls and named them Teddy after President Theodore Roosevelt.

Steiff's creation summed up Neusass. It was a teddy bear kind of a town – a place designed for the soft, unprepossessing side of life where cuddly toys were as commonplace as rampaging journalists were alien.

As the hours went by and the restaurant began to fill up with more people like us looking for the ball and deluded diners looking for a filling but otherwise profoundly unsatisfactory meal, Haller started to think about formalising the negotiations so as to avoid any more trouble. He wanted to talk to everybody about the football's future, but vague notions of honour based on diplomacy, sportsmanship or respect for an Anglo-German 'footballing' royal family were not concepts he wanted to commit himself to. Haller was far more interested in deutschmarks: Wembley stadiums full of them.

By three in the afternoon the English team opposing us had become resentful about a number of minor things: all the Germans in the restaurant; all the other English people in the restaurant; and the restaurant itself. Accordingly, they were quite happy to see all kinds of objects flying around, including the sauerkraut and my camera-laden travelling companion. A plate crashed to the floor and smashed after one of the TV researchers carelessly knocked it over after tripping over the downed waiter (who turned out to be a Ukrainian immigrant and was still writhing hopelessly on the floor and groaning in agony 15 minutes after dropping the sauerkraut).

A signed and framed photograph of a Bayern Munich right-back fell off the wall at about the same time. Nobody knows how that happened, but it was quite dramatic in a 'could that be an omen?' kind of a way. The waiters started to remove the plates of sauerkraut as the regulars began to leave the restaurant shaking their heads in a wishy-washy, ineffectual display of mild disgust.

The cook stormed out from the kitchen and started swinging one of the giant pepper grinders around his head. On a scale of cook temperaments – which normally starts out at idiosyncratic and moody in upmarket brasseries, descending to psychotic and dangerous in the case of Turkish kebab houses – he was somewhere in the middle: unpredictable and prone to violence was how most of us would have described him.

The cook noticed all the bowls of uneaten sauerkraut lying around and began to shudder with rage. 'My creation, my creation!' he yelled, dipping his hands in the messy substance. 'This is how you treat my creation!'

His tone was far from neutral, but this was perfectly permissible because he was from the Ukraine too. Like the crocked waiter, he had used the dissolution of the Soviet Union in 1991 to do something constructive for the country he loved: he had left.

The chef gathered up a couple of handfuls of his creation and flung them across the restaurant. They landed right in the middle of the TV people. Although refusing to be drawn into the fighting, the German media men and women were desperately trying to work out where the real blame for it lay.

'Look, mates. This has to stop,' said a pallid sound man.

The sound of a larger dollop of pickled cabbage – an odd *whoosh* – accompanied by the oompha music and a synchronised display of Ukrainian swearing was all he got in reply. It was a contemporary symphony which would have made Mozart profoundly unhappy, but not half as unhappy as it was making Klaus. He looked me straight in the eye. With a tortured expression and, almost pleading, he exclaimed: 'Tell me it was your countrymen who started it, tell me it was your countrymen.'

I shook my head nonchalantly, pushed my cabbage mound to one side and sliced my over-done, black Kaiser sausage in half at the curve.

'No, Klaus,' I replied. 'You started it . . . you always start it.'

2 · Gain Plan

By 30 July 1966 England had never lost to Germany in an international football match. Accordingly, when Helmut Haller scored the opener in that year's World Cup final he thought his place in the record books was secure. Headlines like 'Brilliant Haller Wins The Day' or even the simpler 'Haller One Nil' both had a suitably predictable, if slightly dated, ring to them. Such cheap but easily understandable phraseology would sustain the ecstatic Bavarian long after the pundits had stripped him of his 'useful midfielder' tag.

Haller pictured himself talking endlessly about his greatest-ever goal on national television. Every time there was a major international tournament his unmistakable bob of gelled blond hair and endearing grin would enliven pre-match analysis programmes. He was already looking forward to recording his greatest triumph in a ghost-written autobiography. He'd make himself available for radio phone-ins and charity events too – for a small fee, of course. Haller would describe how his 13th-minute triumph had been the explosion of brilliance which brought a slow, plodding contest to life and sealed a historic 1–0 win over the English.

The goal, executed with furrow-browed ruthlessness, had been more than worthy of ending Germany's appalling run against the host nation which had started with a 3–0 defeat at White Hart Lane in 1935. For high-minded Germans, once used to duelling to the death over little more than a flippant remark about a Rhine Maiden's unfortunate facial composition, such an abysmal record of failure inflicted as much pain as a flashing sabre. The 31 years of hurt cut deeply into a psyche already ravaged by decades of political instability, economic chaos and war.

Games against the English were about so much more than football. For both sides, they were the supreme test of national character: brutal contests between the strategic and disciplined Teutons and the plucky English relying on vast reserves of improvisation, stamina and down-to-earth wit.

At the beginning of the match, the 26-year-old Haller had lined up with his comrades to be introduced to the Queen. In their distinctive white shirts with black trim and shorts, they had stood proudly as she graciously wished them good luck. Haller had spent as much time manipulating his quiff into perfect shape for the historic occasion as he had perfecting his pleasant if slightly quizzical expression in front of his hotel room mirror.

He had not been entirely impressed when the Portsmouth-based Band of the Royal Marines accompanied his first meeting with royalty by dropping a few notes during their recital of *Einigkeit und Recht und Freiheit* but it was not for him to complain. The German number 8 just shrugged his shoulders. His country's progression into the last two of the ultimate football contest had not been anything to do with responding to such baiting. As a member of a progressive federal republic, with its eye constantly on the future, it was not for him to respond to trivial acts of provocation. When a loutish Argentinian rugby-tackled him at Villa Park, Haller had walked away with not so much as a concerned glance towards the referee. It had been the same at Goodison Park, when a surly Bolshevik scythed his legs away during the semi-final against the Soviet Union.

The eleven footballers who took the field for West Germany under Wembley's twin towers on that rainy summer's day were focused on a much higher plane. They were representatives of a new, conciliatory Germany. They were settled Europeans who had taken the Prussian virtues of order and reliability and refined them to create a new kind of winning machine.

It was not for nothing that they were already the most insured nation on the continent, renowned for booking their holidays a whole year in advance. The West Germans had as much saved in their deposit accounts as their neighbours toiling away in Eastern Bloc steel factories had managed to earn in the past twenty years. The Berlin divide had been formalised just five years before, and the capitalists had already asserted their dominant position on the right side of the wall. A full-back who had been playing his football in the West since 1961 could have bought all 11 Dresden Dynamos with his accumulated win bonuses.

The West Germans' beautifully laundered shirts represented a successful but wholesome beginning. Their 10,000-odd fans among the 93,802 Wembley crowd were expecting another triumph as impressive as the one which had seen the country develop into one of the most successful in the world in less than twenty years. Chancellor Ludwig Erhard had built his side's success on sound foundations, including the 1948 Deutschmark and the Bundesbank. The Christian Democrat was the stocky playmaker who hustled and bustled as an eager apprentice to his legendary predecessor, Konrad Adenauer. Together the pair – an Uwe Seeler and a Franz Beckenbauer – had helped complete Germany's rehabilitation in international life through the free flow of capital and moderate politics.

It was the end of the murderous, collectivist state whose only party had gone to the country with just one manifesto pledge: world domination.

Erhard, an ardent football supporter, was in the living-room of his bungalow in Tegernsee, south of Munich, when his fellow Bavarian opened the scoring. Disliking foreign travel, the Chancellor had opted to watch the 1966 final at home with a TV dinner. He had also avoided the VIP box at Wembley for fear that he might come across any of the large and dispiriting examples of Gallic imperialism which were sweeping Europe at the time, like Charles de Gaulle. The Frenchman was always boasting about his soldiers having finally reached Berlin and it was clear that a Paris-dominated Common Market was his greatest goal in life. Such ramblings had looked decidedly hollow when France failed miserably in their World Cup campaign, but even elimination had not shut de Gaulle up.

But as Erhard stared at the flickering black-and-white figures in front of him, he knew that it was not a time for petty chauvinism. It would be easy to laugh at France's abject inability to dominate one little green field, let alone a vast continent, but the German players at Wembley represented everything that was decent and civilised in their reborn nation. Expertly guided by their manager, Helmut Schöen, the side was the manifestation of a German people which could already afford to spend every August naked on a beach on the Friesian Islands, improving themselves physically and mentally to allow them one day to take their place as head of a Bonn-dominated community of European nations.

With a particular affinity for England, Schöen had said: 'As a small boy I knew about the game in England and matches against them have been among the most important events of my career.'

Helmut Haller was just one of millions of young Germans who flourished in such an internationalist, forward-thinking arena. Where else but in England would he get to meet the Queen? Where else but in Italy would he be able to go to the barber's for a blond Elvis quiff? Certainly not in East Germany where the numerous Stasi agents moonlighting as midfielders at Vfb Leipzig would have described both ambitions as provocative exhibitions of capitalist excess. Haller already felt on the verge of greatness as he flashed his boisterous grin at Her Majesty and squeezed her immaculate white glove firmly but without a hint of ostentation. Just 20 minutes later he held his same right hand high in the air, with palm facing outward in a modest but heartfelt victory salute.

Until the final match itself, the entire 1966 contest had turned out to be one of the most brutal and unpleasant in the history of the game. The German players were among the few who had come out smiling and with their heads held high. As tackles came in hard and late, they hardly put a foot wrong. Their ethos was one of the first truly 'touchy-feely' philosophies. Like Erhard and Adenauer, many members of the West German side were devout Christians whose path through life was subject to intelligent regulation; and not just of the economy or their own worldly vices, but of little thugs from South America or Russia.

When the German captain Seeler was slapped in the face by a Uruguayan in a group match at Sheffield, he left it to one of his team-mates to put his arm around the assailant and lecture him on the errors of his ways. There would be no spitting or hurling of insults. Seeler, ever the gentleman, knew that conciliatory tact was worth a 1–0 headstart in any game as his team aspired to the glittering Jules Rimet trophy.

In a world where Tony Blair had barely finished choir school, the Germans were already propagating a philosophy in which material success and territorial expansion could be accompanied by a social conscience and a respectful commitment to the weak. Erhard and Schöen were the ultimate modernisers. Their philosophy embraced bustling but sensitive playmakers underpinned by immovable rocks at the back.

Haller was certainly never one to abandon his commitment to the weak – especially the kind of weak, non-league header which England defender Ray Wilson placed at his feet in the 13th minute of the first half. It gave Haller the chance to perform his own version of the *Wirtschaftswunder* – the 'Economic Miracle' – which had restored his country from the ashes.

In a few seconds of brilliance Haller felt he had turned into another Erhard – the animator of the despondent face of the German nation. A country which had so recently been shattered and reviled was, in a moment of brilliance, respected and admired. Haller caught the ball with his right foot and powered it past the England goalkeeper, Gordon Banks.

He was delighted at the way his boot seemed to connect so perfectly with the ball to make the score 1–0. Throughout the scrappy opening minutes of the final, international stars had sliced and miskicked like schoolboys. It was as if they were playing on a rain-soaked municipal pitch in front of a few stray dogs and dubious-looking men in Gannex macs, instead of at Wembley in the first televised international tournament, watched by a global audience of 400 million.

Five minutes before kick-off Haller had noticed that the ball was a strange amber colour, and at that moment he knew it was an inspirational tool which had been specially delivered for him to perform his minor miracle.

The ball must have had immense luck attached to make it to the final at all. It was one of 610 made by Slazenger for the competition. Even on 30 July itself, it had been one of eight balls that had been put before the two teams during the pre-match photographs. Haller had watched the match referee, Gottfried Dienst, selecting it. He had pushed its neat panels inwards and bounced it on the soggy Wembley turf a few times to test its durability. The official had been impressed by its weight, shape and feel. Hand-stitched by Yorkshire craftsman Malcolm Wainwright, the ball was more than ready to endure the trials which lay ahead. England, like Germany an industrial giant in its day, had created a world-class product.

But it was the colour which particularly attracted Haller. The orangy shade – one he had never seen before in his life – was quite extraordinary. He was enchanted by the warmth it exuded. It was the colour of conciliation, so different to the grey drabness on the other side of the 866-mile wall between capitalism and communism. It was not vulgar, but muted and stately. In its strange way the ball was a masterpiece.

When the German struck a perfect shot in the 13th minute of the first half, he was sure that it was a ball upon which destiny had already inscribed the legend 'Helmut Haller'.

The ball rocketed into the back of the English net. Dienst blew his whistle sharply, his hand held authoritatively in the air. How impressive and dignified the Swiss referee looked, thought Haller. Like the gracious Queen whom he had just met, the official's stature was almost regal. How appropriate that someone from the most neutral and objective country on earth should be chosen to referee the most important game in the recent history of the world. The man in jet black looked intelligent and refined as he made sure the amber ball was placed on the centre spot for an England kick-off.

The rest of the match would, of course, be a formality. Haller had already earned his right to call the ball his own. It was a German tradition that the player who scored first in any game was allowed to keep the ball. (Bizarrely, leader writers at *The Times* even suggested that Haller was allowed to keep the ball because he was to become the last player to touch it. In fact, the last kick of the game was made by an Englishman.) Dienst – a man who did not just play by the rules but *was* the rules – had already signalled as much with a knowing nod at the triumphant midfielder. It was as if Dienst had agreed to keep a close eye on the mystical amber orb before handing it back to Haller at the end of the 90 minutes.

The symbol of Germany's progression into a conciliatory yet ultimately triumphant phase in its history was in safe, Swiss hands.

3 · Royal Disappointment

High in the royal box, Elizabeth II was far from impressed by Haller's goal. It was not because she was supporting England, and that a German had scored. It was because she disliked football and everything to do with it. She thought it dull, overrated and supremely common, like so much of the 1960s.

The only good thing about the afternoon so far was that her first minister's pipe smoke was wafting downwind two seats away. At one point she thought she might not have to deal with it at all, thanks to a delayed flight from America where Harold Wilson had spent another few hours making us all a bit poorer. If he wasn't giving away large chunks of Africa, threatening to devalue the pound was about all he could be relied upon to do efficiently.

In May the previous year Wilson had told Her Majesty to keep July 1966 clear for the competition. In the same month he had ignored her when she returned from a state visit to West Germany. Despite the Foreign Office asking him to report to Heathrow, he had preferred to spend his weekend at Chequers keeping his pipe stoked. Of course the Queen knew what the cold-shouldering was really all about: as a socialist prime minister he did not want to lose touch with the left-wingers in his party by appearing to suck up to her. But he needn't have made the snub so obvious.

Now, of course, Wilson was more than happy to put her at the centre of a populist extravaganza. The Queen knew what football meant to the Right Honourable Harold Wilson: it meant votes. When Denis Howell, the sports minister, had approached him for £100,000 to pay for ground improvements eighteen months earlier, he had replied: 'What's the World Cup?' Now he was jumping around the ground as if he were Bobby Charlton himself.

The Queen was aware that Wilson liked to think of himself as a man of the people, in touch with the classless Britain he was trying to create. Her Majesty quite enjoyed their weekly chats, and approved of Wilson's social welfare ideas, but thought he had about as much in common with ordinary men and women as her Corgis had with the footballers she was watching. At heart the Prime Minister was a pernickety intellectual; somebody who had never had the privilege of enjoying the pure and simple things in life, like riding a steed across one's realm on a sunlit July morning. His heart was certainly in the right place but, more than just occasionally, she felt it would have been far better –

and safer – if he had stayed put in his dusty Oxford college compiling graphs and writing books about coal.

As the rain clouds gathered overhead, Her Majesty could think of just one sensible use for the 'white heat of technology' which Wilson spent so much time banging on about in his dull, nasal tones. And it wasn't to light his pipe.

The Queen thought she had done her bit when she opened the World Cup before England's tedious 0–0 draw with Uruguay on 11 July. She had stepped up to the microphone and announced: 'I welcome all our visitors . . . I'm sure we'll be seeing some fine football,' with the emphasis on the fine'.

The thought of all those millions of people sitting at home eating their American-style TV dinners as they prepared for the football made her feel distinctly unsettled.

Her Majesty's coronation in 1953 had been the first major event in the country's history to be televised. More than 20 million people, many of whom had bought sets especially for the event, watched the pageantry. There was nothing wrong with that, of course – it was what grew out of it that upset her.

Coronation Chicken – fowl smothered in a mild curry mayonnaise – had been a direct result of the 'TeeVee Extravaganza'. The dish, designed to be eaten in front of the small screen, represented everything that was original but ultimately cheap and distasteful about a mass media industry driven by profit, tackiness and sensationalism. Satire and social realism were creeping out of shoddy magazines and obscure stage plays and on to the television screens appearing in millions of homes across the land. In the early days the medium had been dignified and aloof. It had reflected the essential British charac-teristics of self-control and a sense of responsibility. Now graduates driven by a populist and anti-imperialist agenda were tearing the barriers down, as TV became the lowest common denominator in our cultural life. Ordinary people were stepping into the studio to have their say. The Queen could foresee a day when they would be allowed to unburden their filthiest thoughts and deeds, urged on by loud, vacuous personalities. Everything from sexual fantasies to filthy language and sordid confessions about marital infidelity would be acceptable in the battle for higher ratings. An accompanying deluge of crass advertisements and soap operas would crush any leanings a previously great, innovative people might have had towards original thought or action.

As the Americanisation of Britain intensified, there were so many aspects of the World Cup which were proving to be just as downbeat as Coronation Chicken and TV. There was the World Cup Willie cartoon lion – straight out of the sentimental and thoroughly unBritish cartoon world of Walt Disney. There were those red-white-and-blue baseball caps which some of the Queen's Wembley subjects were wearing, albeit the right way round. Her Majesty had even noticed sausages just like the ones she'd seen smothered in sauerkraut all over Germany during her visit in 1965. They were being served up between slices of doughy bread to create 'hotdogs'. How long would it be before the whole country was full of tacky outlets churning out quick and unwholesome food for the masses? Worst of all was the commercial sponsorship. There was even a huge sign for the *RadioTimes* overlooking the royal box. It was all so foreign to the spirit of unsullied sportsmanship which she and her horses had grown up to love and respect.

The Queen sat in a neat row of blue wicker chairs with Sir Stanley Rous, the President of FIFA; her husband, the Duke of Edinburgh; and the Duke of Kent. Tartan rugs had been placed on each seat, just in case it got too cold. Her Majesty was dressed in the same yellow as Gordon Banks's goalkeeping shirt, with a feathery hat, brooch and big earrings.

When the blond German scored, her face was stern and disapproving. The Queen glared distastefully towards the seat where her first minister was sitting, his Gannex mac to hand instead of a rug. She placed a pair of sunglasses over her regal features and tried to take her mind off things with some polite small talk with those sitting next to her.

Her Majesty did not know enough about the game to analyse Haller's opening strike, and thought it would be disloyal to her own subjects anyway. She did not quite understand why one of her men in red had presented the ball to him, but thought it best not to ask. Instead she passed comment on the most eye-catching and interesting-looking thing on the entire pitch: the match ball itself. 'Isn't it an extraordinary colour?' she said.

It had been a frantic rush from the airport for Harold Wilson. He had been in Washington DC at a financial meeting with Lyndon Johnson, the US President. They had spent hours discussing riveting statistics which included some particularly interesting fiscal growth charts indicating Britain was on the verge of bankruptcy. Wilson had been concerned that the value of the country's gold and currency reserves had dropped to less than $70 million in June, but he would not have missed the game for the world. He had already warned his ministers that it would be a long, hot summer but there was no reason why they could not all put the sterling crisis out of their heads for at least 90 minutes.

A car and four motorbike outriders had met Wilson at Heathrow at lunchtime and he had been rushed to north-west London just in time for the 3 p.m. kick-off. He was delighted to see the England lads playing in Labour red. They had got to the final in white, but the true colour of the Wilson social revolution was now there for all the world to see. His government had been re-elected in

March with an improved majority of 97 seats in the House of Commons. The result had sealed Labour's new role as the natural party of government, but there was still lots of time needed to interpret the figures necessary to reverse 13 years of Tory misrule.

As he tried to steady the new Britain onto a sound statistical footing in one of the most dynamic eras in its history, Wilson's analytical brain calculated that an England victory was worth at least 20 points in the opinion polls.

What was it that Howell, his sports minister sitting next to him, had said about football when he told him about the World Cup around a year ago? Something about it being more than our national game? He'd said it was a sport which could galvanise the power and energy of the entire nation. All classes were interested in it, from the Duke and Duchess of Kent downwards. He'd talked about it in political terms. After the close-run election in 1964, Wilson was glad to hear there was another field of human activity which he could start to examine with his sharp, statistical eye. It would be nice to get something for himself from the people's game.

What a pleasure it was to relax for a couple of hours with his pipe and almost 80,000 potential Labour voters. Most were dressed traditionally in smart, dark suits, and many wore those thick-rimmed black glasses which always appear in Michael Caine spy films like *Funeral in Berlin*. They used slang expressions like 'Blimey' and 'Wotcha' as their metal shoe-protectors kicked up sparks all along Wembley Way. Rattles and rosettes were everywhere, as were bells and hunting horns. Casual dress meant duffle-coats and stripy scarves, and there were plenty of schoolboys wearing their uniforms on that Saturday afternoon. There were thousands of women in the crowd, too, but they favoured headscarves and woolly jumpers rather than Carnaby Street mini-skirts or two-tone dresses. As the teams emerged out of the darkness of the Wembley tunnel, they joined in choruses of 'Come on, England', 'When the Reds Go Marching In', and 'Rule Britannia'. Despite the apparent conservatism of the crowd, Wilson was in no doubt that his government was getting across the message of what the Swinging Sixties was all about. It was about so much more than Little Englander moans about the pound in their pockets.

It was no coincidence that the glamorous young boxer Muhammad Ali had made a trip from America to attend the final. He had just renounced his 'slave name', Cassius Clay, and was ready to defend his world title unburdened by the forces of reaction which had so cruelly held back aspiring young men of previous generations.

Harold Wilson's ethos was all about liberating people. His equal opportunities programme would ensure that everyone, regardless of sex, colour, race or creed, would be able to stand up and be counted on the Wembley terraces. New institutions like the Open University would ensure that further education was not beyond the reach of any of them, not even the bovine-looking ones wearing the red-white-and-blue baseball caps.

Of course, as an economics don, Wilson could not forget about the pound in people's pocket completely – especially as he'd bet Canadian Prime Minister Lester Pearson a pound and 15 shillings that England would win the game. The British Premier calculated that a quarter of the Wembley crowd had paid £5 for a seat and the rest around 10 shillings to stand on the terraces. The hard statistics were that approximately £130,000 in gate receipts were now in the Wembley kitty ready to be charted up in a projected fiscal forecast graph for season 1966–67. Those who had contributed to such a monetary influx – all on an average weekly wage of £13 – were taking part in an economic vote of confidence in Wilson's government.

The football fans were responding to the brave new world which Wilson had forged in the white-hot furnace of technology. It was a time of radical change, but most of all it was time of dynamic young role models who could galvanise public opinion towards electoral advantage. Britain was awash with icons of style, charisma and talent – men like Paul McCartney and John Lennon, at the top of the charts with 'Paperback Writer'. Those boys deserved an MBE, Wilson thought. They were symbolic of a nation which could accept gritty Northerners with flattened vowels from lower-middle-class back-grounds and turn them into superstars, loved and respected for everything they represented, even if it was dry statistics and pipe smoking.

Wilson stared in wonder at the electoral possibilities of the symbols on show right in front of him.

There was Bobby Moore, the golden-haired Adonis and captain, whose looks captivated the gaze of every young woman in the stadium and whose play enraptured everybody else. What a political property he would be. Wilson looked at the huge sign advertising the *Radio Times*. The medium really was the message. They were just two simple words, but they were bold and inspiring and staring right into the face of anybody who had an interest in the game. Millions of viewers watching on their little black-and-white televisions at home would see them. Just imagine if there were a huge sign with the legend 'Vote Wilson' on it.

There was the revolutionary new ball, springing about all over the field. Wilson chuckled to himself at its avant-garde colour – 'radical amber' was how he would have described it. It was so stylish, so upbeat, so modern, so Beatles, so Sixties ... so *people's game*.

'Oh dear,' groaned the Prime Minister. 'A German's kicked the bloody thing into our net'.

Alf Ramsey remained utterly calm and composed as Helmut Haller drove the leather ball past Gordon Banks. The England manager's dark, authoritative features were implacably still as the German midfielder celebrated. Harold Shepherdson, the team physiotherapist sitting on the wooden bench next to him, had already started to fidget and Ramsey did not want to encourage him. He'd be jumping up in the air soon, like some excitable Latin playing for Uruguay.

Ramsey's days in the Duke of Cornwall's Light Infantry had taught him all he needed to know about discipline. Even when he'd been playing for the battalion as a centre-forward, his victory celebrations had never been any more than a satisfied half-smile and a vigorous sprint back to his own half. As he'd watched his 1966 troops downing their scrambled eggs and bacon that morning at the Hendon Hall Hotel, he knew he could rely on them to remain calm and dignified in the face of an early breakthrough by their opponents. His captain, Moore (whom Ramsey had described as a lieutenant he could trust with his life), was already steadying the rest of them as they prepared for the game to restart. Through gritted teeth, the manager had told him that there may be setbacks, but that the team was supremely well equipped to deal with anything that was thrown at them.

Ramsey, dressed in a light-blue tracksuit, white socks and an incongruous pair of black half-brogues, knew that it would not be skill and artistry which won England the World Cup. It had not been creativity or Latin emotion which won his country a huge territory upon which the sun, still absent from the sky above Wembley, never set. Rather, it had been courage and discipline underpinned by tactical brilliance. Soft, highly-strung artists would not have lasted 45 minutes manning the far-flung frontiers of Empire. Those who had formed the spearhead of Britain's dynamic thrust into the outside world had been warriors equipped with sturdy leather footwear and bulldog names like 'Nobby' and 'George'.

Ramsey had forged his team according to the same principles which the young Queen to whom he had sworn allegiance was now watching evaporate in a wind of anti-colonial zeal abroad and snide, satirical feeling at home.

Thoughtful and calm, Ramsey had displayed his own tactical brilliance by negating the wings. His guiding principle had been the same as that used by the infantry officers who formed the unbreakable squares on the field of Waterloo, or the bowmen who brought down lines of French knights at Agincourt. It was to initiate a war of attrition in which elegant cuirassiers and titled nobleman on fiery horses would be left frustrated, vulnerable and devoid of the ability to sustain an effective attack.

Ramsey would never let the opposition outflank his men. Any attempt at wing play would be snuffed out in an instant. Opponents playing wide would be forced back into the centre of the field, where they would be left wrong-footed and exposed to a counter-attack by his Wingless Wonders. Hard, stubby Englishmen like Nobby Stiles – toothless and balding – would finish them off as Alan Ball, a red-headed bulldog whose lifetime's ambition had been to fight for his country, would stifle any foreign build-up and turn it into an English breakthrough.

Winston Churchill had always complained that the great weakness of the British was that they never hated their enemies. Ramsey had tried his best to stir up anger against the Argentinians in the quarter-final on 23 July, but only after the match was won. He described the Latin Americans as 'animals' and refused to let the England players swap shirts with them. The Argentine captain, Antonio Rattin, had wiped his hands on the Union Jack corner flag following an eight-minute argument with the referee after being sent off, but Ramsey had faced the provocation with stiff-upper-lipped disdain.

Even Nobby Stiles, whose final World Cup disciplinary record was to read like a Crown Court indictment, failed to react when he was spat at seven times during that game. A *Sunday Telegraph* headline read 'The Butchers of Buenos Aires make football a farce' after they tried to knock down the door to the England dressing-room, urinated in a corridor and threw a chair through a window.

The FIFA disciplinary committee report said the Argentina team 'brought the game into grave disrepute by their flagrant breaches of the laws and disregard for discipline and good order'.

The ill-feeling between the two countries had already seen a detachment of Royal Marines sent to the Falkland Islands earlier in the year. England and Argentina were disputing ownership of the isolated outpost in the South Atlantic. The way things were going, there would probably be a diplomatic dispute soon, if not a war.

There had been problems with the French, too. When Stiles flattened their captain, Jacky Simon, in front of the royal box on 20 July, it appeared that the Englishman had played his last game for his country. 'He called me Norbert,' was the midfielder's only excuse, but the blazer-clad officials of the Football Association failed to accept it. FA secretary Denis Follows demanded Stiles be dropped and, in an example of his supreme loyalty to his men, Ramsey offered his resignation.

Stiles, a devout Roman Catholic, insisted that he had not meant any harm, and Ramsey replied: 'I believe you. I take your word as an Englishman.' The manager was not one to pander to the French anyway, especially since Charles de Gaulle kept saying *non* to our entry into the new Europe which everybody was talking about. The manager's resignation was refused.

The Germans were a decent bunch, even if they were a bit wishy-washy and non-committal. Ramsey was impressed by the gentlemanly Seeler, who had generously handed Bobby Moore a plaque instead of a pennant before the game, but considered he might lack a bit of steel when it came to the crunch. The way he'd let that Uruguayan slap him in the face had been embarrassing. Schöen had perfect manners, but you had to wonder how much he really wanted to win. Young Beckenbauer looked intelligent and calm on the ball, but he was probably one for the future.

Ramsey could have done without Haller's goal, though.

At 1–0 down the journalists would already be gathering like a threatening tribe of dervishes around a vastly outnumbered expeditionary force. It was no use getting in a state, though. He'd undoubtedly have to tell Shepherdson to 'sit down' by the end of the afternoon, but panic was a concept unknown to an English commander.

Geoff Hurst was looking confident up front, even if his fellow striker Roger Hunt had received a few boos from certain sections of the largely southern crowd. They would have preferred to see Dagenham-born Jimmy Greaves leading the line rather than the Liverpudlian. Instead, the Spurs forward was sitting on the bench in a suit which was more King's Road, Chelsea, than Tottenham High Road. Substitutes were not allowed in 1966, so Greaves wore the look of a Frenchman who had just met Nobby Stiles. Out on the field, Jack Charlton did not look too happy either. He was losing it after Haller's goal and was making all kinds of odd arm movements and pained expressions. They were almost as ridiculous as Haller's facial contortions following his early goal, thought Ramsey.

But within five minutes of the Germans taking the lead, England were playing the ball around with confidence. The amber orb would receive more than a few hard British belts before the afternoon was over.

'We'll be all right,' Ramsey thought to himself.

4 · Sinking Son

As he stared down at the scenes on the Wembley pitch, German TV commentator Werner Schneider was philosophical: 'In England winning at football is treated like winning a battle . . . the English nationalism is more than football,' he said.

Haller fell to the ground like a dispossessed cavalryman whose horse had cantered into oblivion. He clutched his face and ran his fingers through his hair. It was 5.15 p.m. and Augsburg's most famous sporting son had just experienced the most crushing defeat of his entire footballing career. As red-shirted Englishmen ran around him in triumph, Haller was reduced to pulling massively exaggerated sorrowful expressions and shaking his head from side to side.

Instead of contributing the decisive first goal to what would have been one of his country's greatest sporting triumphs and the end of 31 years of despair, Haller had become an abject loser. The misery of the 3–0 defeat at White Hart Lane in 1935 still stood as an unwholesome stain on the pure white spirit of the aspirational Germany. In the fashion of the cruellest of games, Haller was reduced from being a white soccer knight blazing a trail of glory to a sad figure lying unnoticed at the side of the pitch.

Some sporting England fans standing on the packed terraces made conciliatory hand gestures to the midfielder (at least he thought they were conciliatory) but they were not enough to lift his spirits. As he forced himself off his knees and wandered across the famous old pitch in search of solace, tears could be seen rolling down his normally impish face. They cascaded turfwards in the same way that the midfielder's stylish, flowing play had earlier helped to spark the game into life and make it one of the most thrilling ever played under Wembley's twin towers.

The pain of defeat was almost unbearable. As the chants of 'We won the Cup' grew, Haller later confessed that he began contemplating a downhill future running a non-league side in the Harz mountains, or selling shinpads and replica kits. Worse than that, he might even have to spend his retirement doling out pickled cabbage in southern Bavaria.

It had been such a cruel, unnecessary defeat. Hurst's headed equaliser and the follow-up goal by Martin Peters had made the score 2–1 to England, but even then Haller felt his side would still win. With ruthless Teutonic efficiency Wolfgang Weber had equalised to make it 2–2 in the last minute of the game, and it seemed that yet another miracle recovery would ensure a German victory.

Schöen had reminded his players at half-time of all the recent shortcomings of their mighty nation. He told them that they should never forget the disasters which had gone before. The experiences which had reduced the entire population to shame and ridicule needed to be exorcised. Their immediate history had been one in which ignominy had been heaped upon them.

It had been a full 12 years since Germany last won a World Cup final. When they lined up for half an hour of extra time – the first in a final since Rome in 1934 – the Germans had been inspired. They were certain they had enough iron discipline and courage to reassert their dominance. During 1954, the year of their last World Cup triumph, against a team of outstanding Magyars, they had lost to England 3–1 in a Wembley friendly, but this time there would be no such mistakes. Haller, whose name was already set in amber, felt especially certain that victory was still a formality . . . until the 102nd minute of play.

Alan Ball passed to Hurst, standing just ten yards from the nearest German goalpost. The England number 10 swivelled, puffed his cheeks threateningly, and hit a ferocious shot. It hit the underside of the crossbar, spun downwards, appeared to skim the goal-line and then bounced back into open play. Roger Hunt had been poised perfectly to knock it into the open net. Instead he lifted his arms in celebration and began to jog triumphantly back to the halfway line. It was an instinctive reaction by Hunt – one which was to cause unimaginable controversy and create a mystery which remains unresolved to this day.

Wolfgang Weber cleared the ball but play was halted and Wembley was reduced to a deathly hush. The match referee was left to decide whether the ball had crossed the line.

There was no possibility of him awarding a goal, thought Haller. He was too objective, too bright, too refined, too Swiss.

Gottfried Dienst ran over to the side of the pitch to speak to his linesman. Haller knew the short, stocky figure running the line spoke German because he had heard him cautioning players earlier in the game. With his authoritative demeanour, long baggy shorts and Kaiser-sized moustache, he even looked German. There was no chance of him judging that such an ineffectual thump against the crossbar had been a goal. From his position so close to the action he would have been perfectly placed to follow the flight of the ball. It was amber, for goodness sake – hardly the kind of colour anybody could miss.

The linesman lifted his flag and pointed to the centre circle. Dienst pointed to the centre circle.

Tofik Bakhramov, a former soldier from the Soviet republic of Azerbaijan who had once fought Moscow-bound Panzer divisions on the Eastern Front, signalled the end of Germany's assault on the Jules Rimet trophy.

Dienst said later: 'I still don't know if the shot by Hurst in the 102nd minute was in or not. I have to say that I was standing in a poor position for the shot, exactly head on instead of diagonal to the goal. I wouldn't have allowed the goal if the linesman Bakhramov hadn't pointed to the middle with his flag.'

The linesman's massive contribution to the world game later led to an airport being named after him in his homeland (there are few greater honours in Azerbaijan). Bakhramov never expressed any doubts about his decision to award the goal, even after watching it numerous times on television. Although he was touched by the Germans' approach to the game, he knew that England were the better side.

Bakhramov, unusually sensitive and poetic for a linesman, said: 'Dienst rushed towards me because he wanted to clear up the situation. In the mean-time the whole stadium was waiting in profound silence. When, in accordance with my signal, Dienst decidedly pointed to the middle of the pitch, an infernal noise could be heard from the stands. I asserted that the English had kicked their goal in entire accordance with the rules.

'Uwe Seeler, captain of the German team, made a rude remark towards me but later apologised for his inconsiderate behaviour. Though I did not doubt for a moment in the justness of my decision, I felt an unusual burden in my soul. I should have liked it if the German sportsmen had admitted my impartiality.'

By the time Hurst struck his third goal in the final minute of extra time to make it 4–2, the game was long over. Englishmen and women were shouting with joy as the whole nation united in triumph. It was the greatest day in English sporting history.

The Queen turned to Sir Stanley Rous and said: 'How much longer to go?'

At the end of the match, Haller briefly put out of his mind his role as a footballer who had animated the face of the German nation for a glorious seven minutes. He had even forgotten his role as an ideological frontiersman in the eternal battle between capitalism and communism. Instead, his non-committal approach to the jubilant excesses of his fellow Europeans was sorely tried.

Like the rest of his team-mates he was furious at the gross injustice of the defeat. The 4–2 scoreline was an affront to all the qualities of decency and forward thinking which the new, revitalised Germany represented. Hurst's farcical second goal should never have been allowed to stand.

Some Germans were forgetting their roles as non-committal Europeans, prevented by their nationality from making controversial comments. Horst Hottges, Hurst's hapless marker, was the worst offender. He later opined: 'Geoff Hurst had a lot of luck in the game. It wasn't a goal. After the match Bobby Charlton talked to us and said it wasn't a goal.'

As Haller moped around the pitch, he suddenly spotted the amber ball he had so expertly cannoned into the English net less than two hours before. It was still lying at the back of the German goal, abandoned by the match officials to whom he had entrusted its safekeeping. The England players showed no interest in it whatsoever. Nobby Stiles was dancing. Bobby Charlton was crying joyfully, saying, 'She's there.' Alan Ball, just 21, was searching for his dad. George Cohen was kissing everybody in his path. Roger Hunt was hugging his team-mates. Alf Ramsey was gritting his teeth and looking marginally less miserable than usual.

Not even Geoff Hurst, who had scored a record three goals in the game, appeared interested in the discarded lump of leather. Scoring a hat-trick is the prerequisite for any footballer who wants to keep the match ball after a game in Britain. Instead, he was summoning what little energy he had left to climb 39 steps to lift the Jules Rimet trophy.

Haller hobbled towards the amber ball and stooped over it. At that very moment the clouds high above in the north-west London skies appeared to swirl and burst open. For almost two hours they had been full of rain and threatening to send down lightning rods towards mortals who were flagrantly mocking history. But in a few seconds of even greater Wagnerian intensity, bright sunshine lit up the vast green pitch. It was a signal as clear as the sharp blast of Gottfried Dienst's whistle which had bought the 1966 World Cup final to an end. Haller knew that his second legendary moment of that extraordinary afternoon had finally arrived. The sudden heavenly glow was a sign that he had to claim the already famous amber ball for Germany. Their defeat had been cruel and unjust – so unlike his wonderful goal. The ball was a tangible symbol of the outrage which had been inflicted on the new Germany.

With a furtive glance from left to right, Haller picked the ball up and wiped the mud and grass stains off its amber panels using his short-sleeved white shirt. He began to make his way back towards the tunnel and the visitors' changing-room. It was just a short limp away, and he would be able to slip his trophy into his kitbag before the first post-match interview.

A tug on the shirt from the young Franz Beckenbauer – already well on his pedantic way to earning his nickname 'Kaiser' – reminded Haller that he had to make an important detour before sneaking out. As a defeated German it was part of his duty to face humiliation in front of around 80,000 English people.

Haller was ushered by his furrow-browed team-mate back across the pitch and up the steps to the royal box to pick up his loser's medal from the former Saxe Coburg und Gotha. Haller had already fulfilled a lifetime's ambition by meeting the Queen that day, and the novelty was wearing off. Despite her historical associations with the Fatherland, he knew that Elizabeth II's family had not used their real name since George V changed it to Windsor at the height of the Great War in 1917. If they had been ashamed to use it then, they would hardly want to reclaim it after another humiliating German defeat.

It was only the recollection of that most famous of English soccer clichés 'We was robbed' which allowed Haller a half-smile as he went among the victors, clutching his booty under his left arm and supporting it against his side.

Haller, previously a man of impeccable good character, was obviously inexperienced at concealing the stolen ball. As he dragged himself up the steps, few could fail to notice it. He thought of whistling nonchalantly as a means of drawing attention away from it, but still felt horribly exposed. It was as if the ball had grown into a bright amber planet the size of Saturn. Surely somebody was about to blow the whistle on him.

Instead Elizabeth II flashed Haller a perfect smile and said, 'Very well played,' as she shook his hand and presented him with his medal. Haller grunted back, gripping the amber sphere tightly against his sweat-stained number 8 shirt. The Queen's smile appeared to grow wider as she glanced towards the ball with which her loyal subjects had conquered the footballing world. Haller nodded his blond bob and then quickly returned to the pitch. British policemen in their dark-blue uniforms and pointed helmets stood everywhere, but it was left to the man in black to make a last attempt to stamp his authority on the errant German.

Gottfried Dienst was born in Versailles in 1919, the year in which his palatial birthplace became the symbol of another injustice against the Germans. Shocked and humiliated, the country stood by impotently as its king, its navy, huge areas of its territory, much of its material wealth and its entire imperial status in the world were mercilessly stripped away by the Versailles peace settlement.

For years afterwards everything Germany did as a country was under-pinned by the memory of the detested treaty which brought the First World War to an end. Versailles represented lost greatness and honour. The following decades would see everything possible done to try and see it reversed.

So it was with the amber ball. As Dienst confronted Haller, he knew it meant so much more to the German player than a post-match souvenir. It was another symbol of a huge injustice committed against Germany as it strove to assert itself as a decent and successful nation.

'We must have the ball back,' said Dienst, using the royal plural in deference to the young Queen watching high above. As a man born in the shadow of one of the most magnificent palaces in France, he had been brought up to respect the noble families of his ancient continent.

'I replied "Nein" and raced off to the dressing-room,' Haller recalled. 'The ball was lying at my feet so I took it in my hand and ran. The Queen saw that I had it. Later I took it home with me. It was a perfectly normal thing to do.'

Dienst did not bother chasing him. The referee had already done enough that day to ruin the young German's sense of self-worth. He knew that many of his team-mates would already be sitting in a silent changing-room contemplating their defeat. It was an important ball, of course, but the English already had the most important trophy in the world. That expression of tearful resignation on Haller's face had also affected Dienst deeply. There was no possibility of him depriving the young midfielder of his own personal World Cup.

Dienst had been right about the Germans. They were sitting on the wooden benches in the changing-room with their elbows on their knees and their heads bowed. When Haller joined them he spun the ball in the air and let it roll into the middle of the concrete floor.

The ball's understated amber colour captured their attention as a tiny glint of hope appeared to light up their exhausted, sweating faces . . .

For a few seconds the scars appeared healed: White Hart Lane in 1935 (3–0 to England), Berlin in 1938 (6–3 to England), Wembley in 1954 (3–1 to England), Berlin in 1956 (3–1 to England), Leipzig in 1963 (2–1 to England against East Germany), Nuremberg in 1965 (1–0 to England) and Wembley earlier in 1966 (1–0 to England). Even the World Cup final in 1966 was already turning into a memory.

The thought of the inspirational Stanley Matthews demolishing some of the greatest German sides ever – including the 1954 World Cup winners – was fading as fast as that of the toothless Nobby Stiles scoring his only England goal ever in the 1–0 friendly defeat of February 1966. The 31 years of hurt were behind them, and it was now time to think about a glorious future.

'Never again,' said one of the players as he rolled the ball back towards Haller.

'Never again,' said Haller, as he picked it up.

The ball, the ultimate symbol of the most outrageous footballing defeat in

German history, would give them the power and inspiration to make sure such a humiliation was never repeated.

The entire German team vowed that they would never lose to England in a non-friendly for at least another 31 years.

5 · Dog Days

The ease with which Haller slipped the World Cup ball into his kitbag and smuggled it home to Germany surprised no one. As befitting one of the most brutal contests in world sport, the 1966 championships were one of the worst policed in the history of the game.

Never mind that an instantly recognisable German midfielder had been allowed to steal an instantly recognisable, brightly coloured object from right under the gaze of the Queen and her Home Secretary in the most heavily guarded stadium in Britain. Just four months before, the solid gold Jules Rimet trophy itself had been stolen when it was put on display a few hundred yards from Scotland Yard and the Palace of Westminster.

The crime, like Geoff Hurst's second goal, is still shrouded in mystery, but what we do know about it says everything about the lax security in which a committed ball thief like Haller was able to thrive.

On Sunday, 20 March 1966, the World Cup trophy was put on display in Westminster Central Hall. The exhibition of which it was the centrepiece was closed to the public but part of the hall was open for a Sunday school. A security guard checked the cup at 11 a.m. but, as an Old Bailey judge would later hear, at about the same time a man was seen loitering in Parliament Square. By lunchtime the cup had gone and Detective Inspector Leonard Buggy, of the Flying Squad, was on the case.

The following Wednesday, FA chairman Joe Mears received a package through the post at Stamford Bridge, west London, where he was also worked as Chelsea's chairman. It contained the top of the cup and a ransom demand for £15,000. The note said the trophy would be melted down if the money was not paid. A series of anonymous telephone calls followed, which turned out to have been made by 47-year-old Edward Betchley.

Buggy, pretending to be Mears's assistant, arranged to meet Betchley in Battersea Park, across the Thames in south London. The detective used Mears's distinctive Ford Zodiac complete with the number plate CFC 11. (Even in 1966 members of football's hierarchy were unafraid to display their wealth through a personalised registration plate, the rich man's equivalent of a CFC tattoo emblazoned across an impoverished skinhead's forearm.)

Betchley was shown a briefcase containing 30 individually wrapped packages which Buggy claimed contained £500 notes. The pair then drove off to get the trophy.

During the journey Betchley said: 'I've got someone watching the cup to make sure it's safe. I know you're worried about that money but there won't be any violence. There wasn't any violence when we took the cup and there won't be any when I hand it over to you.'

The handover never happened. The car was being shadowed by two young constables. Unfortunately, they had the subtlety of a pair of truncheons crashing against a Chelsea skinhead's skull. Even without their pointed helmets, they looked like policemen. Their unmarked van was never more than two feet from the Zodiac's rear bumper, and every time Betchley turned round he saw the two men sitting as stiffly upright as they had been when they passed out of Hendon a few months before.

Betchley's suspicions were confirmed when he saw the van's driver scribbling down the number plate of a Morris Minor which looked as if it might well be doing 31mph in a 30mph zone. He jumped out of the moving car and ran away. The younger officers were still too engrossed in watching out for speeding motorists to worry about real crime, so it was left to Buggy to sprint after Betchley and collar him as he tried to disappear down an alleyway.

He was later picked out at an identity parade as the man seen at Central Hall, but always insisted that a businessman he called 'The Pole' had offered him £500 to act as a go-between. He was jailed for two years for demanding money with menaces.

Many years later Betchley's widow Marie said he never told her what really happened. 'He carried the can for it,' she said at her home in south-east London in 1996, 'but the full story died with him.'

Despite the best efforts of the Metropolitan Police, it was only thanks to a dog that the Jules Rimet trophy was ever found. A week after the disappearance, Pickles the mongrel was scuffling about under a bush outside the home of his owner, Thames lighterman David Corbett, in Kennington, south London. Corbett was later given a £6,000 reward, and said: 'I saw him sniffing a bundle so I tore off the paper and realised my dog had found the World Cup.'

Things had not ended in the same way as a similar sorry tale in 1895, when the original FA Cup was taken from a Birmingham jeweller's and never seen again, but the incompetence of the football authorities and later the police had been badly exposed. And if it had not been for Pickles there may well have been no World Cup to play for at all. The dog, who became a national hero, was not allowed to go to any of the games but was later invited to join Harold Wilson on the top table of the celebration banquet following the final.

Betchley himself ended up watching the World Cup final in a London prison, where victory was celebrated with as much energy and enthusiasm as everywhere else in the country. In Pentonville inmates commemorated the achievement by smashing up their cells.

The theft was symptomatic of a deterioration in the standards of law and order at a time when football supporters were being allowed to run on to the pitch, and shameless Germans were being allowed to run off it with English sporting treasures.

6 · Shooting Star

It's no coincidence that Geoff Hurst is cockney rhyming slang for a university First. Students who have avoided a Bishop Desmond (2:2) or a Douglas Hurd (Third) usually find themselves with a 2:1 – the standard degree grade for standard pimply youths whose brains have stood up reasonably well to three years of alcohol, drug and daytime television abuse. They might not have much individual flair, and almost certainly can't spell, but a cheap parchment scroll is a perfectly respectable prize for those who eventually see themselves taking on some kind of responsibility in life, like a shirt and tie.

Sadly, in an age when remand homes for juvenile delinquents are amalgamating with open prisons to become universities, first jobs normally don't amount to much more than checking the cleanliness of the toilets in hamburger restaurants every 20 minutes, but at least a formal education is worth a couple of stars on a McDonald's name tag. Recruits from the university milkshake round can also relive the heady idealism of their undergraduate days by wearing trainers and a moody face during daylight hours.

A Geoff, however, really is a glittering prize. It's the gold standard which sets particularly bright students on pedestals and makes up for all those years of being bullied at school. It proves that a seemingly ineffectual post-adolescent with the charisma of a laptop computer was once at the very top of his or her subject, even if it was Ancient Fast-Food Studies with a Cheeseburgerology subsidiary.

The performance which Geoff Hurst turned in on 30 July 1966 really was first class; first class with honours and a hearty slap on the back from the vice-chancellor, in fact. His three goals were pure unadulterated striking perfection. Hurst's was the ultimate goalscorer's performance in the ultimate game, one which was voted Greatest Match of All Time by readers of the Daily Telegraph and the football magazine FourFourTwo in January 1999. It made it to first place above the 1960 European Cup final at Hampden Park in which Real Madrid beat Eintracht Frankfurt 7–3.

Hurst had worked incredibly hard for his success, and it did not matter what came before or afterwards. In the same way that the best students begin their revision the night before, Hurst only began to shine as a world-class striker in the days leading up to the finals. He had not even pulled on an England shirt at all until February 1966. By August he was as important a figure to the people of Britain as the astronaut Neil Armstrong was to become to Americans.

As we begin a new millennium and think about the images which make us feel really good about ourselves as a nation, that famous picture of Hurst scoring his third goal in the closing seconds of extra time is one of the most enduring. It is as emotive a sight as white-spacesuited mortals bobbing around on the surface of the moon. Both are poignant images of pride and glory personified. They are living proof that a country's best can reach for the stars and, in little more than a second, attain heights of success so far removed from the base earth upon which most of us will always remain firmly rooted.

The image of Hurst usually bursts into our consciousness every time we qualify for the finals of a major tournament. It dominates newspapers and TV screens. It shines out magnificently in a media so often obsessed with the ugly and the uninspiring. Etched on to the consciousness of every English football supporter and millions of others, the picture shows Hurst blasting the ball across the furrow-browed and quizzical gaze of defender Wolfgang Overath. It is the last kick of the game, and the England team has finally reached heights which had not been attained before and which have not been attained since.

Those of us who have stared at the image time and again will have noted the studies in concentration which are the players' faces. We will have noted other, peripheral details, like the soon-to-be-altered scoreboard showing the legend England 3 West Germany 2, and the referee trying desperately to keep up with play and the pace of history.

But there has never been any real doubt as to where the focal point of the dramatic scene really lies: the ball. Eagle-eyed Hurst looked like an Olympic marksman as he rifled the unstoppable object past a stationary goalkeeper, but his clean-cut features never became really famous. He would always joke that he used to book a restaurant in the name of Bobby Moore to make sure he got a table. Hurst had no front teeth even though he was just 24, but it was his team-mate Nobby Stiles who was renowned for his upper gumline. Hurst still had a fine head of hair, but it was Bobby Charlton who became famous for parting his above the left ear. (In later life Sir Bobby was asked what prompted him to adopt a drag-a-strand hairdo: 'I don't know. Vanity, I suppose,' he replied.) Hurst's red shirt was also an eye-catcher, but even that was a change strip. England's first-choice kit has always been white.

Wolfgang Overath, his perfectly laundered white shirt still unsullied after two hours of combat, was a picture of Teutonic grace and motion. The 23-year-old inside-left looked authoritative and athletic but, unlike the even younger Franz Beckenbauer, never became a famous name internationally.

There was never any chance of him becoming the focal point in the picture, anyway, because he was a German.

What everybody concentrates on and remembers about the image is the ball: the supercharged ball flashing across the pitch to ensure the greatest victory in the history of English sport. Its power and energy had left dozens in its slipstream, including a Swiss referee tired by 120 minutes of play and the burden of making monumental decisions ready to be debated throughout history; the enigmatic 'was it in, or wasn't it?' ball which had teasingly skimmed across the German goal-line to create a puzzle which would never really be solved properly, not even by brilliant academics with a Geoff in geometry, applied physics or aeronautical engineering; the magic ball which had weaved and dodged its way past defenders and an exasperated German goalkeeper at impossible angles. Even its colour was inappropriately eerie: amber, the colour today of bad-weather alerts at Heathrow and Bakhramov, is an ideal tint for games played in hail, sleet, snow or fog. In a weather-obsessed country like England, anyone could have told FIFA that a mixture of sunshine and showers was the worst that could be expected in north-west London on a July day in 1966.

Despite its colour, it was a real leather ball, solid enough to endure the scuffs and panel wounds of a bitter battle. It was so different to the modern, artificial balls starting to be produced in the new era of throw-away commercialism, where transient logos and crass advertising became more important than the quality of the product itself.

The ball was about so much more than cheap profiteering. It was about pride and greatness. As Hurst gave it that ferocious kick, it was already well on its way to becoming an English icon which would one day be described by The Times as a 'saintly relic'.

Of all the people in the world who remained captivated by the image of the amber ball years after the 1966 final, Geoff Hurst was foremost. After scoring the greatest three goals ever seen at Wembley, Hurst knew that he had played out the principal role on the most glorious summer's afternoon of his life. He joyfully accepted the congratulations of his team-mates. He vaguely remembered people crying and others falling to the ground, but he was in no fit state to retrieve the ball he had just propelled past the stationary Hans Tilkowski.

Hurst's last, magical strike of the amber leather had not even been planned. He had ignored Alan Ball's screaming pleas to pass it to him, and recalled the little redhead shouting, 'You bastard!' as he hit the ball harder than he had ever done in his entire life.

The England striker's own commentary of the scene which captured the imagination of so many people reveals his devastatingly effective pragmatism. His words are worth bearing in mind when you see 'technicians' like former England manager Glenn Hoddle standing at the side of the pitch acting as if they're conducting the London Symphony Orchestra.

Hurst's grand finale was nothing to do with complicated pincer movements or tapping the channels out of midfield. His main aim was to 'welly' the ball as far as possible into the stand so as to give a ball-boy some exercise, and make sure his side held on to the 3–2 scoreline before the final whistle blew.

Hurst said: 'It never entered my mind that I could score. We'd been playing for two hours, and I was completely drained of energy. I wanted to play for time by running to the corner flag, or passing to another red shirt which wasn't being marked.

'I heard a shout from my right. It was Bally. Two Germans drifted across to cover him. Only then did a patch open up for me. The game was over, but the whistle was in the referee's mouth and all I wanted to do was hit the ball with all the strength I had left. If it went over the bar there were around fifty yards behind the goal. It would take vital seconds to collect the ball.'

Instead, the football flew into the top corner of the German goal, accompanied by a commentary far more famous than Hurst's. BBC television commentator Kenneth Wolstenholme said: 'Some people are on the pitch. They think it's all over . . . It is now!'

At first Hurst was not even certain that his last goal had counted. He said: 'Everybody went crazy, but I wasn't sure if it was a goal because the ref seemed to blow his whistle as the ball went in. When I realised it was a goal I was incredibly pleased.'

Hurst was urged by some team-mates to retrieve his prize from the back of Tilkowski's net, but chose instead to punch the air like a maniac and scream, 'Yesss!' The only other words he felt fit enough to mouth were to ask if his third goal-bound strike of the ball had stood following all the arguments. He said: 'The thought that it might have been disallowed was going through my mind the whole time. I knew I would never hit a better shot so long as I lived. Tilkowski had no chance. If I'd had the energy I would have chased the ball into the net and kissed it.'

After 120 minutes of non-stop effort, Hurst was grabbed by his team-mates as he contemplated his afternoon's achievements. 'My momentum slowed. I felt my legs shaking and my whole body droop. I turned suddenly, wanting to giggle. I waited as Ball and Peters came running up to crash into me. They seemed to be babbling.

'Then I noticed the crowds pouring onto the pitch, and saw our players down on their knees or leaping about in groups. The Germans were in little clusters of white shirts and grey faces. It was over.'

Ramsey's strict control of his players ensured discipline was maintained during the celebrations. There were no victory dives, or 'Beer we go!' salutes, or pulling of faces, or pulling on of red-white-and-blue baseball caps thrown from the crowd.

Hurst said: 'Again and again I asked the faces that loomed up in front of me "Did that third one count?" They didn't seem to hear me. Or if they did I couldn't understand their answers. It's hard to describe those minutes – players I knew seemed to be talking in some foreign language. There was a glazed look on every face, nothing seemed quite real or in proper focus. I was conscious only of everybody talking at once, yet saying nothing that made sense.

'I could hear my own voice, but I didn't know what even I was trying to say. One of the England players was swearing, just pouring out the same few four-letter words over and over again. But he wasn't angry, he was laughing. Somebody kept punching me. Somebody else kept leaping in the air and punching his hands together as though he couldn't stop. This was how we all found release from the tension. We just kept on moving, talking and making sounds until gradually control came back.'

Hurst, gloriously happy but utterly bemused, strode up the Wembley steps to collect his gold medal from the Queen. He was lost and not quite in control. Of course, he was supremely happy to have reached a romantic moment in his life, but that did not make the crowds and noise any easier to cope with, let alone the shifty foreigners preparing to pull a fast one.

Cameras were flashing everywhere, press reporters were shouting questions. Television journalists like Jimmy Hill were lining up endless interviews. It was almost impossible to think about anything except escape.

Hurst was is no way acting as if he had just become the first player to score a hat-trick in a World Cup final. He was far more concerned about finding his wife, Judith, whom he had married two years earlier. She had watched the game from the Wembley stands with her father, Jack, who had predicted that Hurst would score three times. 'Geoff and I had no idea that we'd never be able to forget the occasion,' she said. 'It's always being talked about on television nowadays. I remember a milkman asking me just after the 1966 final what it was like to be married to a star. "I don't know," I replied. "I've never been married to one."

'We were so young, like kids, and just took each day at a time. Even though football is all we've ever known, it's only now, looking back, that we realise how special it was.'

Back through the Wembley tunnel some England players were already sipping beer from the Jules Rimet trophy, but most remained shocked and confused.

'In the dressing-room the reaction set in for some of the team,' recalled Hurst. 'They slumped, just staring at the wall. I remember George Cohen saying: "It's bloody ridiculous. I don't feel anything. I don't, I really don't." The noise was deafening, but through it I heard someone, an FA official, shouting in my ear: "It counted, Geoff ... it counted." But still I walked out up the tunnel before we left to take a last look at the stadium and up at the huge scoreboard. "England 4 – West Germany 2" it said, and now I knew.'

By that time Haller was washed, changed and had the amber ball neatly packed in his kitbag, ready to smuggle it back to Frankfurt the next morning.

7 · Little Britain

Tired and more than slightly bemused by his day's exertions, Geoff Hurst took his place on the red-and-cream team coach on its triumphant journey back to the Hendon Hall Hotel. The England players then travelled into central London, around Hyde Park and Kensington Gardens, and on to a reception at the Royal Garden Hotel that evening.

All along the route there were people shouting and waving. Car horns blared as dizzy motorists made their contribution to the carnival atmosphere. Hundreds of banners were unfurled together with Union Jacks and Cross of St George flags. Traffic was brought to a standstill all over the capital as an AA spokesman announced: 'It's like VE night, election night and New Year's Eve all rolled into one.'

At the formal meal, at which all the England team wore red carnations, Hurst barely noticed Helmut Haller. With Pickles the dog and Harold Wilson present, there were too many other distractions. The way the chocolate marzipan on the football-sized Bombe Glacé was demolished by the guest of honour was hilarious. Pickles' table manners weren't much better, and everyone burst out laughing when the dog began sniffing around the Prime Minister's shoes.

Hurst vaguely remembers Haller sitting at one of the neatly laid tables, but did not speak to him. He was more concerned about Judith who, like all the other wives and girlfriends, had been excluded from the main celebrations. Haller passed the ball to Bobby Moore, Bobby Charlton and Uwe Seeler and they signed it. Later Pelé would add his signature, but Hurst was not asked.

When Moore took the World Cup trophy out on to the concrete-and-glass balcony of the hotel, the entire winning team realised for the first time just how much the victory had meant to the people of England. There was an eruption of joy among the massive crowd who chanted 'We won the Cup' and 'God save the Queen'.

A cordon of 60 policemen held the masses back. They stretched all the way along Kensington High Street towards Kensington Palace, the birthplace of a woman who had once painted huge chunks of the globe the same colour as Hurst's Wembley shirt.

All the England players were deeply moved to witness the kind of scenes that had been a regular occurrence during the reign of Queen Victoria. Popular triumphalism had been as commonplace as bugle calls in the heyday of Empire.

All over the globe, those whose lives had once been touched by British majesty were still celebrating the World Cup triumph. In Uganda, the fledgling nation cleared its entire TV schedule to run and re-run England's victory after the tapes were flown from Heathrow to Kampala. James Bwogi, the director of television in the country, watched the afternoon's entertainment on the British High Commission's set. Sadly, the huge enthusiasm displayed across the African state for the match did not extend as far as Idi Amin, a former sergeant in the King's African Rifles. He later had Bwogi murdered.

Such atrocities were not uncommon as psychotic dictators began to take over the British Empire, parts of which by 1966 were being given away as cheaply as tickets to an amateur trumpet recital.

The English people had very little to celebrate. India had gone in 1948, followed soon after by Pakistan, Ceylon and Burma. Most of Africa disappeared after Harold Macmillan's 'Winds of Change' speech in Cape Town in 1960. At the time Britain ruled most of East Africa from Cairo to the Cape. British troops had been stationed in Egypt since the early 1880s but the Suez Crisis of 1956 destroyed any lingering illusions about the extent of British power in the region.

By the end of the 1960s all our African colonies and protectorates had gone completely, with the exception of the self-governing Southern Rhodesia which announced a unilateral declaration of independence in 1963, and caused untold trouble for Harold Wilson's government.

A White Paper of February 1966 had abandoned the strategically crucial port of Aden as a national consciousness underpinned for hundreds of years by supreme confidence was replaced by emptiness and self-doubt. Being kept out of the Common Market – our entry had been vetoed by France three years before – was further evidence that we could no longer take anything for granted.

Instead of a united entity celebrating Britain's role as a world power, the Queen presided over a mishmash of dependencies, dominions and colonies. We were cascading towards third-division status, fit only to be snubbed and patronised by arrogant Frenchmen like Charles de Gaulle and to draw with Eastern Bloc countries like Poland in dire World Cup qualifiers.

Only in July 1966 did we really have something to be truly proud of. Our celebration of ultimate victory at Wembley was not about cheap jingoism or any kind of provocative excess. The pleasure of the English people was simple: winning the Jules Rimet trophy was nothing to do with the brutal subjugation of spear-wielding tribesmen, or disease-ridden concentration camps, or the melancholy heroism displayed by British infantrymen needlessly slaughtered on endless forays towards foreign guns. It was nothing to do with the stiff-upper-lipped chauvinism and murderous excesses occasionally displayed by those rallying under the battlecry of 'King, Country and Free Trade' in tiny colonial outposts whose names were known only to stamp collectors.

Our victory was about the best parts of our imperial legacy. It was about a steady and dignified evolution which had given rise to the Mother of Parliaments, the best legal system in the world and the most envied civil service. It was about exporting such institutions around the globe, together with the richest and most comprehensive language ever created. It was about a talented and hard-working population uniting under a wise and unflappable monarch.

By 1966 Britain had produced the very best in every field of human life – from history's greatest poets to its greatest generals. It was through such men and women that a race once isolated by its island position had become the most influential on earth. Our joy at now having produced the world's greatest footballers was sincere and heartfelt.

Faced with such ebullience, Hurst's personal loss seemed irrelevant. The rest of the weekend went by in a haze, giving him no time whatsoever to track down his lost ball. Jack Charlton left the Kensington hotel with £200 cash and a card in his pocket saying 'This body is to be returned to suite 508, Royal Garden Hotel.'

Some of the players went to Danny La Rue's nightclub in Hanover Square. There they were treated as national heroes: the cabaret act came to an abrupt halt, the band struck up a chorus of 'When the Reds Go Marching In' and they were presented with a cake.

The next day's visit to Elstree Studios – when Alf Ramsey famously announced that he would not take any questions from journalists because it was his 'day off' – was another brush with celebrity. There had been earlier squad meetings with Sean Connery, Britt Ekland and Norman Wisdom. That weekend there was also a special appearance on a TV programme hosted by Eamonn Andrews.

It was a glamorous two days for the Golden Boys of 1966, but it finally came to an end with a greasy supper at a motorway service station as they all returned from the BBC studios in Shepherd's Bush, west London. Lesley Ball, Alan Ball's 18-year-old fiancée, was living with her parents in Lancashire, and had never been to London before the final. She fainted when Wolfgang Weber equalised with 15 seconds of normal time to go. 'I remember we stopped for egg and chips at the service station, all clutching our World Cup winner's medals,' she recalled. 'Then we just arrived home, saying: "Oh, we won the World Cup," and that was it. People didn't go overboard like they do today.'

Hurst's reluctance to search for the ball was typical of the modest, unprepossessing sportsmen who won the World Cup for England. Even victory did not lead to airs and graces. The England team knew their places in life just as well as they knew their positions on the field of play. They had no expectations of anyone or anything.

Hurst, earning £10,000 a year, was back training with West Ham within two days of the World Cup final. His only real souvenir of the occasion was his gold winner's medal, a small, sentimental token of one of the greatest moments of his life, second only to his marriage to Judith.

Most of the players consigned the red-and-black boxes to bank vaults or a safe in the loft. Jack Charlton kept his in a steel cabinet locked inside 'something seriously secure'. He admitted that he only brought the medal out once every four years 'to show to family and friends'.

Further small, sentimental tokens of the game followed. FA secretary Denis Follows sent all the players a thank-you note and a £1,000 win bonus, reduced to £664 after tax. Sponsorship deals were almost unheard of, although Bobby Moore was given £500 by Radox Bath Salts for being the best player in the tournament.

While England and club sides like Manchester United now change their strips as regularly as most of us take a shower, there were no branded products in 1966. The Humphrey Brothers firm, founded in 1924 and using the trade name Umbro, made all but one of the 1966 team kits and prided itself on its unfussy, non-acrylic designs.

Unlike the playboys of today, some of the Boys of '66 were surviving on club fees of less than £100 a week. Financially, their expectations were as modest as the way in which they presented themselves. Instead of the designer crewcuts, diamond earrings and unlikely-lapelled suits so common among the young millionaires who play for their country today, the Golden Boys wore short-back-and-sides, and paid in cash as they stopped off at motorway service stations for egg and chips. With their proud posture and military gait, they looked ready to be shipped out to some distant foreign field within a bugle blast. Their clipped accents – straight out of films like *Passport to Pimlico* – were a direct and efficient means of communication which befitted working men renowned for their restrained humour and gentle tolerance. Even nowadays

Hurst still calls everyone 'sir' and qualifies every statement with self-regulating phrases like 'as far as I can ascertain' and 'it would be fair to say'.

Deference was something which all the 1966 players had grown up with. Almost all were born during the Second World War, and knew that conceptions of honour and respect to other people, especially those higher up the social order, was what was expected of them. In times of war, when orders were there to be obeyed and blackouts observed, they were a matter of survival.

When the 1966 England team lined up to meet the Queen before the World Cup final, many bowed their heads because they did not think that their monarch should be expected to look into mouths full of gaping holes instead of teeth. The image of Bobby Moore wiping his hands on the velvet surround of the royal box at Wembley is another study in working-class deference. The England captain knew his hands were covered in mud after an afternoon spent toiling on a boggy field, and was anxious not to soil the young Queen's spotless white gloves when he went to shake hands with her.

Celebrity came very gradually. There were no money-obsessed agents or analytical media pundits forcing monosyllabic players to spill out their innermost feelings about everything from their last haircut to their latest pop-star girlfriend. 'It took a long time for what we had achieved to sink in,' said Hurst. 'There wasn't the hype that you get today. A week later we were training for the next season. There was no time to sit back, relax and enjoy what we had achieved.'

While Hurst lived in Essex, most of the side were gritty Northerners. They had learned their trade kicking scuffed tennis balls with steel-heeled school shoes which sent sparks flying whenever they connected on the pavements of the streets where they grew up. Their homes were in rows of terraces on bleak, industrialised hillsides. It was from these streets that Britain had also drawn a workforce and exported its industrial products across the globe as it forged its mighty empire.

One of the supreme ironies of the 1966 tournament was that the Brazilians – who had learned their beautiful game juggling balls on palm-fringed beaches – should be based in Liverpool. The brilliant Pelé was kicked out of the game as he tried despairingly to come to terms with one of the most hard-working and grey industrial centres in Britain. Pelé had been injured in Brazil's opening game against Bulgaria, was carried off against Portugal and missed the match against Hungary. Sensitive and supremely gifted, he eventually returned to South America feeling hopelessly out of his depth. He had simply not been able to cope with the hard, brutal demands of the modern game.

The England players, in comparison, had been. They coped because they were a family who all looked after one another. If one was being picked on as Pelé had been, they would all go to the rescue. As full-back George Cohen, explained: 'When the call came, Bobby simply picked up the ball and said, "Let's go."'

There was no special psychology involved. Their approach to the game – as to life – had nothing to do with counselling or psychobabble of any kind. Before the greatest day of their lives, the team prepared by going to the Hendon Odeon to watch *Those Magnificent Men in their Flying Machines*. Ramsey deliberately announced the team selection in the foyer of the cinema so that all the players would have a good night's sleep, untroubled by the possibility that they might end up as rejects. Nobby Stiles involved himself in some personal reflections of his own, attending Mass on the morning of the final.

When it all ended, Hurst was determined that he would never change. He did not want to end up as a former has-been, endlessly recalling the past. The England number 10 was more than satisfied with the way his professional career turned out. In 49 matches for the national side he had scored 24 goals. For West Ham he scored 250 times in 500 games. His trademark puffed cheeks – they always appeared on the verge of bursting when his boot connected with leather – became synonymous with shots as hard and true as his second and third goals in the '66 final, but in fact it was in the air that Hurst was most effective. Brian Glanville was just one of the journalists who had noted Hurst's overall contribution to the national game, writing: 'England's chief weapon continued to be the glorious leap, the skilled aerial deflections of Hurst.'

In the 1970s the striker went on to play for Stoke City and West Bromwich Albion, and spent time managing Chelsea and Telford. He had also been the first future World Cup winner to play first-class cricket, scoring nought not out in a match for Essex against Lancashire in the County Championship of 1962. As well as a right-hand bat, he was a wicketkeeper and an outstanding fielder.

Hurst's approach to life, like his football, was all about moving forward. The ball was lost and, for the moment, it was part of history. He was to become the antithesis of the retired player living on former glories. There was never any possibility that his hat-trick would condemn him to sullen twilight years propping up the bar in tacky west London nightclubs telling bored barmen and teenage starlets how he had once played in front of the Queen at Wembley.

Of course there were always people who wanted to talk about the World Cup, but Hurst would never make a fuss about it. Family holidays abroad were invariably punctuated by foreigners pointing at him and asking him what it felt like to score those three goals. The Germans were the worst. Hurst recalls one coming up to him when he was on holiday in Spain and saying: 'When you score zat goal, I kick in zer front of my television.'

And, of course, there were the numerous concierges in Italian hotels who could recite the names 'Banks, Cohen, Wilson, Stiles, Charlton, Moore, Ball, Hurst, Hunt, Charlton and Peters' as easily as 'John, Paul, George and Ringo'. Hurst concentrated instead on building a sound financial future for Judith and his three daughters, Claire, Joanne and Charlotte. 'My philosophy has changed over the years. When you have three daughters at private school you are certainly a saver. Now I don't have the responsibility of school fees, I can afford to spend a bit. But I am still saving for my retirement.' Hurst bought a 19 per cent share in a company, Motorplan, and numerous shares, through unit and investment trusts. He went into insurance, eventually becoming a divisional managing director underwriting almost £6 million for London General Holdings.

In 1964 the Hursts were living in a semi-detached bungalow in Horn-church, Essex. By the 1990s they were in a detached five-bedroomed house with half an acre of garden in Walton-on-Thames, Surrey, surrounded by company directors with chauffeur-driven Jaguars, wives who lunch and pony-riding daughters.

As Hurst, a golden hero of 1966, lived out his respectable Middle England dream, he kept in close touch with Martin Peters. His former West Ham and England team-mate was by now guiding sales teams in the corporate world, as well as being a non-executive director at Tottenham Hotspur. Peters lived with his wife, Kathy, and two children in Shenfield, Essex. He drove a white Rover and would hang his blazer off a hook above the back seat.

Unlike the gritty Northerners of the World Cup winning team, Geoff and Martin were Southerners through and through. Even their soft, suburban Christian names indicated men who drape C&A sweaters across their shoulders in Home Counties pubs. They conjured up images of businessmen golfers enjoying a few swift bitters – 'Just a couple, love, I'm driving' – before returning to their spotless domestic castles for roast beef and Yorkshire pudding. Sunday would always mean time for the family before they seized their Monday-morning briefcases for another excruciating week of dull figures and even drabber clients.

Both men had worked long hours to advance lives in a society where status was decided by letters on a car registration plate and the number of foreign holidays they could afford each year. They fitted in perfectly with former Prime Minister John Major's eulogy to a safe, secure Middle England; an over-populated south-east full of people obsessively building up the funds to support a life where nothing much happens except for material advancement. Hurst and Peters were in the centre of the world Major had alluded to when he spoke of 'long shadows on county grounds, warm beer, invincible green suburbs, dog lovers and old maids bicycling to Holy Communion through the morning mist'. As he enjoyed the limited free time paid for by a hugely successful second career in finance, Hurst would often think back to a period when life was about so much more than uncompetitive cricket matches, lifeless pints, suburban back gardens, spoilt Labradors and Orwellian grannies. He knew there was a world far beyond the boundaries imposed by school fees, mortgages, health insurance schemes and prestige company cars with 'GH 1966' number plates. Sitting in his armchair in Walton-on-Thames, he could vividly recall a time when he was still living in a bungalow on £10,000 a year. It was a time when life was unpredictable and financially insecure ... It was a time when life was truly awe-inspiring.

Hurst would stare down at his gold World Cup winner's medal – a respectable symbol of the most triumphant day of his life. It represented the formality of the match: the shaking of hands with the Queen; the pre-match photographs; the exchanging of plaques and pennants; the walk up the 39 steps to the royal box; the formal dinner at the Royal Garden Hotel.

What Hurst missed was something which represented the other side of that incredible day: the skill and aggression; the heart-stopping excitement; the never-say-die attitude; the gallons of blood, sweat and tears; the crunching tackles; the filthy language; the intense pain; the sheer unpredictability of a game which had left 11 men disconsolate and shattered, and 11 others feeling as though they had reached life's pinnacle.

Hurst missed his amber ball.

8 · Family Tie

News of our descent on Germany was the most stirring piece of news Geoff Hurst had received since Alf Ramsey took him aside in the foyer of the Hendon Odeon on 29 July 1966 and told him he was to play in the World Cup final. As he sat in an Italian restaurant in Surrey, on Thursday, 25 April 1996, he was overwhelmed by memories.

The 54-year-old insurer privately recalled the triumphs of an earlier, far more romantic stage of his life. It was the young men who had shown him such loyal support all those years ago who were uppermost in his mind. Alf Ramsey had always taught him to treat them like a family. To Hurst, they were so much more than the Wingless Wonders who had run themselves into the ground to make sure that the amber ball was placed in his path for him to score the most important goals of his career. They were men of immense character and ability, whom he had counted as his best friends.

Looking out of the restaurant window onto a grey, pedestrian scene, Hurst thought of all their young faces lit up by the golden light of an early evening in July following the greatest triumph of their lives. The united family of Banks, Cohen, Wilson, Stiles, Charlton, Moore, Ball, Hunt, Charlton and Peters flashed through his mind in less time than it took for the ball to leave his boot on one of its unstoppable flights past Hans Tilkowski.

The death of Bobby Moore in 1993 was the saddest sign that the years had passed by all too rapidly for the Golden Boys of 1966. Players like Bobby Charlton were still household names, but most had long since lost their youthful appeal. By now all were middle-aged and contemplating parting their hair above the left ear.

Despite being given a knighthood in 1967, Sir Alf Ramsey felt badly let down by the Football Association. He had been sacked ruthlessly following the 1–1 draw against Poland on 17 October 1973, a game which had ended England's hopes of qualifying for the following year's World Cup finals in West Germany. As he began a modest retirement in Suffolk, Sir Alf also expressed his sorrow at not receiving his own medal after the 1966 epic.

His wife, Lady Vicky, said: 'It's too late now. Nothing anybody can do would make up for how he has been treated. Alf wants to be left alone, to play his golf.'

Some of the 1966 team were honoured with official titles, but only on prime ministerial whims years after the final. For Sir Alf's family, hard times came very quickly indeed. Personal tragedies afflicted the vast majority as they tried to settle into ordinary life.

Gordon Banks's outstanding goalkeeping career ended prematurely when he lost an eye in a car crash. His mesmerising one-handed save of a Pelé header in the 1970 World Cup and OBE in the same year had sealed his reputation as a footballing legend, but by 1996 he was working in corporate hospitality and living in Keele.

George Cohen suffered a crippling knee injury in 1968 and was forced to retire from football. Lengthy spells of even more serious illnesses followed, including cancer. Cohen struggled to make ends meet in the building trade and was later forced to auction his World Cup medal for £80,000 so as to afford a pension plan. He also sold his most prized international cap for £11,500 and put up for sale three West German shirts he had acquired over the years. One had been worn by Lother Emmerich during the 1966 final.

Even Bobby Moore, the Golden Boy of Golden Boys who became an OBE in 1967, found life beyond Wembley's twin towers fraught with problems. Before his death from cancer in 1993 his formerly glittering career sank to the depths of Oxford City. Even though he was surrounded by the university town's golden stone, the sight of one of the most charismatic and talented players in history managing a team of non-league amateurs was full of pathos. Things got even worse with a series of disastrous business deals, including a country club which burnt down in the middle of the night. Whether this was as serious a disaster as Moore's later incarnation as 'Mooro', sports editor of the *Sport* newspaper, is open to debate.

Ray Wilson became an undertaker following a crippling knee injury, but his decision to go into such a mournful industry was nothing to do with his 13th-minute header to Helmut Haller. He took up a post in his family firm of funeral directors before retiring to become a virtual recluse with his wife and their three dogs on a smallholding in Halifax. Wilson had also made some money from his World Cup mementoes: he auctioned an envelope sealed with a World Cup stamp and signed by Alf Ramsey.

Nobby Stiles managed Preston North End and later joined the hackneyed but lucrative trade of after-dinner speakers, making jokes about his tackles being later than the 8.15 Connex South-East service from Maidstone to Victoria. His speeches to red-faced businessmen stuffing themselves with Bombe Glacé were funny, but never produced the same sense of satisfaction as his days spent shackling foreigners with odd-sounding names. As a young man Stiles had twice reduced Eusébio, the top scorer in the 1966 tournament, to tears: once in the 26 July semi-final against Portugal and again in a Manchester United v. Benfica European Cup tie. Stiles's gritty enthusiasm for such youthful achievements was lucidly expressed by the title of his autobiography, *My Battlefield*.

Roger Hunt ran a road haulage firm in Bolton and helped out on the Pools Panel, choosing home wins, away wins, score draws or no-score draws when matches were rained off. Compared to scoring goals for Liverpool, let alone leading the England line with Geoff Hurst, it was mundane work.

Alan Ball, the youngest member of the 1966 team, lost some of the huge respect he had acquired as a player through disastrous spells in management, especially with Manchester City. At one point, Ball became so disillusioned with football that he took time off to run a pub in Stoke. He enjoyed relative success by taking Portsmouth into the old First Division for one season, but was later sacked by them (twice). Nothing could match that glorious summer when he was just 21 years old and already a World Cup winner.

The Charlton brothers fared better. Bobby was knighted in 1994 after an OBE and a CBE, and became a director of Manchester United. Personal triumphs included producing a new generation of skilful young players at his summer schools, as well as the BBC weather-forecaster Suzanne Charlton. Big Jack, who was awarded the OBE in 1974, led Ireland on two World Cup campaigns before devoting his retirement to his love of fly-fishing. Like Hurst (an MBE in 1977) and Peters (an MBE in 1978), the brothers also enjoyed regular appearances in the media.

But none of the footballers who had played their hearts out for their country received anything they had not fought for. In most cases, they received far less. Ball, Cohen, Hunt, Stiles and Wilson were still without any official decoration whatsoever by the start of the new millennium – a full 34 years since their finest two hours.

After July 1966 all were still expected to scurry and scrap for any half-chance life threw their way. Serious illness, financial ruin, family bereavements, non-league football and all the other heartbreaking realities of everyday life were as relevant to Alf Ramsey's Wingless Wonders as they were to the rest of us.

9 · Hard Time

Just as life had changed dramatically for the England team of 1966, so it had for the country in whose name the players had lifted the World Cup.

Like that of so many others, the players' recollection of the era has always been bathed in the bright sunshine which filled Wembley Stadium after hours of rain at 5.15 p.m. on 30 July 1966.

The 1960s have been endlessly mythologised – a decade perfectly summarised by short, snappy expressions like Wingless Wonders. The Swinging Sixties were the era of The Rolling Stones, the King's Road, The Beatles, Mary Quant and mini-skirts.

Just three months before the World Cup final, on 15 April 1966, Time magazine announced that London was the centre of the style world: 'This spring, as never before in modern times, London is switched on,' said the American publication. 'Ancient elegance and new opulence are all tangled up in a dazzling blur of op and pop. The city is alive with birds and Beatles, buzzing with mini-cars and telly stars, pulsing with half a dozen separate veins of excitement.'

Pop music, television, fashion and modern art were providing welcome relief from everyday problems. Like football, they were the means by which people escaped from the hardships of their day-to-day lives and the terrifying global problems of the late twentieth century. In the Britain of 1966, distraction was not a luxury. It was essential.

The Soviets, whose nuclear arsenal was a far greater threat to England's future success than their towering goalkeeper Lev Yashin, chose 1966 to stick a spacecraft on the moon. If a superpower with a political culture diametrically opposed to England's had the ability to propel its new technology beyond the stratosphere, you had to take its potential for mass destruction pretty seriously too. Our own military chiefs confidently predicted that Britain would be obliterated within three minutes of the first strike arriving from Moscow. It was reassuring to know we had such efficient strategic analysts on our side.

The Russian warheads could create a single explosion 20,000 times more powerful than that which destroyed Hiroshima – equivalent to 400 million tons of TNT. Less than a week after the 1966 World Cup final, Swedish scientists recorded a massive explosion in the Soviet underground nuclear test area in Semipalatinsk in central Asia. Thoughts of instant destruction within little more than the blast of a referee's whistle certainly put relegation worries into perspective.

The Iron Curtain, which Winston Churchill had coined in a speech in March 1946, symbolised the ideological divide between capitalism and communism. Both sides were involved in a silent war of attrition which could, at any moment, end in Mutually Assured Destruction (a defensive strategy developed by the same kind of military analysts who worked out how long it would take for the Russians to kill off all our hopes of ever winning a World Cup again).

Such a scenario instilled in the whole population the kind of fear which surpasses the uncomfortable, slightly windy stomach-churning which goes on before internationals against Germany. We were absolutely terrified.

Other disturbing international developments included the Cultural Revolution in China. Its first 30 days coincided with the start of our World Cup and did far more to worry Harold Wilson than an early Helmut Haller goal ever could. When Maoist red guards burned down the British embassy in Peking, diplomats found sinister little effigies of the Labour Prime Minister hanging on trees. These were sent back to London for analysis and the Chinese characters scrawled on the back were found to have said 'Down with Wilson' and, even more hurtfully, 'Wilson is a bastard'.

Our economic situation was as dire as President Johnson had warned Wilson the day before the World Cup final. The country was gripped by strikes and a financial crisis. In July 1966 James Callaghan, the Chancellor, introduced the pay freeze which had prompted his Prime Minister's dash to the USA. The minutes of a special cabinet meeting a few days before read: 'The prevailing lack of confidence in the British economy is due to a persistent doubt about our ability to pay our way.' A state of emergency was to be called because of the crippling 47-day Seamen's Strike. Wilson blamed it all on communist agitators.

In fact, the agitation was nothing to do with ideology – that was the whole point. Britain had suddenly lost an empire and there was a distinct lack of ideas about what to replace it with. Workmen who had so recently been acclaimed as the best in the world found themselves facing unemployment and the kind of poverty seen in the Eastern Bloc. The pound was far too strong to sustain the former workshop of the world where competitiveness with other countries – particularly Germany – was declining. Wage increases became illegal for six months. Government expenditure was cut. There were restrictions placed on loans. Nobody could take more than £50 out of the country, including the royal family.

After England's World Cup quarter-final against Argentina, the British embassy in Buenos Aires received hundreds of abusive phone calls, including fire-bomb threats. Britons were attacked by chanting and swearing youths at a trade fair. When Prince Philip was sent to try and diffuse the situation by attending a polo tournament to mark the 150th year of the Argentine Republic, 'special arrangements' had to be made to allow him to bypass the strict currency regulations.

Students all over Europe were giving up any hopes of attaining a Geoff and concentrating instead on anti-establishment violence. Instead of writing long, theoretical essays about US foreign policy, they took to the streets to beat up the police in protest against it.

The US military presence in Vietnam was quadrupled to 400,000 troops in 1966, prompting violent demonstrations all over Britain. An anti-Nam gathering outside the US embassy in Grosvenor Square in 1968 led to 300 arrests and 90 police injuries. There had also been punch-ups at Campaign for Nuclear Disarmament rallies, including the famous Aldermaston march. Interestingly, James Callaghan, who was Home Secretary by 1968, blamed German students for introducing 'new and more violent' tactics.

One of the most dramatic episodes in our 1960s decline came with the devaluation of the pound on 18 November 1967. One of the great symbols of British power and prestige – introduced when the Exchequer first came into being during the 1080s – fell from $2.80 to $2.40 in an instant. Wilson tried to fudge the issue by pretending that sterling devaluation would not affect the 'actual pound' in our 'actual pockets'. It did. Our 'actual pound' in our 'actual pockets' was worth 14 per cent less than it had been. James Callaghan, who had presided over the World Cup austerity programme, left his post 11 days later.

By the time Britain reached the 1970s, it did not even have the mystical qualities of the Swinging Sixties to see it through its troubles. Such indefinable comforts had evaporated in one too many clouds of marijuana smoke, Bob Dylan protest songs and Charles I hairdos. Even The Beatles – in their heyday Scousers as warm and affable as Roger Hunt – had turned into hippies on the verge of a drug-enhanced deterioration reflected in lyrics which were becoming more and more pretentious and flares which were becoming wider and wider.

The decade of the Wingless Wonders gave way to the decade of 'Chopper' Harris, Norman 'Bite Yer Leg' Hunter, the Sex Pistols and 'Anarchy in the UK'. It was a crass, destructive ten years within which England failed to qualify for the World Cup at all, except in 1970 as former winners.

Wilson blamed his defeat in the general election of that year on our 3–2 loss against West Germany in the World Cup quarter-final held two weeks before. By that time he had not been able to pacify workers like the militant seamen by implementing Barbara Castle's White Paper *In Place of Strife*. Trade unionists obsessed with petty bureaucracy, rigid time-keeping and mandatory tea-breaks really were running the country.

The economic malaise continued as Conservative Prime Minister Ted Heath was forced to introduce a three-day working week at the end of 1973. Powercuts meant that stadium floodlights could not be used and hundreds of midweek games had to be postponed. Desperate policies fitted in perfectly with the vision of a third-rate England which was not even good enough to make plans beyond Wednesday teatime, let alone our next World Cup appearance. Others felt 'Grocer' Heath's decision to sign our fortunes over to the European Economic Community was another sacrifice to those who believed Britain was long past its sell-by date.

The slide continued. There was an oil crisis. Taxes and unemployment continued to rise, and inflation reached double figures. In another of the most humiliating episodes in our history, the government was forced to borrow money from the International Monetary Fund. We'd gone cap in hand to the US Treasury in 1945, but at least then we had the excuse that we'd just taken part in the most destructive war in the history of the world. In 1976 the only war we'd been through was against would-be Gottfried Diensts whose power relied on beer and sandwiches at Number 10 and block votes from the 1960s student thugs now running CND.

By the end of the 1970s we really had reached rock bottom. The government completely opted out of their key ties with the unions as the 1978–79 season's Winter of Discontent turned into a time of personal discomfort and national humiliation which remained unprecedented until *Royal It's a Knockout* the following decade. There was no post, no fire service, no electricity, no rubbish collection, no hospital porters and no decent football. The most glamorous and exciting thing in the game was the trumpet fanfare on the *Match of the Day* theme tune and Jimmy Hill's beard.

The 1980s were the decade of Margaret Thatcher. It was appropriate that she had first been elected to Parliament in 1966. When she won the General Election of 4 May 1979 she immediately began implementing a Nobby Stiles approach to modern politics. The unions were hacked down as mercilessly as Jacky Simon. Britain became Thatcher's battlefield as she tackled anybody who got in her way. Her watchwords were 'personal responsibility', which meant everybody had a personal responsibility to get out of the way when her studs went flying in.

Thatcherism offered a choice to everyone: like it or lump it. All Thatcher was really interested in were those who were ready to lump it, or those who were prepared to learn how to lump it. You did not have to be weak and ineffectual to fall victim to her game plan. By the early 1980s unemployment was at an unprecedented post-war level of three and a half million and Britain's economy was still deep in recession.

We had become a standing joke and the whole world was laughing at us – even the Scandinavians. When a national side managed by Ron Greenwood lost 2–1 to Norway in Oslo on 9 September 1981, a local commentator's observations were broadcast all over the world. He shouted: 'Lord Nelson, Lord Beaverbrook, Sir Winston Churchill, Sir Anthony Eden, Clement Attlee, Henry Cooper, Lady Diana, Maggie Thatcher, can you hear me? Maggie Thatcher, your boys took a hell of a beating.'

If it had not been for the Falklands War in 1982, Mrs Thatcher might well have been substituted after the shame of Oslo. Instead she had talented but ruthlessly arrogant Argentinians like Antonio Rattin to thank for her ascendancy. The causes of the war in the South Atlantic – in which British power and prestige were briefly revived by a successful military adventure – could directly be linked to England's quarter-final victory just 16 years before.

In August 1966 Michael Stewart, our Foreign Secretary, wrote: 'Most Argentinians quite sincerely believe that the way the whole tournament was managed, or mismanaged, was a dirty business and a stain on the British reputation for sportsmanship and honesty.' He said many in Buenos Aires had described the appointment of a German, Rudolf Kreitlein (described by Brian Glanville as 'a compulsive taker of names'), to referee the game against England as a 'blatant conspiracy to defraud the South Americans'.

On the field, our trouble with the Argentinians included the 1977 friendly in Buenos Aires when Trevor Cherry had his teeth knocked out by Daniel Bertoni. Cherry was sent off. In Mexico in the 1986 World Cup we went out to Argentina. Their goals against us included the notorious 'Hand of God' tap in when Diego Maradona blatantly cheated to put his side ahead.

Had it not been for the Thatcherite lifeline of North Sea oil (it provided nine billion pounds a year in the early 1980s – equal to 8 per cent of tax revenue) Britain may well have been bankrupt by 1983. In 1987 there was a crash on the stock-market which saw share values drop by 20 per cent in two days, bottoming out at 36 per cent below their peak value. Not until 1993 did the volume of trading fully recover.

Worst of all were the thugs. Kenneth Wolstenholme's seemingly exaggerated claim that the Michael Caine lookalikes running on to the pitch in the closing seconds of the 1966 World Cup final were hooligans did not, with hindsight, appear quite so misinformed.

A proliferation of people with CFC tattoos across their forearms all contributed to the problem. By the 1970s the odd crowd disturbance had turned into stabbings and full-scale riots, as crumbling stadiums provided a perfect environment in which fans could fight.

By the 1980s football was facing a crisis. There was the Heysel disaster of 1985 when stampeding Liverpool fans forced hundreds of fleeing Juventus supporters up against a wall. It collapsed, killing dozens of Italians. In England there was the Bradford Fire disaster and then, in 1989, the Hillsborough tragedy when 96 Liverpool fans died in a crush during their team's FA Cup semi-final against Nottingham Forest in Sheffield.

A publishing industry began to spring up around the beer-swilling, violent supporters who were kicking the game to death. Academics drew a correlation between their behaviour and Britain's industrial decline. They created unconvincing theories about hooligans' alienation from a modern industrial process plunged into recession and failure by the unions, Ted Heath and James Callaghan. Sick paperbacks appeared in bookshops with titles like *Psychofan* and *Terrace Slayer*. Saturday-afternoon yobs were portrayed in television documentaries as cunning leaders of men with nicknames like 'Nightmare' and 'Nutjob'. TV investigators sketched a cartoon world full of 'generals' and 'foot soldiers' co-ordinating their violence via mobile telephones.

What these sensational caricatures failed to convey was that there was nothing vaguely complicated about football hooliganism. It was caused by lads who like beer and fighting. Britain is full of lads who like beer and fighting.

Portsmouth was one of many clubs blighted by a following of notorious 'commuters' throughout the 1970s and 1980s. In the case of the Hampshire side they called themselves the 6.57 Crew, because they always took the 6.57 a.m. train to London for away games. Sociologists, writers and investigative journalists loved the tag, and they were instantly granted notoriety as a sinister new cult. In fact, the 6.57 Crew were no different from the kind of young men Portsmouth had produced for hundreds of years. Most of their fights took place in or just outside pubs, just as they had done in the time of Charles Dickens. He was born in Portsmouth on 7 February 1812 when it was one of the most violent and unpleasant places on the south coast, full of perpetually drunk men who had fought in the Napoleonic wars. Many had been pressganged into the Battle of Trafalgar and others would fight at Waterloo in 1815.

Nowhere in England was particularly safe in the time of Dickens, least of all the ports and the overcrowded slums of industrial cities like London and Manchester. Throughout the centuries, Britain has been swarming with lads who like a drink and a punch-up. The only difference by the 1970s and 1980s was that thousands of them had latched on to the affordable distraction of football. There was nothing else to get excited about and, because there was no longer an empire, we did not have a big enough armed service to give them a sense of direction in life.

The egg-and-chip culture of the terraces became loathed and feared, especially in the Middle England towns inhabited by men like Geoff Hurst and Martin Peters. Football fans had become the lowest common denominator in British society – an unfortunate sub-class herded every weekend or weekday evening towards their crumbling stadiums with their stinking toilets and vile hotdogs. They were body-searched for sharp instruments before tedious 0–0 draws, and demonised by social commentators.

Like so many aspects of post-war Britain, there was nothing discerning or bright about watching football. You simply turned up. Football was cheap – sometimes as cheap as jumping a turnstile and never much more than the price of a pint of lager and a packet of salt-and-vinegar crisps.

Hurst sensed the game which he loved with such an innocent passion as a young man was turning into an ugly beast – the kind of cousin who's always there in the background but you don't really want to talk about, especially when you're holding down a senior position in an insurance firm.

The World Cup ball, lying deflated and discarded in some faraway cellar, did not fit into the picture. It represented a side of football and a chapter in England's history which was optimistic, heart-stopping and glorious.

When home had turned into something so unpleasant, it was almost fitting that the ball should stay as far away as possible.

10 · People's Gain

Then, in the 1990s, something changed. Just as the fall of the Berlin Wall in 1989 had signalled an end to the bitterness and hatred of Cold War rivalries, so there was a revival in the fortunes of Britain and in English football.

The fall of the graffiti-covered ideological divide was followed in 1991 by the collapse of the Soviet Union and the death of communism. The Iron Curtain was gone and strategic analysts were left trying to make sense of the numerous new republics staking a claim to representation in the world's major international football tournaments. What was most important, though, was that we all suddenly had a very good chance of avoiding sudden termination in a giant mushroom cloud of nuclear energy.

Britain's economy began to boom as students settled down to their essays about television and fast-food. Riots still went on occasionally, but were limited to London and centred on relatively uncontentious issues, like the domestic rates. Even the wars we involved ourselves in were clean ones, fought against hopelessly ill-disciplined Arabs or Slavs carrying Second World War carbines against our space-age missiles and planes.

The horrors of Hillsborough and Bradford led to Lord Justice Peter Taylor, a lawyer who had supported Newcastle United as a boy, nursing the game off its sickbed and getting it on its way with a new image of respectability. His report into the Sheffield tragedy led directly to the creation of smart all-seater stadiums complete with video-camera security systems, clean toilets and little Italian bistros serving ciabatta and Chianti.

The only reminders of the kind of conditions supporters had suffered for decades were the grease-laden fish-and-chip caravans, hotdog stands and those inbred-looking men called Sidney who always seem to be in charge of the match-day carpark.

Taylor's report changed the decaying, nasty and cheap culture which was destroying the game into something which was sophisticated, bright, entertaining ... and very, very expensive.

Rupert Murdoch, the billionaire Australian media baron, became a benefactor in the same way that John Moore's Pools empire had provided a huge cash injection into football during the 1920s. Murdoch had not been instilled with a deep love for the game inspired by a joyous childhood cheering on the Melbourne Colts, or even an Australian World Cup run. Instead, his decision to invest millions in football coverage through his satellite TV company Sky was inspired by a deep-seated love of money. He was keen to rake in as much as possible and needed the national game to launch his kind of TV.

By the last decade of the twentieth century, there was a lot of spare money in England. The country was richer than it had been since the First World War. Entrepreneurs were thriving and everywhere there were personalised car number plates, four-holidays-a-year families and cuddly pound signs hanging from Jaguar rearview mirrors. Unlike the late 1980s, it was real wealth, too; not just based on ludicrously inflated house prices and the fortunes of a few thousand computer operatives working in the City of London. Taxes were down to well below 50 per cent. People from all over the country were going on dream trips to places like the Seychelles, Bali and Barbados.

Britain was becoming a nation of small investors as millions of ordinary people funded takeovers of companies including British Telecom and British Gas. We were queuing up for financial products – unit trusts, pensions and personal equity plans – and critical illness insurance for the day we became so stupendously dull that we needed a charisma transplant.

Instead of bashing out the useful little products which had bankrolled our empire, we were dealing directly in money. By the early 1990s we were the fourth biggest economy in the world after the USA, Japan and, inevitably, Germany.

In 1990 England reached the semi-finals of the World Cup. We went out, inevitably, to Germany on penalties, but it had all been an incredible turnaround.

Football – the stuff of Boys' Own comics and sporting heroism in the 1960s – had gone through a difficult two decades before maturing into a safe, money-spinning and successful commercial product. Just like Britain itself, fans changed. Instead of clubs being forced to rely on the standard pool of retarded gardeners and unemployed pub bouncers to fill the stands, football was now attracting the professional classes: men and women who wore shirts and ties to work (and often, especially during weekday evening matches, to the games themselves). Some were people with 'Geoffs' from the better universities. As well as being bright and articulate, they had bank accounts, pensions and a vote at general elections. Even those excluded from Britain's electoral process, like members of the royal family, were taking a keen interest. Prince Harry, third in line to the throne, was regularly seen in the VIP box at Arsenal together with his friends from Eton and the legions of north London barristers who had season-tickets at Highbury. As he leapt about with his red-and-white scarf, cheering on all those 1–0 wins, Harry's joyous face provided a stark contrast to his grandmother's bored expression throughout most of the 1966 final. While the Queen had looked as though she would rather have been cleaning out a horsebox than watching 22 grown men chasing a ball, the Prince's face was always a picture of delight.

News of Prince William's birth in 1982 interrupted the World Cup match between Brazil and Russia. Prince Charles and Princess Diana's first son, who is destined to become king one day, also grew into a supporter of the game but tried very hard to keep his allegiances a secret for fear of alienating future subjects. When he was just 12 it was rumoured that he had started following Middlesbrough, but it was probably just a stage he was going through before full-blown adolescence. In the same way that juveniles are liable to go through moody and quiet spells, so Middlesbrough phases are not unheard of. With so much interest in his development, William had an extremely difficult childhood. When he was about 16 he was pictured going to a party in Gloucestershire wearing an Aston Villa bobble hat. As William approached his majority and began going out with girls, he was also linked with a string of fashionable London clubs including Chelsea and Tottenham Hotspur.

Despite such rumours, it was in fact the Villa to whom William had pledged allegiance at a very early age. Pennants emblazoned with the Birmingham side's motto – 'Prepared' – covered his bedroom wall at Eton together with a large poster of All Saints, the girl pop band.

There was nothing élitist or even inversely snobbish about football. The game made a mockery of England's traditional class divides. Whether you were living on the 16th floor of a council block or in a suite of apartments at St James's Palace, you could legitimately pull on an offensively coloured, starchy shirt and become a real supporter. The new fans were the Acrylics – a united people unconcerned with the traditional divisions of history, whether they were manifested in place of residence, regional accent or type of woollen headgear.

Murdoch's Sky Sports was beaming matches into homes all over Britain for a subscription which worked out at considerably less than a pint of lager and packet of crisps per game. If you enjoyed all those third-division play-off matches they showed on a Sunday morning, the cost was even less than a packet of crisps.

New fans could call themselves Everton supporters even if they lived in Billericay. If they were Manchester United supporters it was almost expected that they lived in Billericay. Satirical magazines called fanzines were produced by supporters at every club. Humorous TV shows like Frank Skinner and David Baddiel's *Fantasy Football* won cult audiences. Established figures like Melvyn Bragg, a peer and an Arsenal supporter, began applying their distinguished brains to the game, rather than to the over-long documentaries about obscure poets and lesbian filmmakers which normally occupied their attention.

Almost every celebrity supported a football team. There was Sir Richard Attenborough of Chelsea and Hugh Grant of Fulham. Men of God provided a spiritual lead and sealed the game's new-found respectability. The Archbishop of Canterbury, George Carey, was an Arsenal fan. Cardinal Basil Hume, the Archbishop of Westminster and the spiritual leader of Britain's Roman Catholics, was a Newcastle fan. As church attendances dropped, hundreds of thousands of people found their spiritual release at the new, all-seater stadiums or watching third-division play-offs on Sunday morning TV.

The glory game of the 1960s became a Glory, Glory Hallelujah game. It represented all the religious values of hard work, teamwork, strength of character, respect for others and lucrative collection plates. It was about togetherness and love – especially between those on high enough salary levels.

Players began writing touchy-feely autobiographies, books about loving hugs and tears. When Paul Gascoigne broke down and cried during England's World Cup semi-final against Germany in 1990, he was metaphorically embraced by a million counsellors who already provided a sensitive ear to an increasingly emotionally drained and misty-eyed population.

Off the field, retired professionals built careers in the media. Men like Gary Lineker were refined and bright. They were able to provide an analysis of the game which was as thoughtful and well articulated as that of New Chelsea fan David Mellor, a barrister and former government minister. Presenting *Match of the Day* on 29 January 2000, Lineker described how Mark Lawrenson and Trevor Brooking were preparing to 'eulogise' about the day's games. He described the tie between Premiership side Sheffield Wednesday and underdogs Gillingham as 'a quintessential FA Cup tie'. The ex-player's language was free of all the old 'half-time banter' and 'at the end of the day' clichés which had seen the profession pilloried for so long. Like many of the new Acrylics, those behind the game of football looked smart and respectable, and sounded as though their education had extended far beyond the confines a grass field.

11 · Blair Play

Foremost among the new class of football fan was an aspiring young politician called Tony Blair. On 30 July 1966 he had been on a foreign holiday with his family. It was his last summer of freedom before starting public school, but he would rather have been at home.

'I have many, many things to thank my parents for but their holiday plans for the summer of 1966 are not among them,' said Blair. 'We were in France. Like any 13-year-old without a ticket, I was glued to the television and driven by adrenaline.'

Even as early as his first teenage year, the young Blair was influenced by the short, snappy phrases which later became eternally associated with the contest being played out on the flickery black-and-white television in front of him. Of Kenneth Wolstenholme's famous 'They think it's all over' line, the future Labour Prime Minister said: 'One of the most famous soundbites of all time is born and the country erupts into street parties and wild celebrations.' He went on: 'The fact that I could only imagine the scene did not prevent me from sharing the delirium.'

Although the Conservative-voting Leo Blair had first taken his seven-year-old son to Newcastle United's St James's Park, one cannot imagine that football played a particularly important role in the traditional middle-class upbringing of a classic British public-schoolboy. At Durham Cathedral Choir School Blair's energies were directed towards the more traditional activities associated with aspiring young choristers, like singing. He also excelled at Latin, rugby and cricket.

There was certainly no football at the place he went to after the 1966 final. Kimmerghame, Blair's boarding house at Edinburgh's Fettes College, was more a training ground for the battlefields of northern France than a relaxed home-from-home where teenagers could chat about the Magpies' FA Cup prospects over the latest edition of *Shoot!* magazine. It had no carpets, the walls were whitewashed and unwelcoming, and the dormitories were so cold and draughty that boys often wore their rugby shirts in bed.

Fagging was acceptable, and the young Blair found himself 'dedicated' to Mike Gascoigne, later to became a senior partner in a firm of Edinburgh solicitors. Blair would 'blanco' his army belt and polish all the brass buttons on his uniform. 'He was willing and efficient,' Gascoigne later recalled, in the sinister tones of a mature Flashman.

It was at Fettes that Blair developed an upper-crust accent which allowed educated locals to differentiate his classmates from boys who went to Watson's or Broughton, the other exclusive schools in the area. Although he later adopted a mode of speech which socio-linguists would probably dub 'Refined Estuary' – more Des O'Connor than Leslie Phillips – it is unlikely that Blair's excited teenage voice would have gone down very well on a packed St James's Park terrace during the grim days of the early 1970s. The thought of the Fettes scholar joining in the joshing and banter after a disputed goal in a north-east derby match against Sunderland is an unlikely one. 'Now, look,' Blair would probably have said. 'I didn't go into football to put up with ludicrous decisions like that. I don't care that it is a referee we're dealing with, I'll be doing everything I can to reverse the worst effects of his abysmal record of failure.'

At St John's College, Oxford, Blair wore a Charles I haircut and formed a rock band called Ugly Rumours. He listened to Dylan, Led Zep, The Beatles and The Rolling Stones. For a long-haired '70s student, university was all about analysing the class system over endless cups of black coffee in ancient rooms smelling of aromatic candles and stale socks. Sweeper systems and flat back fours played no part in Blair's three years of gilded privilege beneath the dreaming spires.

Even in Paris, where he spent a year after Oxford, there were no Saturday-afternoon excursions to Gallic football matches. His flirtation with traditional working-class lifestyles only extended as far as serving Kir Royales to American tourists, and small glasses of *anise* to moody Frenchmen in one of the single-figure-*arrondissement* bars. Like so many other young Englishmen before him, Blair also used his time in the French capital to experiment; not so much with existentialist thought and women called Cherie around the Bois de Boulogne, but certainly with flared jeans and pretentious lyric recitals in Montparnasse.

The legal Bar followed, but in Blair's day barristers' leisure hours were more likely to involve long country walks with wet-nosed Labradors called Biffer than north London derbies between Arsenal and Tottenham Hotspur. An early marriage to Cherie Booth and the duties of fatherhood meant even less opportunity to concentrate on football, even had he had the inclination to attend games in the first place.

There was never any time for football but, throughout his early life, Blair epitomised a period when popular culture began to challenge the traditional

British values of conservatism. As he grew up, discreet understatement and an overriding respect for authority were replaced by self-expression and an over-whelming need for millions of people to make themselves heard.

The kind of grey, middle-aged politicians who had sat around the VIP box at Wembley smoking their pipes and cigars in between boring, statistic-based speeches and two-day-long cabinet meetings did not have a part to play in Blair's vision of a new Britain. As a child he had been far more interested in Bobby Moore and Uwe Seeler than Harold Wilson or Ludwig Erhard.

As he was to announce in Stevenage during his 1997 general election campaign, Blair was a product of the rock 'n' roll generation; a man who could embrace the finest aspects of the new, swinging culture and produce a Cool Britannia which the world would look up to – even the arrogant, Gitane-smoking young men on scooters who used to come into his Paris bar to patronise him.

By 1996 Blair was leader of Her Majesty's Opposition and just a year away from his landslide election victory. It was a time when he realised that the revitalised sport of football was all about the new Britain he represented – it was respectable, aspirational and affluent and, most important of all, it was popular.

Aside from a few outings to St James's Park and his adulation of the 1966 England team in front of a crackling French television, Blair's greatest footballing influence was his close friend and official spokesman, Alastair Campbell. Unlike Blair, Campbell was a thoroughbred, old-fashioned football fan. Not even a Cambridge University education had dimmed his passion for Burnley. Throughout the egg-and-chip days of the 1970s and '80s he had stood on crumbling terraces, gnawing away at meatless pies while violent hooligans with stinking, alcohol-filled breath stood by. Campbell had relieved himself in urine-flooded communal toilets, scraped layers of police horse manure off his Doc Marten boots and watched as skinheads with BFC tattooed across their forearms had laid into other fans whose only crime was that they had been born in Walsall.

Like all fans of the era – especially those whose side had not won the Championship since 1960 – Campbell suffered the indignities of his chosen leisure activity with a quiet humility. On 9 May 1987 he had stood open-mouthed as Burnley beat Orient 2–1 to avoid dropping out of the professional game completely. Campbell's nerve endings did not receive a similar onslaught until a decade later, when he became one of the architects of Labour's general election victory.

Although occasionally finding solace at the bottom of a wine or whisky bottle, Campbell never became involved in the vandalism and organised fighting so prevalent when terrace culture was held in less esteem by the British public than almost any other part of day-to-day life, including armed robbery and the financial services industry. Instead he only got involved in the occasional punch-up through his work as a tabloid-newspaper journalist. It was while working for the *Daily Mirror* in the House of Commons that Campbell landed one on a bald know-it-all from the *Guardian* whose accent would have gone down well at Fettes in the late 1960s. With one well-placed smack to the jaw he finally had a right of reply to the thousands of self-indulgent essays churned out by the woolly-scarved misfits who patronise and sneer in the name of British liberalism six days a week.

Campbell knew that the language of the terrace was not just the only one *Guardian* journalists would understand. He also knew it was the one which the whole of Britain could understand. The Prime Minister's official spokesman was a man of the football world who knew how to fight hard, talk hard, drink hard and play hard. He was to teach the more sensitive Blair how he could take the best aspects of terrace culture and turn them to huge electoral advantage.

Like Denis Howell in the 1960s, Campbell saw football as the people's game. The difference was that under New Labour it really did become the people's game. Campbell's genius was that he thought in tabloid headlines. He embraced the power of football in exactly the same way as he had embraced the power of the popular press: to influence people, to make them feel wanted and to win their support.

Blair was told that there was far more to being a football supporter than taking part in contrived photo opportunities heading the ball to Kevin Keegan. Campbell taught Britain's first Labour prime minister for 18 years how to talk football. Out went the Fettes drawl to be replaced by the Refined Estuary twang, with plenty of dropped Hs and answers which trailed off into nothing if interview questions became too hard. He taught Blair to say 'Now, come on' a lot, as if he'd been asked if he was about to snap up that big Italian centre-half we'd all heard so much talk about.

Blair learned to wink and smile his huge, cheeky grin whenever the word 'speculation' was bandied about. He displayed mild annoyance with the words 'Now, look' and used cheap, easily understood phrases like 'So yer pays yer money and yer takes yer choice'. There were also plenty of references to 'getting us out of this mess' and sentences which started with 'Now, the fact of the matter is' and 'Frankly'.

Blair spoke of 'fairness' in the same way that football commentators, notably Ron Atkinson, use the expression 'to be fair' a lot. He used the word 'inclusiveness' in the same way that chirpy football managers promise all their players are members of the squad, even the over-paid Italian centre-half with the ridiculous ponytail and attitude problem.

Blair had no wish to style himself as an international statesman in the style of Churchill and Adenauer, or, to a lesser extent, Wilson and Erhard. He was an 'ordinary dad' who took his 'football-crazy kids' for Saturday-morning kick-abouts. He was proud to alter the legend 'Football's Coming Home' to 'Labour's Coming Home'.

He did not just talk a good game either. Campbell taught Blair to be as ruthless and firm as a BFC skinhead faced with an unvandalised and unpoliced British Rail compartment on a train travelling from Burnley to Swindon.

His huge, flashing white teeth and no-nonsense language came into their own at the Winter Gardens, Blackpool, in October 1994, when he abandoned Clause 4 of his party's constitution, so ending its commitment to nationalise 'yer means of production, distribution and exchange'.

I was standing at the back of the auditorium with an Old Labour official representing a branch of the TGWU near Birmingham. As Blair began to savage the centre of the union man's world, the small, bespectacled figure beside me collapsed on to the red carpet below him and began to weep. The thin black moustache on his upper lip appeared to crumple onto his deathly white face, as he let out a hysterical shriek. It was a display as pitifully sad as the sight of a Ukrainian émigré who had come to grief under on a bowl of steaming sauerkraut. I looked from left to right, desperately wondering what to do, but everyone else in the huge room was engrossed in Blair's speech and completely ignored him. After a couple of minutes I gave the union man's Gannex raincoat a gentle kick. He got up, looking as sheepish as he had done before he fell down.

Of course, the whole point of Blair's football-speak was that everyone, including over-emotional trade union activists from the Black Country, were in his team. His politics were about creating a society to which everybody belonged: one completely united, irrespective of accent or facial hair.

Football was a perennial theme in Blair's vision of a united Britain. Even when he went on his annual holiday to Tuscany, the people's game was uppermost in his mind. In deference to all the massively rich Arsenal-supporting barristers from Islington who also spend their summers in that part of Italy, Blair once took part in a five-a-side game against the local police. It was in August 1997 and, appropriately enough, he was wearing a number 10 shirt when he turned out on a ground close to his hideaway villa in the Tuscan hills, near San Grimignano. His 13-year-old son Euan wore a number 10 shirt too in the colours of Helmut Haller's old club, Bologna. It had been signed by

Roberto Baggio, whose penalty miss in the 1994 World Cup final meant Italy lost the World Cup to Brazil. Blair's second son, Nicky, aged 11, also played and watched his father score two impressive goals in a game which ended 5–5.

Then there were penalties. Incredibly for an England side playing abroad, the Blairs did us proud and we tied 7–7.

More than his election win in 1997, the zenith of Blair's devotion to football came at the 1999 party conference in Bournemouth. Again I stood at the back of the auditorium, next to a shiny-suited computer programmer from Bracknell this time. Blair admitted lying awake at night worrying about the really important things in life, like the state of the economy, the impasse in Anglo-Irish negotiations over Ulster, the Balkans bombings . . . and Newcastle United's relegation prospects. Despite what seemed like an unstoppable run by a people's prime minister surging forward in the name of the people's game with his people's press secretary behind him, I still had grave doubts about Blair's true love for football.

I was also in the Trimdon Labour Club, bang in the middle of Blair's Sedgefield constituency, on the night of the Labour landslide at the end of the 1996–97 season. Locals, mostly Newcastle or Sunderland fans, had always been a bit suspicious of his footballing credentials, so I carried out some independent research of my own. I spoke to ten constituents, ranging in age and social type from a 42-year-old unemployed miner to an 84-year-old pensioner, asking them a series of questions about the man who had been their MP for 14 years. They offered supportive, positive answers to the predictable, dull questions like 'Do you think Mr Blair will be good thing for the economy?'. When, however, I asked them which team Blair supported, seven did not know, or thought he supported Sunderland. One even said Coventry City, but he was called Sidney and looked as though he might be in charge of the carparking at St James's Park. Just 30 per cent of Blair's own people knew which team he supported. My worst fears were confirmed.

When I told the 84-year-old grandmother how wrong she had been, she replied: 'Well, he's just like all the politicians.' When I asked what she meant by that, she replied: 'He's a crafty little booger.'

For the entire previous month I had been sitting on Blair's Battlebus, a coach which toured the country trying to whip up electoral support in between stopping at depressing lay-bys somewhere near Wolverhampton so that we could all have picnic meals involving even more depressing tuna-and-diesel-fume sandwiches.

I was introduced to the would-be prime minister for the first time at a reception held at Birmingham's Hyatt Hotel on 13 April 1997. Instead of a suit and tie, Blair was dressed casually in an open-collared check shirt with a Man At C&A jumper thrown casually over his shoulders, as if he was in a Home Counties golf club bar. He was sipping Budweiser from the bottle as John Williams, who was then political editor of the *Daily Mirror*, said, 'Peter, let me introduce you to Tony. Tony, this is Peter.'

'Hi, nice to see yer,' said Tony, lifting his beer bottle cheerfully and nodding pleasantly.

'Hello,' I replied, twisting my mouth awkwardly into a half-smile.

There was silence for two seconds before Blair furrowed his brow and exclaimed, 'Bloody hard work, this.' He was trying the Bill Shankly on me – gritty and in control.

There was another two-second silence.

I'd spent three weeks listening to Blair giving an average of six speeches and a dozen interviews a day. He'd ranted on for hours and hours about the profits of the privatised utilities and class sizes for five-, six- and seven-year-olds. He'd used the words 'Now, look' over and over again. He'd furrowed his brow. He'd showed off his huge teeth with the slight chip on one of the forward molars. He'd run his fingers through his hair.

There in front of me was the future successor of Pitt, Lloyd George and Attlee. He was the statesman who would be guiding my country into a new millennium. He was a future world leader whom I could not think of a single thing to ask. We stared at each other for what seemed like two Parliaments.

I vaguely thought of bringing up the future prospects of Britain's eight-, nine- and ten-year-olds, but thought that would be disrespectful. Blair's brow was getting closer and closer to the lower half of his face, and his teeth were beginning to sink deeper and deeper into his lower lip. He stared from left to right in a rather statesman-like way, considering he was locked into a vaguely embarrassing social situation in a hotel bar in central Birmingham.

Then it happened. I looked into his eyes, smiled a full-blown, Tony Blair kind of a smile and said: 'What about your team, Mr Blair, how are they getting on?'

Confident and ever in command, he steadied himself and began to pontificate in the style of Alex Ferguson. 'Oh, I think they're coping very well,' he replied, appearing to warm to me. 'It's been a tough few weeks for them but the big test isn't too far away now and they're all ready for the challenge. Now, look, I'm not saying this thing is going to be easy, but we're organised and ready for anything come May.'

I thought this an odd answer, considering that at the time the Magpies had as much chance as Dynamo Dresden of rising to an end-of-season challenge like the FA Cup.

Then it dawned on me. He wasn't talking about Newcastle United but about Alastair Campbell and the young shiny suits who were guiding him on every one of his dreary motorway miles to 10 Downing Street.

This was a man who spoke football, who acted football, who even played football. What he was not, however, was a man who *felt* football.

In spite of such disappointments there was no doubt that Blair was at the forefront of football's newfound respectability; a new fan maybe, but one who would be embraced by all who had the game's best interests at heart. In towns like Walton-on-Thames the new class of football fan was never more obvious. Men and women who had previously spent their weekends playing golf, pottering around in their half-acre gardens or adding up their personal equity, were instead following the fortunes of Premier League sides and the national team.

Geoff Hurst, who was still regularly being interviewed by the press and broadcasting media, said he was delighted with the way the game had developed. 'As far as I can ascertain the future is looking very good indeed for football,' he said.

Hurst said the revival might even give England the confidence to win a major competition in the coming years. An eternal gentleman, he said he was grateful for all the good things the game had given him, and that he would not have changed a minute of his professional career, nor anything which came afterwards. Except, that is, for one thing.

When he was interviewed by *Total Football* magazine, Hurst said that there was one huge blot on an otherwise golden past. For the first time in 30 years, he admitted that he had lost something which meant the world to him. He had not seen it for 29 summers and he had no idea where it was. It might sound silly to some, said Hurst, but his numerous goals, medals, trophies, shares and unit trusts could not cover up for a gaping hole in his life.

The loss of his amber ball had caused as much sadness in Geoff Hurst's life as it had once caused an entire nation.

12 · Ball Story

Helmut Haller was able to look back on 30 years of English failure with a feeling of immense satisfaction. Those despondent German faces in the Wembley dressing-room had indeed been revitalised. The amber ball's epic symbolism had seen them animated into an expression of joy which can only come from ultimate success.

The entire nation had worn exactly the same expression of smiling ecstasy when the young Kaiser, Franz Beckenbauer, held the new World Cup trophy high above his head at the Olympic Stadium in Munich in the summer of 1974. Just eight years after the country's unjust humiliation in London, West Germany had re-established its rightful position as the finest team on earth.

In the ensuing years success followed upon success. There were more famous victories in World Cups and European Cups, as the legendary white shirts became associated with late equalisers and scrambled winners in extra time. Their last reign as world champions had ended as recently as 1994. Germany's win in Italy in 1990 had been a typically hard-fought, scrappy but ultimately successful battle against a mob of pugnacious Argentinians. Again it had been Kaiser Franz – once a prodigy like Mozart but now a steely-eyed manager with rimless spectacles and a check jacket – who had presided over his team's second World Cup final victory in just 16 years. They had also been finalists in 1982, against Italy, and in 1986, against Argentina.

Best of all, though, had been the successes against the English. They had started unspectacularly with a 1–0 win in a friendly in Hanover in 1968, but had got better and better as the 1970s, '80s, and '90s progressed.

The pledge made by 11 weary Teutons in front of an amber talisman glowing in the half-light of their Wembley changing-room in 1966 steadied them through some of the bitterest contests ever seen in the history of the international game. The games were still about so much more than football, and Haller was convinced it was the historic ball's power which made the difference as 31 years of hurt were wiped away.

How else could Germany have come back to win 3–2 after being 2–0 down against an England side still managed by the indomitable Alf Ramsey in Leon, Mexico, on 14 June 1970? The 1966 winners had been well on their way to retaining the Jules Rimet trophy. They still had immovable defenders like

Bobby Moore at the back and, even when Gordon Banks was replaced by Peter Bonetti, there appeared no possibility of them losing. Something far more mysterious than the familiar German goalscorers Uwe Seeler, Franz Beckenbauer and Gerd Muller had ensured a German recovery. Their spectacular triumph in the searing Mexican heat really was nothing less than a miracle.

Geoff Hurst, who had not been anywhere near the amber ball for four years, described the game as the low point of his career: 'After I left Leon I drove back to Mexico City and spent seven hours thinking. Even when I got there I had not taken it in. We were two up. Coasting. And yet we were out.'

And what was it that gave the Germans the almost supernatural power to win the first leg of the European Championship qualifier at Wembley on 29 April 1972? Ramsey marshalled his English lions superbly, but still the Germans won by three goals to one.

Then there was that night in Turin on 4 July 1990 when an England victory in the semi-final of the World Cup had seemed inevitable. Gary Lineker's equaliser to made the score 1–1 had been a magnificent contrast to the lucky deflection which ensured Germany's opener. What was it that caused two talented and intelligent England players to miss hopelessly during the penalty shoot-out after extra time and allow Germany to go on to win their third World Cup?

Haller knew the amber ball would ensure a German triumph in that summer's European Championships because it was within the 31-year time limit, but he still felt uneasy. There would be further games against the English in the new millennium, and who knew how they might turn out.

Despite its unquestionable power, Haller had always felt uncomfortable in the ball's presence. He was happy about what it represented and was more than glad that he had brought it to the Fatherland, but did not like to spend too much time in front of its majestic glow. In fact, after flying from Heathrow to Frankfurt the day after the defeat, he made sure that it did not play any part in the open-topped car drive around the city. Hundreds of thousands turned out to cheer the heartbroken German team, but few of the 11 players felt like celebrating and were more likely to comment on the missing Jules Rimet trophy than the missing football. Later Haller stuck the ball in a discarded hold-all and left it with a pile of studless football boots and old magazines in a cupboard in his home.

On 8 August 1966 there was a brief shock when Sir Stanley Rous, President of the International Football Federation, said he wanted to buy the ball from Germany for £5,000. Sir Stanley said he was going to auction it and give the proceeds to Oxfam, the overseas aid charity. Haller knew the ball was worth a lot more than that, especially with the pound on the verge of being devalued. He declined the offer through the German FA and, somewhat surprisingly, Sir Stanley was incredibly gracious about the whole thing. The Englishman agreed that 'in accordance with custom' it should remain with the losing side who had scored first.

Every time the Hallers moved house, he had got a removal man to carry the hold-all for him. He would watch intently to make sure that the ball was treated with due reverence, especially in Italy where removal men have as much respect for treasured family possessions as did the Visigoths who sacked their capital city thousands of years before.

Twice the ball had been tossed around Bologna and Milan as if it was involved in a cup tie between ancient civilisations, but Haller always made sure that he was a fitting custodian for such a historic treasure.

Whenever they could, cleaning ladies would give the ball a rub with a cloth. No polishing agents were allowed, just in case the leather was harmed any more than it had been on 30 July 1966. Haller was also contantly worried about the signatures, including those of Moore and Seeler. He'd only had a cheap hotel pen on him at the gala banquet after the final and, inevitably, the ink had begun to fade as the years went by. The amber glow, however, had not.

The year after the 1966 final, Haller had presented the ball to his son Jurgen as a present for his fifth birthday. This did not, of course, mean the boy was allowed to take it out of its hold-all and start playing with it, but Haller thought his child was old enough to start appreciating its significance in the illustrious career of his modest father. It would be something he could look up to when he started going to school. *Gymnasiums* were not solely about dull maths classes and turning out a new generation of technocrats ready to dominate Europe with their forward-thinking know-how. Little Jurgen would also be taught all about his dad's appearance in three World Cups, his extraordinary club form and, of course, the Wembley opener of 1966 which moved an English queen to hide her regal scowl behind a pair of dark glasses.

In 1967 Haller stared down at the little boy desperately trying to take the amber ball into the back garden and play with it. 'Nein,' snapped Haller, gently telling his son off. How could he think of playing with a piece of history? Did he think fifth birthday parties were all about trite games and childish revelry?

As Jurgen grew up, his father told him more and more about the ball. He made it the centrepiece of what seemed like a thousand long-winded recreations of the best goal ever scored at Wembley. It also figured in infinite explanations of other personal triumphs and numerous anecdotes drawn from an illustrious professional career spanning three glorious decades and a hat-trick of World Cups.

But as Jurgen got older he could tell there was something about the ball, now hidden in the family's cellar in Augsburg, which worried his father. It was something about the way he never wanted to see it, let alone play with it. Jurgen recalled his childhood tears when he had been so keen to produce a goal of his own using the amber ball, even if it had been between two jackets in the local park. Later, the rapidly maturing teenager sensed in his father an over-bearing antipathy towards using the icon for a game of headers and volleys in the garden. His father, a firm but fair disciplinarian, always used uncharac-teristically harsh language to make sure the ball was kept well out of sight.

It reaffirmed Jurgen Haller's niggling belief that, for the population of an entire country, it might have been far better in the long term if the ball had never been anywhere near Helmut Haller at all.

The English had to hand back the World Cup in 1970. The Jules Rimet trophy was given permanently to Brazil to mark their third outright victory in the championships, but before it could be presented to them, it had been stolen and melted down. That kind of thing happened all the time in shoddy, second-rate countries, thought Haller, but it was sad that a nation like England should be deprived of a tangible and awe-inspiring souvenir to mark the most important triumph in their history.

For the country of the great Queen Victoria and Albert, her German prince, life had been bleak and uninspiring for far too long. And, just as Britain had begun to emerge from a slump, so the Germany of the 1990s was experi-encing serious problems of its own. The country's post-war economic miracle had led to standards of living undreamt of outside the USA, but Erhard's *Wirtschaftswunder* was long gone. It had been replaced by an economy hampered by enormous social costs. The federal republic was struggling to support an overweight and whinging population who were living beyond their means and not working hard enough. Their aspirations towards brash consumer goods made the hopes and dreams of over-sentimental Americans sound like those of a friary full of Franciscan monks. Worse than that, the new Germans wanted long holidays and retirements within which to enjoy their turbo-charged dishwashers and computerised cabbage-cutters.

Many of the pampered student rebels who had brought so much discord to Germany and the rest of Europe in the 1960s were now in positions of power. They had been only too happy to preside over the liberalisation of society, encouraging free thought and self-promotion. 'I want to make the world a better place for me to live in,' became the rallying cry of the new Germans.

Their contemporary philosophy was centred on a handful of inalienable rights – principally index-linked state pensions, profit-sharing schemes and six weeks' holiday a year. In Bavaria alone there were an extra 14 public holidays as well, including one to celebrate the end of the Thirty Years War.

The German worker, for so long the most expensive in the world, was becoming fatter and lazier. In 1993 his average hourly rate was £16.45. Workers in Britain were charging just £9.80 an hour. The previous year Mercedes Benz had announced that its profits were down by 45 per cent. Its executives were alarmed to discover that their production costs were 35 per cent higher than they would have been in Japan. Yet the paternalistic firm was still buying church dresses and blazers for the children of its Roman Catholic employees who were getting confirmed. Gross domestic product began to tumble as unemployment rose. Periodic slumps meant tax increases to try and combat the gaping budget deficit. Revisionists were already starting to put the blame on 'Rubber Lions' like Erhard who, they claimed, had initiated stop-gap economic solutions for which the whole country was now paying. The situation prompted Helmut Kohl, the Chancellor, to announce in 1993: 'A successful industrial nation, which means a nation with a future, doesn't allow itself to be organised as a collective amusement park.'

Worst of all, there were the 'Ossies'. These were the eastern hordes who swarmed over the Berlin Wall when it came down in 1989. They came over faster than defecting Olympic athletes of the old East who regularly sprinted across No-Man's-Land with a heavily armed detachment of the Friedrich Engels Honour Guard urging them to shave a few seconds off the 200-metre record. With the collapse of the Soviet Union two years later, there had been even more of them, desperately relying on prosperous Westerners like Helmut Haller for their future well-being. They were becoming the workforce of the new Germany, taking up menial jobs as moody cooks and bumbling carpark attendants.

The cost of absorbing 17 million East German citizens, many packed into Trabant cars, and millions of other immigrants was unimaginable. West Germany had grown by 40 per cent, but most of the new territory was grey, bleak and inhospitable. The people were even worse.

When 144 members of the East German Parliament took their place in the Bundestag there was not a single smart check jacket or pair of rimless spectacles to be seen. Instead, the Ossie politicians turned up in imitation leather jackets imported from Turkey, stonewashed jeans which looked hand-made, and chunky trainers straight off the terraces at Dresden Dynamo's home monolith. They soon became known as 'concrete heads' in recognition of their contribution to the disastrous state they had presided over when they had tried to force 'Real Existing Socialism' on a workforce, members of whom did not know what many kinds of fruit looked like, let alone a turbo-charged dishwasher or computerised cabbage-cutter. Imagine trying to explain the subtleties of Stalin's branch of Marxist communism to an Ossie who had not yet got to grips with the banana.

When nostalgic Easterners spoke about the good old days, they recalled an era of murder and forced labour on an untold scale. As a state, East Germany would have won the World Cup for human misery. Its economy was bankrupt after years of producing very little apart from millions of overpaid spies not qualified to do very much except watch out for indications of capitalist decay, like Dutch pornographic magazines and Italian football videos. The Stasi told everyone to keep quiet about everything, particularly their average annual wage which, at £4,000 at the end of the 1980s, was not enough to qualify for tax in the West.

Their towns and cities weren't just old in an atmospheric, guidebook kind of way; they were falling down. Some western economies might have experienced galloping inflation, but the East had been all about galloping dilapidation. Litter lay everywhere. Fresh concrete, of which there was much, would be covered in graffiti before the night curfew had been called. Traffic-calming methods were unheard of, mainly because the cars could barely reach 30mph. Even at top speed they would get stuck behind an armoured convoy on its way to suppress a frisky satellite state. The Ossies did not bother with pooper-scoopers because the piles of dog excrement everywhere made no difference whatsoever to the overall ambience of the place.

Although the fall of the Berlin Wall on 9 November 1989 was a welcome end to the Cold War, it meant an influx of millions of the poor, blighted, hugely expensive Ossies. People like Ukrainian chefs and waiters who had previously derided the West as decadent and weak were now signing up for the jobs and welfare packages which would finance their first banana.

There was a genuine fear that Germany was well on its way to becoming a *Kaput* nation, just a few years away from the monetary collapse, mass unemployment and even more demonic terrors which had grown out of the impotent politics of the Weimar Republic.

Helmut Haller, once a shining soccer knight blazing his country's determined path into a brave and ultimately glorious new era, was only too well aware of its apparent slide into mediocrity. Already there was a downturn in the number of people eating out. Normally, Haller could only attract around ten people for a hearty plate of sauerkraut followed by a thick wurst sausage at lunchtime. It wasn't a crisis yet, but national consumption of brains and offal was down as well. Haller's pension fund was getting smaller and his share options were plunging, too. Staff were becoming more expensive to hire, and even those whom he could attract appeared to be unstable psychopaths obsessed with swinging pepper pots around their heads.

The ball had provided so much in terms of footballing power and prestige. Was it possible that, in some strange way, it was helping to contribute to the current decline? A shiver went up Haller's back. It was as tingling and meaningful as the apparent charge of electricity which passed through the fingers of Martin Peters when he scored a goal 13 minutes before the final whistle of his greatest-ever match. The England midfielder thought the shiver meant his team was on the verge of winning the 1966 World Cup final.

For Haller, the feeling was far more unsettling.

13 · Second Coming

By the time the eternally modest Geoff Hurst made his first public comment on the missing ball, it was the summer of 1996. The European Championships, the biggest and most prestigious football tournament apart from the World Cup, was to be held in England. A worldwide audience of seven billion would be watching, compared to the 400 million who watched the World Cup when it was played here.

Unlike 1966, when Harold Wilson funded the whole thing with money we did not have, this time the Football Association would be paying. The Queen would be attending her first football competition for 30 years and presenting the trophy at the final. Politicians including John Major and Helmut Kohl would be putting pressing political problems to one side and going to as many games as possible. The Royal Garden Hotel in Kensington would be the main base for the competition. When the Italian team tried to reserve their favoured hotel near Manchester, they found the Germans had had it booked since the year before.

For the second time in history, the home of football would once more be at the centre of the international game. The country needed a pertinent symbol of its greatest sporting triumph, a symbol of the new order within the game and the new fans who were supporting it. The amber ball fitted the bill perfectly. What better representative of English football than an English football itself? Not just any ball, of course, but the most famous and inspired ball in the history of the game. The people who could return Hurst's ball to its rightful home at such an important time in its history would be tapping into the *Zeitgeist* of the entire nation. Millions of overpriced-season-ticket holders and armchair fans would be looking up and taking notice. Whether they were Labour leaders or unemployed miners who thought their Magpies-obsessed MP was a Sunderland supporter, they were all wearing the same replica shirt. A victory on behalf of Geoff Hurst would be a victory for Acrylics high and low, rich and poor.

Broadcasters had also become obsessed with the sport. Television and radio knew it was the key to huge ratings made up of audiences from every social group, especially ABC1s with large disposable incomes. Like Tony Blair, they realised there was far more to football than sheepskin-coated commentators droning on about how difficult it is to go to Norway in September and get a result, or saying, 'What was that all about?' as an England player lay crumpled by the side of the pitch following an off-the-ball incident with an Argentine defender. Regular news bulletins on the BBC and ITN started to feature football stories and big-match build-ups for the first time – often as their lead items.

Newspapers had always been loyal. They had stuck to the game through the dark days of the 1970s and '80s when football was a cheap, beer-stained pastime associated with stinking fast-food and non-flush piss trenches. Its renaissance simply increased excitement on the back pages and convinced editors that they had been right to support the sport for so long. With the new, more sophisticated fans reading as much as they could, however, editors knew it was no longer enough to provide dreary match reports, laboriously describing the motion of balls through the air as they travelled goalward. News stories, issues and talking points became just as important.

Football was becoming one of the most interesting forms of human activity in Britain, which was not difficult considering how bland everything else had become. Despite an upturn in fortunes, consensus politics had replaced the radicalism and divisive issues of the three previous decades.

On 31 March 1990 a march on Downing Street had turned into a riot in which more than 130 people were injured. The baying mob of 50,000 also found time to cripple 20 police horses, damage 40 shops and destroy millions of pounds worth of property. All kinds of people took part, including the pampered sons and daughters of the 1960s student radicals who had turned such formerly respectable names as Grosvenor Square into bywords for anti-establishment mayhem. But this time there was a huge difference. Instead of a violently expansionist American foreign policy or weapons of mass destruction, the political protesters of the 1990s were complaining about something far more mundane. The riot which centred on Trafalgar Square had been a mass explosion of popular dissent – aimed at the way in which people funded local council services including refuse collection, street-lighting and keeping the pavements free of dog excrement.

The so-called Poll Tax riot was the clearest signal that England had become exceptionally bland and pedestrian. We were all starting to agree about everything: the type of economy we wanted, the way we negotiated our salaries and working conditions, the acceptable levels of force we could use against Ukrainian caterers claiming political asylum.

Traditional Labour voters were finding themselves in agreement with the Conservative Party over almost everything apart from pinstriped suits and double chins. Traditional Conservative politicians were finding themselves in agreement with the Labour Party over most things too, apart from combat trousers and cycling helmets.

Tony Blair, whose father Leo had tried to bring him up in a Tory household, found the socialists' plain women and gnome-like activists with ginger beards a little bit offensive too, but that did not stop him leading his adopted party to power. Liberals were so confused at the new consensus that they changed their name around a dozen times.

Military triumphs which had traditionally stirred the nation to wild celebrations outside Kensington Palace were by now exceptionally sad. It was no longer a question of not showing enough hatred towards our enemies, it was a question of feeling sorry for them. An officer who led his men on the big push towards Kuwait during the 1991 Gulf War described the Iraqis defending their desert positions in front of him as 'sad and vulnerable'. He made them sound like the kind of homesick Arab mathematicians you see standing by themselves in the corner of union discos at provincial universities.

When we eventually secured our oil supply using an armoury which made the zapper beams on the *Starship Enterprise* look outdated, victory was greeted with a mass outpouring of 'I hope they're going to be all right' platitudes. Instead of returning home to a land fit for heroes, our professional soldiers were offered counselling and the possibility of financial compensation for the psychological discomfort they had suffered.

The young radicals of the 1960s were now in positions of power and influence. They provided large second homes and trust funds for their off-spring to express themselves through small hallucinatory pills and techno music with no discernible lyrics except for 'Boom, boom, boom. We like to party'. They created a lethargic generation of affluent young people who had neither the energy nor the inclination to change anything in the world, least of all their bed clothes or the PIN on their parents' cashcards.

Those who did try to make inroads into the world concentrated on chartered accountancy. Their ultimate aim in life was to become bean counters, adding up the merits of alternative photocopying paper and sending off internal memos starting with sentences like: 'I am becoming increasingly concerned at the amount of forks which are going missing from the staff canteen.'

When people stepped out into the streets in the Britain of the 1990s they expected pavements to be undamaged and free of animal excrement. They expected street-lights to work and rubbish to be collected on time. With soldiers wanting wars to be violence- and stress-free, other people's aspirations also grew massively. If anything went wrong in life, huge payouts were expected for the suffering and inconvenience caused. If you tripped up on a crack in the pavement you could expect £5,000 from your local council. If you fell in a mound of dogshit at the same time you could expect £10,000. If you went for the hat-trick by claiming sexism or unfair dismissal as well, £100,000 would not be out of the question.

A proliferation of negligence litigation and advertisements starting 'Have you had an accident recently?' saw Britain turning into the ultimate nanny state. Huge payments were handed out for everything from unwanted babies to unhappiness at work. Unpredictability and a change of routine was no longer something which people yearned for, they were concepts for which you were compensated.

Even going abroad did not provide the romance and mysticism of the past. Cheap package tours meant that Sky football matches, English pubs and egg and chips were as easily available under the Spanish sun as they were in Bolton. Professional holidaymakers like Judith Chalmers sipped cocktails on far-off beaches and urged us to concentrate our talents and ambitions on securing dream holidays within overpriced Caribbean compounds or former African colonies full of native barmen and cleaners.

The Queen had been right about TV. By the 1990s its output was far from original and inspired. Instead, the medium was constantly churning out images of the most miserable types of human activity. The never-ending stream left many viewers unable to differentiate between African safaris, African famines and studio confessions by overweight divorcees divulging every sordid detail of their nights of passion with African barmen.

The most popular programmes were soap operas: bland parodies of ordinary life spiced up by adultery and frantic dashes to hospital emergency wards. Their obsession with shallow, suburban dramas punctuated by tragedy-inspired histrionics were there to provide us with light relief from our shallow suburban lives punctuated by tragedy-inspired histrionics. There were very few starry-eyed radicals drawing inspiration from anything, not even Che Guevara posters or flickery recordings of Bob Dylan concerts. We were all too busy watching Dirty Den filing for divorce on *EastEnders* on our walnut-panelled widescreen televisions.

Real life provided very few opportunities to punch the air, wince maniacally and scream, 'Yessss!'

Against such a background, football thrived. It was one of the few things about the new Britain which was still unpredictable and exciting. Passions were inspired on almost every day of the week. Footballers were the living players in a genuine drama involving pain and hardship, hope and glory. There was the romanticism of games between big-city giants and provincial underdogs, stirring cup runs and cruel, extra-time defeats. Managers and players were sacked ruthlessly when things weren't going a team's way. Football meant something, and people cared. T-shirts emblazoned with the legend 'Football Is Life' summed up the nation's obsession.

What other single event in the bland, post-imperial Britain could come close to matching the penalty shoot-out in Turin on 4 July 1990 when England were playing Germany in a World Cup semi-final? Almost 30 million – more than watch each episode of *EastEnders* – saw the drama unfold. More than half of the country's adult population were inspired by Gary Lineker's late equaliser, and moved beyond sadness by Paul Gascoigne's tears. When Chris Waddle and Stuart Pearce missed their penalties and Germany won 4–3, there was a mass outpouring of emotion, the like of which had not been seen for decades.

Students, who had got up in time for the game's evening kick-off, hugged their tutors. Chartered accountants and other office workers embraced in ways they had not done since being humiliated at long-remembered Christmas parties. Emotional crowds assembled in cities, towns and villages all over the realm. The German embassy in London was plagued with abusive phonecalls. Volkswagens, BMWs and other German cars had their badges stolen.

Despite such minor excesses, that night in July 1990 really was a turning point for England. On show for all the world to see was the innate desire of a subdued and once-great people to unite in a countrywide display of feeling. It was a night for zapping the off-button on Judith Chalmers and Dirty Den. It was a time for passion and emotion; a time when ordinary mortals once more felt that it had been possible to reach for the stars.

Newspapers thrived on such emotion. If England won and were playing well, managers would be fêted with positive headlines and column feet of praise. They would be described as Churchillian figures who had inspired their English lions to play out of their skins for John of Gaunt's gleaming gem set in a jewelled sea. If we failed to qualify for another World Cup, lost 2–0 to the United States, and began going 1–0 down to teams like San Marino, a manager would be called a turnip and urged to go home to Watford.

Football had to be explained in terms of people's innate desire for glamour, romance and excitement in their everyday lives. Its journalistic coverage therefore had to be bright, intelligent and occasionally inspired. When editors heard that the most influential striker in the history of the English game had lost the most influential ball in the history of the English game, they too were inspired. The potential for popular excitement and national triumph which it represented was as large as the Soviet nuclear arsenal had been during the Cold War. All vowed to do everything in their power to bring the ball home.

14 · Global Views

Following the report in *Total Football*, there were claims of sightings of the ball all over the world. Geoff Hurst's agent was contacted by scores of people saying they had spotted it at some stage in their lives. In the same way that the Vatican regularly receives claims of miracles made by Catholics looking for a divine revelation – weeping statues, Celtic fans buying a round, that kind of thing – so sightings of the ball were reported in places as unlikely as Leamington Spa and Wigan.

Every newspaper in the country received information. Often it was hard to differentiate from the 'I've found a new planet' calls which newsdesks receive a dozen times a day, but when the ball was mentioned callers had to be taken seriously. With the start of Euro'96 less than two months away, and editors desperate for the best possible stories, no blade of grass was left untrampled as the search continued.

Readers of the *Sun* had always been adept at looking out for things on behalf of their favourite newspaper. Their 'shop-a-scrounger' campaigns of the early 1980s were supremely successful. They pinpointed thousands of lank-haired students whose liberal, non-materialistic parents had taught them to make as much money as they could from the Welfare State so as to contribute to the upkeep of the family's second home in Gloucestershire.

The caller from Leamington Spa said he had won his amber ball in a local radio competition during the 1970s. Another, a used-vacuum-cleaner salesman from Fulham, said his bright orange ball had just 'kind of fallen off the back of a skip' some 30 years before. Reporters who inspected it found it was a resprayed white ball, probably done 20 minutes before they turned up to the businessman's fifth-floor apartment on the Clement Attlee council estate off the North End Road.

Tipsters from all over the world began to get involved. In Italy the kind of freelancers who usually filed short stories about police being called to a monastery because of a punch-up between monks, began to think football. There were unsubstantiated claims that the ball had been sold to an Italian restaurant in Wembley, close to the pub where the 1966 World Cup crossbar is now on display.

Amateur scientists who said they were from a new university near Bradford (formerly a washing-machine repair centre) claimed the ball would have internally combusted soon after such a fiercely fought contest.

A freelancer from Australia said the ball was in a wine bar in the Outback, one which did not have a telephone. Days before, the same journalist had filed a news-in-brief item about a man who scrubbed himself to death in a car-wash, so we weren't unduly concerned by his claims. There are hundreds of stringers getting very rich by filing dubious news-in-brief items from Australia. It's so far away, and the time difference so enormous, that their validity is seldom checked out. It is unlikely that a foreign editor sitting in London would look up and casually remark to a reporter: 'Nice one here about a fellow being mangled up in a car-wash in Adelaide. Can you just nip over and take a look?'

Within a few days of Hurst's confession, German correspondents started to show a strong interest in the story. The rumour that Haller had walked off with the ball was as strong as ever, and there was a firm belief that the ball was indeed 'somewhere in Germany'. The words 'somewhere in Germany' sounded ominously like the opening words of a cheap and predictable spy novel which you buy at Sunday-morning markets for 50p, but they were to inspire almost every journalist in England over the coming days.

Papers including *The Times* and *Daily Telegraph* received frantic calls from their German stringers. They ran speculative pieces about the whereabouts of the football – upmarket 'Spot the Ball' analysis articles is probably how their executives would have defended them against accusations of dumbing-down.

Experts on television joshed each other about 'that ball' between expertly analysing tackles and throw-ins. Everybody found a new friend on a news-paper with *Allgemeine* in the title. Vast tip-off fees were offered to any German journalist who could come up with a location ...

A Wolfgang Gywer from Düsseldorf said his father had given him the ball. The correspondents working for British newspapers began to roam.

One was a serious-minded TV producer called Klaus who topped up his salary by filing the occasional few paragraphs to the British tabloids – snippets about German pigs making the ultimate sacrifice for European unity by being castrated to appease British housewives who did not like the smell of male pork, that kind of thing. As British foreign editors began to grill him on the subject of the ball, Klaus recalled stopping off at his local restaurant near Augsburg a few months before. The sauerkraut and sausage had been excellent, and he remembered getting into a conversation with the famous international footballer Gerd Muller. Over a steaming bowl of pickled cabbage they had discussed the restaurant's owner, Helmut Haller, and his colourful past.

Klaus was more used to producing worthy but dull TV specials on Bavarian milk quotas than initiating classic journalistic scraps, but he could not ignore the suggestion that Haller kept Geoff Hurst's 1966 World Cup final ball in his cellar. Klaus had furrowed his Germanic brow and narrowed his eyes behind his rimless glasses. Calls to daily newspapers in Britain followed.

As Klaus phoned London, he knew that he was on to a massive story, and that there would only be two sides in the game. The *Daily Mirror*, with more than two million readers, and the *Sun*, with a circulation of over four million, were part and parcel of the English national game. Both hugely rich and influential papers were willing to invest as much time and effort in soccer stories as their circulation figures deemed necessary. Just a few weeks earlier, a marketing consultant had telephoned the *Mirror* newsdesk to try and get a commission for a six-week survey into exactly who the newspaper's target readers were. He was one of those eager media types who are normally called Gus or Sophie and who use your first name as if they are your best friend. In this case he was even nicer, mainly because he was offering the scientific research at a price of £10,000.

'But we know exactly who our readers are already,' replied an assistant news editor. 'They're lads and lasses who like football and beer.'

Despite the new type of football fans all over Britain, the game's roots had not been ignored completely. It did not matter at all that many of the new lads and lasses who liked beer and football might also be university-educated and qualified as lawyers or doctors. It did not matter that they might be members of the royal family, or future prime ministers who drank bottles of Budweiser in Birmingham hotels. Everybody in the country had reached the level of the football fan, and had become a target readership.

Newspapers and their headline writers were obsessed by the country's twin obsessions of football and beer. The *Sun* came up with the Great Carling Quiz – presented under the 'Beer We Go!' headline – in which readers could win a case of lager if they could come up with the answer to their trivia test. The inevitable question was 'How many goals did Geoff Hurst score in the 1966 World Cup final?'

When Klaus called London he unleashed a contest of (according to the *Sunday Times*) 'high farce and no rules'. Two football-supporting giants were competing for the ultimate prize in the world of journalism: Geoff Hurst's ball and the circulation that went with it. Its capture would represent a massive triumph to impress Acrylics everywhere, whichever mass-market daily tabloid they supported.

Like the 1966 World Cup final, there could be no defeat, only victory.

Those who won the bitter contest between the fiercest rivals on Fleet Street would receive a massive boost to their prestige and future prospects of success in one of the most cut-throat, competitive industries in the world. Failure could only mean humiliation and unpleasant jokes, as mean and vindictive as the 'Turnip Head' jibes aimed at former England manager Graham Taylor.

Klaus called the Sun newsdesk first, because he thought they would have a better chance of success. They had more money to spend, a better record of provoking the Germans and dozens of reporters on standby to move at a moment's notice. He telephoned Wapping, the east London headquarters of Rupert Murdoch's News International, at around 3 p.m. on Wednesday, 24 April 1996.

The Mirror did not receive their call until around two hours later. By the time Klaus's tip had been investigated, and Haller's whereabouts located, it would be too late to catch a flight to Munich that day.

As the two sides contemplated their game plans, they worked out the best way to locate the ball and get it back to England. What was clear to both sides, even at this early stage, was that the quest would involve large amounts of money. It would have been churlish to expect otherwise. Football had become a huge, money-spinning business. Players with short careers were eager to earn as much as possible, especially retired players who had made next to nothing from contests as famous as the 1966 World Cup final.

Geoff Hurst's red number 10 shirt from the 1966 final had been valued by auctioneers at £1 million. The number 6 top which Bobby Moore did not even wear at Wembley on 30 July 1966 was sold at auction for £44,000 on 22 September 1999. All the players had two shirts, and Moore gave his spare one to Harold 'Sit Down' Shepherdson, who had been awarded an OBE in 1969. The money made at auction, paid by an anonymous telephone bidder, eventually went to the team physiotherapist's widow, Peggy.

Moore's entire collection of medals – including his solid gold winner's medal, 43 England caps, Footballer of the Year trophy and silver salver to mark his 100th appearance for his country – was estimated at £2.5 million when his family considered selling it after his death in 1993.

Roger Hunt eventually managed to get £17,250 for his red shirt after he put it up for auction along with that of Wolfgang Weber, with whom he exchanged his spare shirt. It was sold to a man who had gone along to the 1966 game as a 12-year-old. Gordon Mouschino lived in Virginia and also bought a telex report of the match for £977. (Were it not for the fact that his details were confirmed by the auctioneers, one might have expected Mr Mouschino to be filed under the category of dubious news-in-briefs.

Perhaps those freelancers in Australia and Italy aren't making it all up, after all.)

Jimmy Greaves, the spare striker at Wembley, even managed to sell himself to the Sun. His weekly 'Greavsie' column is rumoured to cost the paper at least £100,000 a year. Even the Union flag flying above Wembley fetched around £1,000 when a friend of Bobby Moore's sold it.

Britain in the 1990s had enough spare money to pay Winston Churchill, a double-chinned and already extremely rich Conservative in a pinstripe suit, £12.5 million for the real Winston Churchill's private papers. They were already in the country, anyway, and of interest only to academics.

Sun journalists prepared to leave Britain with thousands of pounds in used sterling, which could easily be converted into Deutschmarks later. Murdoch was more than willing to invest a tiny proportion of his billions to get the ball back.

Despite its vast profits and healthy circulation figures, the Mirror's editorial department was not bankrolled in quite the same way. Ever since Robert Maxwell had fleeced the Mirror Group and its employees' pension fund of millions of pounds, money had been guarded better than the Sunday-for-Monday exclusives hidden in the newsdesk computer system. Management claimed they did not trust their staff with large sums, fearing that their fiscal naïvety could get them into serious trouble. The company was in the hands of the banks, and shareholders expected maximum profits rather than vast outlays on journalistic projects. When journalists went on a foreign trip they were normally lucky if they didn't have to pay for the flight themselves.

Of course, this did not mean that executive editors were not keen to pursue the big ones. They realised the potential of Geoff Hurst's ball very early on, and were prepared to hand out as much upfront financial support as the accountants signing off internal memos about missing canteen forks were prepared to allow. When I set off to Germany on the Mirror's behalf they gave me £50-worth of sterling traveller's cheques, with the promise of a commission-free buy-back for all unused notes from the Thomas Cook Bureau de Change at Heathrow's Terminal Two.

The Sun unleashed its team of reporters and photographers that Wednesday evening. Drops were made all over Germany, with one team touching down in the capital itself. They believed the ball might be in Berlin following a bogus call from a Mirror sympathiser who had used an 'Allo 'Allo accent to claim a bright orange spherical object had been found by builders digging up Potsdamer Platz.

The main part of the *Sun*'s force headed straight to Munich, however. There they split up into three, so as to cover Haller's restaurant, his home and his sports shop in Augsburg. All were *Sun* veterans: newsgatherers who had served for years in the newspaper's heartlands, from the crime-ridden council estates of southern Essex to the villain-infested *costas* of southern Spain. They knew exactly what their mission was and how to implement it. They checked their equipment (including their camera lenses and tape recorders) and made sure that all of it was well hidden from the prying eyes of German customs officials.

By the time they got to Germany it was dusk. Klaus's call had come too late for them to arrive in daylight. The foreign legion decided to billet down and prepare their main assault for the next morning. They thought of going straight in, but their vast experience made them err on the side of caution.

On all doorsteps the best results are invariably obtained at first light, when people are optimistic and preparing for the day ahead. At night, they will be moody and cautious. If you ask them probing questions they might well swear loudly and threaten violence. (Because of the dangers of night-time assaults, newsdesks invariably only send green reporters on nocturnal manoeuvres. With the stupidity of youth and inexperience on their side, they will be unafraid of risking personal abuse and physical pain.

A supremely keen young colleague was once sent to find the ageing Old Etonian and penal reformer Lord Longford on a freezing cold, moonless night. In daylight hours the peer was usually happy to provide long-winded explanations as to why old lags should not have to spend their twilight years behind bars, but during the night he was normally tucked up with a hot-water bottle and a pair of novelty convict pyjamas.

As with most members of the aristocracy, he also had about ten addresses around Britain making finding him even more tricky. After around three hours of searching, my colleague knew things were looking hopeless, but pledged he could not give up. He was a Hitler Youth-style cub reporter who approached stories with a fiery glint in his eye and a tenacity bordering on the demonic. Covered in sweat and shaking with cold, he eventually turned his attentions to a large house in Holland Park, west London. It was owned by Lord Longford's daughter, Lady Antonia Fraser. The novelist lived there with her playwright husband, Harold Pinter, another 1960s icon whose thick-rimmed spectacles and dark suits would have fitted in perfectly on the terraces at Wembley on World Cup final day.

The reporter woke up the household and eventually confronted an alarmed-looking Lady Antonia, whose years locked away writing weighty historical tomes about Mary Queen of Scots and the Gunpowder Plot had not prepared her for confrontations with a fanatical freelance journalist.

'You Lady Antonia?' asked the reporter.

'Yes. What do you want?' she demanded.

'I'm looking for yer old man,' came the reply.

Lady Antonia's subsequent behaviour would not have been misplaced in one of her chapters describing how Catholics were treated during the Reformation.)

For the Sun team in Germany, there could be no such mistakes. Too much depended on this mission of all missions, and every one of their movements would have to be executed with perfection.

They would attack at first light.

The Sun's editor was taking a special interest in his journalists' mission. Stuart Higgins was celebrating his fiftieth birthday at the end of the week and had organised a lavish party at the Kensington Roof Gardens, an upmarket club in west London often hired out by millionaire showbusiness stars. As with all editors, Higgins was constantly under pressure and knew that a personal celebration was best enjoyed when his newspaper had something to celebrate. Major celebrities including actors and footballers had been invited to his party, as well as dozens of politicians, businesspeople and vaguely friendly rivals from other newspapers. Rupert Murdoch, Higgins's own boss, had poured millions into reviving English football through Sky. If necessary, the Australian would provide millions more to revive the fortunes of the ultimate English football, so there could be no excuse for failure.

Higgins, who had been a cub reporter in the West Country when England won the World Cup, wanted to make sure that the most stirring present he could ever hope for took pride of place at the hugely expensive party. The sight of the amber ball would ensure that champagne corks would not be going off solely in his honour, but providing a stirring fanfare to mark the continued dominance of his newspaper over all its rivals.

As his troops began to move around Germany, Higgins telephoned them constantly. Reporters used to the unrelenting 'Where are you?' and 'How's it going?' calls from frantic news editors had to put up with an interrogation from the big chief himself. When he blurted out suggestions like 'Have you tried the neighbours yet?', all knew that his desire for success was as keen as Alf Ramsey's had been 30 years before.

The false Berlin tip was ruled out by Wednesday evening. There were more than a thousand builders digging up Potsdamer Platz, but few were German. The reporter and photographer spent two hours standing with six British plasterers and hod-carriers staring down a huge hole next to the old Reichstag building. They smoked a few cigarettes and had endless cups of tea and sausage sandwiches before calling it a night.

Then the *Sun* men began to redeploy to the south of the country. It would be a long, tedious drive along hundreds of miles of bland autobahn, but there would be no sleep for all those taking part in a mission of such magnitude. Every spare man would be needed for the morning's assault.

15 · Last Orders

As the main opposition tossed and turned in their hotel beds around Munich and Augsburg, I was sitting in the main bar of the Builders Arms pub in Kensington, just a short dribble from the Royal Garden Hotel where the 1966 win had been celebrated with such vigour.

Like that of so many of the Wembley stars, my last-minute call to play a part in history had been completely unexpected. In fact, my selection to go to Germany was as surprising as the dropping of Jimmy Greaves for the World Cup final.

Throughout that Wednesday I had been working on an investigation which had as much chance of making the pages of a national newspaper as the Irish bar manager of the Builders Arms had of playing in goal for San Marino. It involved trying to track down a well-meaning but dim peer of the realm who had spent his summer holidays clubbing ducklings in Australia. We had video evidence of the alleged atrocities, but the only view of the 33-year-old was a pair of upper-crust brogues next to a fledgling mallard. The picture editor considered our evidence too graphic for publication, and the Old Etonian had absconded to one of his shooting-lodges in Scotland to orphan a few more wide-eyed birds.

One of my colleagues on the Mirror, however, had spent the entire afternoon and evening telephoning Germany. His main job had been to find out if Klaus's tip was a sound one, or whether those rimless glasses were hiding the personality of a deranged manipulator prone to wearing awful check jackets and luring people to his homeland at vast expense for no particular reason. For around a week the journalist had done almost nothing but work on the World Cup ball story. Ever since Hurst's confession in *Total Football* magazine, he had been assigned to the project full time. He had gone through half the telephone directories for Berlin and Greater Munich. He had managed to get an odd-sounding waiter from the Villa d'Este on the telephone, at first under the pretence that he was trying to order a takeaway sausage-and-sauerkraut pizza. After listing a few more fillings, he had casually dropped in a mention of the 1966 World Cup ball.

The reporter eventually got Helmut Haller himself on the phone and got him to say 'Nein' at least 35 times, which was really pretty impressive. He also spoke to Jurgen Haller and got him to say 'Nein, Nein' in quick succession approximately 40 times.

My colleague was putting in the mind-numbingly boring graft that underpins any successful story which appears in a national newspaper. Countless phone calls and tedious list-checking are just part of the hard work which goes into the best journalism. You also have to spend hours hanging around in the cold and rain, wearing dirty raincoats and risking being arrested on suspicion of lewd behaviour. Like the footballer who spends hours jogging and practising his maniacal victory runs, so any ambitious reporter knows that single-minded dedication is as important as natural talent on the way to the top.

That Wednesday, my fellow Mirror journalist had played his heart out for the paper. He had the skill, tenacity and technical ability of a Jimmy Greaves. While I was lounging around with friends in the Builders Arms, he was making sure he did not put a foot wrong as he harassed and wore down the opposition. As I sipped pints of beer, he badgered the Germans for hours on end – constantly provoking them to furrow their brows and snap at him. At around 10 p.m. he made the final call which just about established the exact location of the ball. He punched the air maniacally and shouted, 'Yesss!'

Then he remembered he had booked a dream holiday in a Caribbean compound and was due to fly out with his girlfriend the following Saturday.

After hours of dedicated effort by somebody else, I slipped in to take on the Germans. The night news editor, Anthony Harwood, called me on my mobile telephone and ordered me to fly to Munich the next morning.

One of the biggest problems of being a journalist is your journalistic friends. Usually it's only other journalists who understand the long, anti-social hours you work, not to mention your odd habits of hanging around in public places wearing dirty raincoats while you wait for complete strangers to approach you. Combined with the cunning required to get and protect exclusives, you often find that it's only other journalists who will speak to you, anyway.

That Wednesday night I knew I was being sent on one of the biggest jobs of my career but did not want to make the importance of my task too obvious to the three other reporters from rival papers who were drinking with me. I considered telling them I was on my way to somewhere like Norwich, but then thought this might raise more questions than it answered. News journalists have to have a very good reason for going to Norwich. Apart from quirky features about farmyard animals and retired potters, the only events of general interest in the region are grisly murders, usually involving peers of the realm and retarded gardeners. Instead I casually mentioned that I would be going 'abroad'.

'Whereabouts?' a friend asked.

'Oh, nowhere important,' I said, displaying an impressive lack of commitment.

Eventually we moved on for a Chinese meal in a small restaurant on the corner of Kensington Square. There we managed to get through an entire Golden Samurai special for four without once mentioning the words 'football', 'World', 'Cup' or '1966'.

As I got up to go, one of my colleagues asked me if I spoke any French.

'No, I'm going to Germany,' I replied.

I felt like Chelsea fan Richard Attenborough in the film *The Great Escape*, when his status as prisoner-of-war on the run is advertised by his friend Gordon Jackson after a Gestapo agent speaks to them in English as they're getting on a bus.

My friend's tactics had been brilliantly effective. 'Sneaky bastard,' I thought to myself.

A car picked me up early the next morning to take me to Heathrow. Hammersmith Bridge had been shut down by the police following an attempt by the IRA to blow it up. It was, I thought, quite a dramatic reason for arriving late at the airport.

The sharp end of Irish nationalism in fact came very close to ending any hopes I had of playing a role in a great victory for English nationalism. The terrorists had planted the biggest bomb of its kind ever seen in mainland Britain – 32lbs of Semtex split into two devices, each in a briefcase-sized box. They were planted three feet below London's oldest suspension bridge, but the devices failed to explode when their detonators went off without triggering the Semtex. The bombs had been planned as a 'spectacular' to mark the anniversary of the 1916 Easter Rising in Dublin, which began on 24 April.

It had been the second IRA attack on the 109-year-old structure. The first came on 29 March 1939 when the Provos had used exactly the same training manual. Then, however, it was foiled by a hairdresser from Chiswick who saw smoke and sparks coming from a lighted bomb fuse. He threw the bomb into the Thames, sending a column of water 60 feet into the air. A second device went off, causing girders on the west of the bridge to fall down and shattering nearby windows.

As I sat in the back of the taxi looking over to Hammersmith from Barnes I was thankful that the inevitable problems caused by a cataclysmic explosion had been avoided. At that moment in time I really could have done without jagged chunks of metal flying through the air, raging fires and tailbacks all along the A4.

I live north of the Thames and did not forget to ask the chirpy cabby how we had come to cross south of the river before attempting to cross back to the north again. I also wanted to know what we were doing in Barnes, when it was nowhere near the A4.

'Don't worry, mate,' he had replied reassuringly. 'It's all on the meter.'

I met photographer Mike Moore at Heathrow. After an uneventful flight to Germany, we were soon involved in a perennial feature of all unexpected arrivals at foreign airports: an argument with the car-hire man.

'No Mercedes,' said the officious Hertz underling, as he confirmed he had nothing left with any kind of badge worth stealing.

Moore, who was well on the way to a free weekend Mondeo on his Hertz loyalty card, was furious. He threatened to cancel all future business trips unless we got a car worthy of his status as the owner of more than 2,000 bonus points built up through years of determined collecting, often on bullet-holed roads in international trouble-spots miles from the nearest Blue Boar service station. We ended up with an Opel Kadett diesel.

As we made our noisy way to Neusass on the main Augsburg road, it was time to put our car-hire frustrations behind us and show our first piece of initiative on what would turn out to be a very long day. The desk had been keen for us to 'nip over' to Jurgen Haller's office in Munich before turning up at Helmut Haller's restaurant. They thought the younger Haller might smooth the way to securing an interview with his father. The instruction was typical of London-based desks who think that everywhere is just a short hop away. 'You're not far from the Rio Grande, are you?' they'll say as you cover a trade summit in Acapulco. 'Can you just grab yourself a poncho, nip over the border and knock out a piece on how the Americans deal with their illegals?'

(Even in smaller countries, 'nipping over' instructions can cause horrendous problems. In their desperation to get a story, desk editors are seldom put off by the more obvious obstacles which can make foreign travel so difficult, like vast, inhospitable landscapes. They frequently forget that the Greek islands, for example, are divided by large spaces of water and usually linked by no more than one Olympus flight a day, or even just a ferry which takes eight hours to get anywhere and is crammed with goats and touchingly adventurous Australian backpackers looking for a revolving kebab heater to spend their summer alongside. I was once told to 'nip over' to Corfu from Athens to ask Helmut Kohl about the effect his castrated German pigs were having on the

English pork market, or something like that. Again, improvisation became the key to the assignment. This time the flights were full up with goats and overweight politicians attending the 1994 European Summit on the island, so the journey took around two days longer than expected. By the time I got there Kohl had returned home, so I was left to improvise. I filed a dubious story about the Chancellor – like Ludwig Erhard before him, a Eurosceptic's Euro-sceptic – having had a Kaiser-sized bed imported from the Fatherland for the summit, because he did not consider the foreign beds on offer sturdy enough for his robust frame. The tip had been given to me by an Athenian journalist who spent all his time filing lucrative news-in-brief paragraphs. The foreign editor was, however, so impressed by my improvisation that he asked me to get pictures of the bed. He also wanted full interviews with the impoverished Greek chambermaids who had to pull a fresh duvet across it each morning while the enormous German worked out further ways to ruin Britain's economic future. Sure enough, I found the hotel, and pictures were taken of me being dwarfed by the bed's epic proportions. It was further proof that those foreign 'nibs' aren't all made up, and that improvisation can get you a long way in journalism.)

Even driving the way photographers drive hire cars, we would have been hard pushed to make Haller's restaurant by early afternoon. There was never any doubt that the retired footballer was going to be the key to getting the ball back to Britain. Accordingly, we ignored the rush-hour traffic in central Munich and drove straight towards Augsburg. Technically, we were defying orders, but the stakes were too high to worry about offending anybody, par-ticularly some irritable weasel stuffing his face with king-sized chocolate croissants and tubfuls of caffellatte in London. Full of bravado, we even considered telling our superiors how small-minded and misguided their instructions were becoming.

Then we remembered that we were driving an Opel Kadett diesel.

16 · Working Punch

We got to Neusass just before noon. The bald Sun doorman standing menacingly on the porch was the first person we saw. He recognised us straight away from numerous previous encounters. We normally got on extremely well on so-called pack jobs when journalists from different papers cover the same story. The doorman was usually amiable and not in the least bit aggressive.

On this occasion, however, the rules were very different. There was only one ball available and only one side would be bringing it back to England. It was an exclusive, one-off ball, and the doorman would stop at nothing to make sure it was his own paper's exclusive, one-off ball. This made him rude, cantankerous and prone to violence. As we fought our way into the restaurant, the nastiness got even worse.

There was nothing personal about the unpleasantness; it was professional unpleasantness, all in the line of duty. Just as you have institutionalised nastiness on the office floor – the kind of behaviour which involves excluding somebody from your complicated coffee run, or talking about their irritating voice when they wander off for a lunchtime throat lozenge – so you get on-the-road nastiness; a kind of on-the-road rage. Usually it's directed at diminutive Croatian hotel owners who can't get their 1930s telephone system to link up with your Mark XII Futureshock 2000 multi-computer, or a Tunisian taxi driver who's slow, unhelpful and, worst of all, can't speak a word of English.

Severe journalistic aggression is also periodically aimed at consular officials who won't drop everything to help you find an English subject caught up in the armed insurrection currently engulfing the British embassy grounds around them and spilling dangerously close to the swimming-pool area. As murderous revolutionaries threaten to maim everybody in the building, it's important to get a reaction from a British person, and if your local representative can't help you, frustration inevitably spills over too. From their desks in London, journalists will scream down the telephone at such unhelpful minions until they pull themselves together.

Particularly impressive displays of on-the-road rage came on the Tony Blair Battlebus before the 1997 general election. I watched admiringly as an

ITN correspondent berated one of Tony Blair's young spin-doctors during a stop-off at Sussex University. The would-be prime minister admitted that he had not visited Brighton since the 1970s when he went to see Shakin' Stevens perform live at a time when Cardiff meant rock 'n' roll. The spin-doctor continually underplayed the political significance of the visit, as the ITN journalist probed for more details. Eventually the spin-doctor sauntered off with one of those mildly confrontational swaggers which only spin-doctors are capable of.

'Come back here, you smarmy bastard,' shouted the incandescent ITN man. When the Labour youth refused to return, the TV journalist screamed out: 'Get out of that shiny suit and fight me.'

A *Guardian* reporter spent a day on the bus and her upper lip began quivering when the photographers started to download pornography on their laptop computers. She made an official complaint to the Labour Party and then expressed her on-the-road rage in one of those snidey, underhand columns which *Guardian* writers do so well. What did she expect bored photographers to produce – poetry?

When it comes to real on-the-road rage, however, you really can't beat the lensmen. Their fights are some of the finest set-pieces in modern journalism. Normally the punches start when a stray object, like a 'hairy dog' TV sound boom, or an innocent passer-by, wanders across their camera's field of vision. They will also frequently lay into each other when somebody has encroached upon the four-inch-square space they've saved for themselves in a pack waiting outside a door or a carpark. Touch their aluminium ladders or tripods and your chances of spending the rest of your life with an unbroken nose will be very small indeed.

I'll never forget my first photographer fight. The scenes outside Marylebone registry office in central London on 8 July 1993, when Countess Raine Spencer married Count Pineton de Chambrun were unforgettable. Her Rolls-Royce and his Range Rover were held up behind a bus, so they both got out and walked. They were immediately swamped by a vast crowd as the cameramen abandoned their hard-won places next to the steel safety barriers on the steps of the registry office. The lensmen all began cascading towards the couple wandering up Marylebone Road. The photographers were taking pictures and throwing punches simultaneously.

The Countess had chosen a strange combination of bright red frills and ruffles for her third marriage but was still easy to miss as she disappeared under a sea of flaying limbs and motor drives.

'We want to get married,' pleaded Raine, stepmother of Princess Diana, in a high-pitched squeal. Her voice rose even higher as she again screamed: 'Please let us get married!'

Tourists began taking pictures from coaches as the professionals started wielding their aluminium ladders and tripods and hitting each other over the head. Yolanda Connor, the marriage witness who had introduced Raine to her Count, remained calm throughout – but had been deeply moved. 'It was very emotional and I cried. It is a day I will never forget,' she said afterwards.

The *Sun* men appeared to be on the verge of similar behaviour when we arrived. They felt the entire morning had been wasted. Despite an early start, they were no closer to prising the ball away from Haller. Higgins, their editor, was making ever more frantic telephone calls, and the opposition was growing all the time.

I was introduced to Haller and his son by Thorsten Riedel, a German goal-keeper who was overseeing the negotiations. Haller, the legendary midfielder, seemed to be enjoying his role back in the centre of the action as he taunted the English with jokes which they had no hope of understanding.

At first the *Sun* men had ignored Riedel and kept asking Haller where the ball was. He had been studiously ignoring them as he sipped a glass of whisky in the centre of the restaurant and tapped his fingers to the oompha beat.

Apart from Riedel – who was not saying a great deal – all the Germans were talking in German. This is something which infuriates English journalists. Verbal communication in any foreign language infuriates English journalists. (Photographers are even worse. A pack was once working in Rennes and were desperately looking for a French-speaker to persuade a woman to pose for them. They were frustrated that their normal 'Come on, love, give us a smile' was having no effect in a traditional provincial French community. They began to bicker. The photographers had been huddled around the woman's garden gate for around 20 minutes when one decided to calm things down by offering 'a few words in French I learnt at school which'll break the ice'. He marched purposefully up the pathway, followed by ten of his colleagues, and banged as hard as he could on the front door using his tripod. Within a few seconds the shocked Frenchwoman answered and stared out suspiciously. The English visitor stuck out a friendly hand and announced enthusiastically: '*Au revoir!*')

After the initial skirmishes in the foyer and some food-throwing by the Ukrainian chef, Haller decided it was time for us all to gather together and start talking. It was nothing to do with the spirit of European unity, sadly. He was concerned for the safety of his regular diners. Accordingly, Haller decided that we should all move somewhere else to begin our negotiations.

Aware that we would be discussing something of no lesser magnitude than the most important icon in English sporting history, he chose the concrete-and-grass alleyway at the side of the restaurant where the Villa d'Este waiters emptied the bins and smoked their cigarettes.

Riedel, who led us out the back as Haller poured himself another whisky, was six foot four and wore a standard Henry Plantagenet hairstyle together with the kind of ill-fitting sports-casual clothes which only central Europeans can get away with. Well, they don't exactly get away with it, it's just that most of them present themselves exactly the same way so nobody really stands out. Haller's haircut was very similar to Riedel's, as was his crumpled T-shirt and badly cut trousers. Jurgen Haller, at 34 the same age as Riedel, wore a black waistcoat, a tie and a pair of stonewashed jeans: the equivalent of wearing evening dress with an acrylic football shirt.

As Riedel began to take charge of the negotiations, it became clear that he was the real playmaker. While Haller would probably have been happy to hand the ball over for a reasonable price and then slip off for a well-deserved nap, Riedel was making sure that he got the very best deal for his friend. Like all Germans who play at the back, he was cold, calculating and impossible to break down. There would be no sign of the ball until money had been exchanged and all were confident that they would not be cheated.

Goalkeepers always make life complicated. They're an odd social group prone to long spells of depression caused by loneliness and the insulting fans who stand behind them at away games. It's no coincidence that literature's most famous keepers are Albert Camus and Vladimir Nabokov – fine authors but fundamentally flawed in their personal relationships. In the changing-room the goalkeepers will always be the ones who are quiet, reserved and won't lend you their soap. They are always sulky and rude, and they won't join in with the games of cards on the team coach either.

(Once, when I was feeling pretty alienated myself on an obscure local newspaper, I had a particularly bad experience involving goalkeepers. In between writing stories about sheep straying over the border from Norfolk into Suffolk, I had to fill up the weekly 'What's On' column with small announcements – 'The witches coven will be holding a cake-making course in the village hall at 3 p.m. on Thursday', that kind of thing. One tedious Friday I inadvertently replaced 'Meeting of the Little Snoring Goat-Keepers Guild' with 'Meeting of the Little Snoring Goalkeepers Guild'. Apart from the inevitable complaints from the custodians of local goats, I later learned that at least three lonely goalkeepers had turned up at the village hall with their gloves and green shirts. They had been expecting a serious discussion about how to deal with unusual bounces, or whatever it is that goalkeepers discuss when they get together socially.)

Outside the Villa d'Este the atmosphere was becoming more and more strained. Negotiations in journalism are always difficult, but this was impossible. We were trying all the tactics known to us, but none was having any effect.

The wearing-down approach to negotiations had obviously been a failure. The Sun had been there since 7 a.m. and their persistence had done nothing to move things on. Normally, if you telephone somebody enough times, or stand outside their home for long enough, they will usually concede something, even if it is just their intention to call the police.

But like the German referee Rudolph Kreitlein, who was harassed continually by Antonio Rattin after the Argentine captain was sent off against England in 1966, Haller was having none of it. He appeared to have all the time in the world. After almost 30 years of looking after the ball, he did not see any reason to rush into giving it away rashly.

In between his laughing and the joking, Haller would aim odd stares at us. He appeared particularly intrigued by the Sun men, who looked tired and worn after going to bed so late and getting up so early. They had maintained their discipline, but the looks of worried commitment on their faces reminded Haller of the North Korean team of 1966 – they had lived in barracks and taken vows of celibacy for two years before travelling to England for the championships.

The happy-go-lucky approach to negotiations was always a non-starter. Haller was smiling the whole time and seemed to be enjoying himself. Riedel was grim-faced and furrow-browed, but he would have looked like that if Groucho Marx and Woody Allen had turned up to try and cheer him up using the Monty Python material the BBC had considered too funny to broadcast because of the grimness of the 1970s.

Every time we tried patting Haller on the back, drawing an imaginary ball in the air and then putting a thumb up, the German would fall about laughing. We'd even tried putting both thumbs up in the air, and playing air guitar while clicking our heels like Italian gigolos. Like funny hats and slapstick comedians, absurd and ultimately meaningless air displays filled Haller with mirth, but he would soon calm down. He then simply carried on smiling and looking at Riedel's face, which was still a picture of gravity. No football had ever been charmed into the net by the force of a striker's personality. To negotiate the ball back to England was going to require subtlety and extremely hard work.

17 · Nein Field

We started the bidding at £25,000. So what, I thought. It's not my money. Haller probably wouldn't give up the ball, anyway, so we would all return to England together; without the football maybe, but with our heads held high, as they said about San Marino when they managed to put one past England for the first time since the fourteenth century before their 7–1 defeat in 1994.

Our pride would be intact and a German goalkeeper would have presided over another tactical stalemate. With any luck it might soon start pouring with rain and somebody wearing a blazer and sitting on the Pools Panel like Roger Hunt could decide what he thought the score should have been.

We had started the serious negotiations at around 1 p.m. By 2.30 they were no nearer a conclusion. Instead, we were still pacing up and down the alleyway to keep up with the giant, strutting Riedel, who kept averting his eyes from ours to stare inscrutably across a nearby field. He had probably said *nein* around 250 times by then.

As his ear became accustomed to the language we were speaking, Riedel began to converse with us in an exaggerated upper-class English accent. His sentences were occasionally ungrammatical and had an almost colonial pomposity about them. He sounded affected, but frighteningly in control. He was assured, supremely intelligent and knew exactly what he wanted out of life. Riedel sounded just like Alf Ramsey.

When we tried to convince Riedel that the ball did not even belong to Haller, the German goalkeeper urged us to seek legal representation. He knew such a complicated case would probably take around 16 years to get through the courts. In Britain you can keep somebody else's house if you've been squatting in it for more than 12 years. Haller had held on to the ball for almost 30 years. If we were successful, the decision in our favour would probably be overturned by the European Court of Human Rights anyway.

Riedel kept emphasising the dubious German football convention that the scorer of the first goal gets to keep the ball. He backed this up by quoting the German FA rule-book inside out from memory. He told us that Rule Two, as in England, was that a ball must be 'spherical'.

We all looked at each other quizzically. Then we furrowed our brows and nodded our heads furiously, as we tried to sound impressed by Riedel's expert knowledge of the regulations governing the international game.

'In Germany vee alvays play by zer rules,' said Riedel. 'Zer iz nothing random or irregular about our approach to life. Vee play togever, and vee play to vin. Vee play according to zer rule-book. Herr Haller vas vun of zer greatest players in zer history of zer game. He alvays played by zer rules. He iz a good, honourable man and vill continue to verk according to zer rules in his dealings viz you, or anybody else who iz involved in zis venture.'

We furrowed our brows again, and nodded our heads eagerly in agreement with all his affirmations. 'Pedantic prat,' said one of the Sun men under his breath. Another called him a 'fugger', which is not as offensive as it might sound. The famous banking family had been obsessed with money and had financed many of the buildings in nearby Augsburg.

My telephone was continually ringing as executives from London asked to speak to the Germans. I handed my mobile to Haller as a senior editor said something like: 'Ah, Mr Haller. So nice to meet you – albeit by telephone – after all these years. I've always been a great admirer of your work, especially since you scored that marvellous goal at Wembley during your early career.'

The tone was all wrong. Haller examined my phone as if it was one of those little devices with which you called Scottie before being beamed up to the *Starship Enterprise*. Haller would probably have been even more astounded if he had known the person attempting to communicate with him in an alien tongue was calling from a desolate landscape called Canary Wharf, at the entrance to the Thames estuary, miles from the civilisation of central London.

'Just tell him to sound polite,' I begged Riedel to tell Haller.

I was concerned that he might hurt the feelings of one of my executive colleagues; a colleague who could have a significant influence on my chances of future happiness in life, a colleague who had the power to recommend constructive relocation to Norwich, or even constructive dismissal to the scrap-heap of life.

Other executives in the Mirror office were more sensible. They began sending faxes of old Sun stories which portrayed the newspaper in a less than pro-German light. The cuttings included rude references to senior politicians, industrialists and footballers. There were exaggerated claims about Germany's cynical plans to achieve European hegemony through a single currency, as well as numerous references to a former chancellor who wanted to create a Berlin-dominated and fully integrated European super-state which would last for a thousand years. There were, of course, lots of references to wars as well as plenty of weak jokes, mainly involving beer-swilling Bavarians, towels by the pool and lederhosen.

Another inspired move by the Mirror executives included persuading 'experts' to join the negotiations on our behalf. (Sometimes this can backfire, as I found out when I once persuaded a self-styled Friends of the Earth activist to telephone a major food manufacturer whom I suspected of selling products riddled with a carcinogenic pesticide. The woman's soiled denims and exotic odour made her appear distinctly friendly with the earth, so I had no reason to doubt her credentials. She bored the company's media office for hours with long-winded explanations about how chemicals were destroying the food chain and exposing the whole population to terrifying health risks. Her cataclysmic explanations contained vivid details of the internal damage humans can suffer from the residues eating away at our meat and vegetables, especially the chilli con carne ready-meals sold in 24-hour garages. When the woman had finished haranguing the firm on my behalf, they said they would be prepared to test their foods if she could present them with scrolls to back up her academic credentials.

'You have got professional qualifications, haven't you?' I asked the pungent eco warrior.

'Yes, of course,' she said. 'Grade C Biology O-level.')

This time the Mirror top brass chose the right person. They got Jurgen Schneider, a *bona fide* official from the German embassy off Belgrave Square, to get in touch with Haller and persuade him that the ball really should be returned to England.

Herr Schneider sent faxes saying as much, telling Haller that the selfless act of sending the ball back to London would enhance Anglo-German relations and portray him in a very good light. Aware that large amounts of money were involved, Schneider even suggested that Haller should accept money for the ball and then make a very large charitable donation. Haller gave the suggestion some thought, as he helped himself to another large whisky.

Klaus the TV producer was also erring towards the Mirror. His conscience, but mainly his soiled check jacket, had persuaded him that we were the team to follow because we now looked the more likely to succeed. He would whisper the odd, choice comment in German ears about how the Mirror was trustworthy and worth working with. He made particular play of the fact that I did not have a nervous twitch or cross-eyes. By 2.45 p.m. the price of the ball had reached £50,000.

'You mean lire, of course,' smiled one of the Sun men, who was hoping that the touchy-feely approach to negotiations might still be effective. Not even Haller laughed at that one.

The Sun hacks knew they were not dealing with their usual cast of big-hearted truckers and gymslip mums who would normally sign away their life's memoirs for £500 before you could say 'How are we going to fill up that hole on page 14?'

Tough, hard words seemed the only way to attract Haller's attention. The *Sun* hacks were becoming angrier and angrier. '*Mein Gott*,' one blasphemed in the only German he could mimic, if not understand. He was the one who had been up all night driving from Berlin. His hair stood on end and his face was ashen. He was the owner of a false eye and thought nothing of popping it out during impromptu efforts to shock. In places like Ilford the trick sometimes helped to move negotiations on. In Germany, however, there seemed to be nothing that he could do to get Haller to hand over the ball. His grimacing and shell-shocked features were caught by both TV crews, who sold the shots on to England where they appeared on BBC and ITN broadcasts. It was one of the most vivid and frightening examples of genuine on-the-road rage ever to be caught on camera. More German journalists turned up, and all were astounded by the scenes of chaos outside the Villa d'Este. Herbert Schmoll, of the *Augsburger Allgemeine*, said: 'It was like standing in the middle of an auction. They were quoting astronomical figures…some were fighting.'

It was a few minutes after the *Sun* man's televised outburst that his news-paper's attack began to appear a bit lacklustre. Their defence also looked very vulnerable. After long journeys from London and other parts of Germany for the away tie, all were becoming extremely irritable. They began falling out with each other, blaming each other for the lack of progress in negotiations. The impasse saw the slick, organised and ultra-efficient *Sun* task force reduced to a ragtag of frantic individuals already thinking about foreign assignments on far-flung beaches, well away from the aggravation of provincial Germany. Journalists don't normally spend too much time working on the same subjects. Long, ponderous investigations are designed for academics and philosophers, not reporters. Compared to most trades, journalistic results are almost instantaneous. Lawyers can wait up to ten years for their cases to come to court, let alone come to a conclusion. Doctors can spend up to 60 years on a patient and still not get it right. Accountants and bank workers simply keep the wheels of capitalism turning, without ever waking up and thinking, 'I'm glad that's all over,' unless they're finally cashing in their pension plans and preparing to watch their final years tick by on their gold-plated carriage clocks. Journalists hate getting bogged down with anything which is long-winded, cumbersome and difficult to understand, like European Union agricultural policy or Thorsten Riedel.

By now the *Sun* men had been locked in negotiations for a full eight hours which, in journalistic terms, is the equivalent of around three months. There had been no punches in the air. There had been no cries of 'Yesss!'. There had not even been a decent lunch. The pressure from London was becoming more intense by the minute. All the *Sun* journalists got calls from Higgins who demanded to know what was going on, why things were taking so long, and had they tried the neighbours' relatives yet.

One of the photographers shook his head and went off to do a bit of shopping, a sure sign that the intense pressure was turning into a crisis. The reporters went off to make phone calls to anybody they could think of, as long as it wasn't Stuart Higgins. For a few crucial moments the entire *Sun* team had taken their eyes off the metaphorical ball. As yet, they had not even set eyes on the real one.

I was left standing in the alleyway with Haller, his son Jurgen and Riedel. Seeing that the *Sun* men had wandered off, the three of them beckoned me back inside the restaurant through a side door. The television journalists and local print reporters had their pictures and stories by now, and stayed in the alleyway to file their copy.

The Germans led me through the kitchens and down to a dingy cellar. Jurgen remained upstairs on guard as we descended some wooden steps. The basement was dank and smelt unwholesome. It was clearly where they kept the sauerkraut.

Private negotiations were going to start now, I thought. Haller wanted to isolate me from the *Sun* opposition so that he could force the price of the ball up and up. There would be another long-winded three hours of discussions, with Haller and Riedel doubling their *nein* totals before we all went home, disillusioned, upset and still hungry.

Then something totally unexpected happened. They produced the amber ball.

For the whole afternoon Haller had insisted the ball had been kept in a safe guarded by security guards at his house in Augsburg. He knew how vulnerable it would be at the restaurant and had kept insisting that it would not be produced until he was happy that a deal had been struck. He said that he would telephone the private security guards who would deliver it in an armed convoy.

When I eventually came to file my copy later that afternoon, he asked me to claim the ball was kept at his house. He was terrified that people might discover that the most famous football in English history had been left in a restaurant cellar along with perishable foodstuffs. At any moment it could have been skinned, pickled and served up as a tasteless Bavarian delicacy.

'Friend,' grinned Haller, impressively expanding his English vocabulary by another word.

The Germans trusted me. Maybe they felt guilty about the brutal way I had been greeted on arrival at the Villa d'Este. Maybe it was something to do with my status as the timid underdog. Maybe they were impressed by the fact that I could be worth a lot of money to them.

'It iz important that vee are all happy and that vee have all seen zer ball. Now is zer time ven vee can see zer ball,' said Riedel, who was lifting his chin high and expanding his pupils in an awesome display of Germanic seriousness. Even his Alf Ramsey syntax and pronunciation sounded more protracted than earlier.

Haller reached down into an old brown holdall. Inside there was a heavy, metal container which appeared rooted to the floor of the cellar. It might even have been concreted in. It had two padlocks on it and a security lock with a serial number. Riedel began entering the combination.

'Bound to be 1966,' I said, trying to diffuse the tension. Neither Haller nor Riedel smiled back.

The pair looked from left to right, which seemed an odd thing to do considering we were in an airless cellar with no windows, 15 feet below ground. Sweat was running down their foreheads as they reached into the metal container and took out an object covered in old newspapers. Haller began to unwrap it slowly.

'Getting the ball out makes me feel as though I'm back at Wembley again,' he said. He gave it a polish with his elbow. The ball was scuffed and stained but unmistakable. With a showman's smile, he held it in front of me.

I had located the amber ball with which Geoff Hurst had powered England to World Cup glory in the summer of 1966. The ball which Banks, Cohen, Wilson, Stiles, Charlton, Moore, Ball, Hurst, Hunt, Charlton and Peters had used to deadly effect in the supreme contest of footballing might.

There it was: the ball which had sent an entire nation to levels of ecstasy not seen since VE Day and the heyday of empire; the ball which had prompted the Queen of England to remove her sunglasses enthusiastically when it caused four bulges in the Germans' net. The ball which had caused unparalleled joy to every patriot in England from schoolchildren in Aertex shirts to Chelsea pensioners who still had their prickly khaki smocks from the Boer War.

The perfect symbol of English greatness was there before me: the ball which symbolised an event not far behind Magna Carta and the Civil War in terms of our historical development. It symbolised the kind of event which, according to our current national curriculum, should be taught objectively without any recourse to outdated and nationalistic displays of triumphalism.

My country's pride and joy was made manifest. Like a bugle packed into the Lion Mound at Waterloo or a bow preserved in the rich soil of Agincourt, this was a living symbol of epic proportions.

'Anybody got a pump?' I asked.

I touched the 30-year-old piece of leather in the same way that Gordon Banks had done when he got his first touch of the ball at Wembley. Like all goalkeepers, Banks had held the ball to his chest and caressed it as a mother would a new-born baby, testing it for weight, size and feel ... Goalkeepers are like that.

As I spun the ball around in my hands, and threw it up in the air I knew instinctively that it was the right one. There were still the scuffs and tears from the epic 1966 contest, but the leather had aged well and, if anything, it looked mellower and had even more character than it did the day it captured the imagination of the whole world. Even the scrawled signatures of Bobby Moore, Bobby Charlton, Uwe Seeler and Pelé, hastily scribbled across its panels with a give-away hotel pen, were just about decipherable. Best of all, the colour of the ball was almost unchanged. Its perfect amber glow was as warm and welcoming as the day Geoff Hurst broke German hearts and lifted the whole of England.

18 · Desk Yob

'What does it all mean?' is a question which lies at the heart of all journalistic endeavour. If you accept a loose definition of journalism as explaining to others something which you don't understand yourself, its complexities are made even more obvious.

When a news editor dispatches a team to some obscure German town no one has ever heard of, he doesn't do so because he's suffering the adverse effects of his high-pressure job. He may have given up all hope of a reasonable family life and happy retirement – let alone a proper night's sleep – to spend the prime of his life guiding gibbering incompetents, but there is still some kind of rationale underpinning his behaviour.

He sends people to distant places because he believes there's a good reason for it. The problem is that when the instructions are given, he has little real idea what the reason is. It's only when the day progresses, when barriers are broken down, and when a number of photographers are physically abused, that the reason why starts to emerge.

That's why a news editor is always at his most foul-mouthed first thing in the morning. During the first editorial conference of the day he has to stroll into The Editor's office and sound as though he's completely in charge of the situation. As well as knowing about every event which is happening in the world at any given moment, the news editor also has to list them all in order of importance. This is not as easy as it might sound.

When The Editor stares down at the news list and says, 'Why are we in Germany? Come on, I haven't got all day,' the news editor needs to reply nonchalantly, and without a hint of hesitation.

'Ah yes, we're currently in Neusass. It's in southern Germany and we're trying to interview a German footballer about a ball. I currently have a strong team down there and the moment Herr Haller starts speaking we'll be alongside him.'

It's when the impatient Editor asks what the German footballer will be saying, and why he's been stuck at the top of the news list along with the biggest IRA bomb on the British mainland ever, that the news editor really starts to earn his place in a high-backed executive chair complete with pump-action cushion and lumbar supports.

Accordingly, especially just before the conference, news editors have to telephone their reporters constantly. They swear profusely and scream: 'What does it all mean? What does it all mean?'

It's when The Editor administers his Big Bollocking of the day and starts making personal comments about his senior newsman's resemblance to a delinquent carpark attendant that answers have to emerge.

That's the whole point of journalism. It's unpredictable, disruptive and often very embarrassing and bad for the health. There are no right answers to anything. There are no obvious solutions, or places to go, or ways to act. That's what makes it all so incredibly difficult. The idea that the media is full of shifty-eyed ideologues and fanatical academics working on their 'agendas' is farcical.

Like the historian A.J.P. Taylor – who believed in the cock-up theory of history as opposed to the conspiracy theory – so real journalists believe that getting stories out is far more important than implementing a grand design. Students sitting down to analyse the workings of the press and television on their media studies courses should take a lesson from Geoff Hurst's third goal at Wembley. It was brilliant and brutally effective, but there was no rationale behind it whatsoever, apart from a hopeful hoof. News editors try hopeful hoofs every day. If they come off it's great for everyone involved. When they don't, he and his staff just start hoping that the Norwich office is well staffed up.

When I picked up my mobile telephone and told my newsdesk in London that I had located the 1966 World Cup ball, their reaction was predictable.

'Right, you've got the ball,' said an assistant news editor. 'You're in Bavaria and you've got the ball. Good ... good. Well ... well ... hang on a minute. You've got the ball and you're in Bavaria.' He spoke in such a literal fashion that I thought he might be working for the Germans.

I was handed over to another assistant news editor. Assistants on the desk are prone to passing the receiver on almost any big story they stumble across as they mope around the newsroom during the course of a working day, especially if The Editor has shown a particular interest in it.

'Hello, mate,' he said in a chirpy voice. 'How are you, mate? Having fun? You have so many foreign trips they'll be calling you Thomas Cook soon. Whereabouts are you this time?'

I remained silent.

He said: 'Right, well, hang on, mate. I know you're on a big one. Er, I think Derek wants a word.'

The other assistant news editor whom everybody thought would want to speak to me had momentarily left his desk to do something potentially more rewarding in life, like placing £20 on the second favourite in the 4.15 at Newmarket.

I got yet another assistant, who was a few more rungs up the editorial chain of command. 'Right, so you've got the ball. Well, I . . . I think that . . . At least I think that's what we want you to do. Hang on, I think there's someone here who wants a word,' he said.

All of them sounded vaguely stunned. I felt more than vaguely stunned. I felt like a striker standing in front of the net with the goalkeeper lying sprawling at my feet and not a defender in sight. Now was the time to shoot hard and low. To score the killer goal which would end any hope the opposition might have of getting back into the game. I needed an unexcitable Alf Ramsey to start shouting calm, authoritative words from the touchline, a voice of simple wisdom in a massively complicated world.

What I got instead was two minutes of vague 'ers' and someone asking after my health. I asked to be put through to somebody who had some experience and common sense – John, the newsdesk driver.

Newsdesk drivers are some of the most important people in newspaper offices. They're the crucial link between editors and on-the-road reporters; always ready with a friendly and well-informed word of unfussy advice about career prospects. Drivers are often on first-name terms with senior executives, so they'll know exactly how your contribution is being discussed in the sinister command bunkers found on the perimeters of all newsrooms. If things are going well, they'll tell you as much with a bit of cheeky banter thrown in to lift the spirits even more. As you fumble around the world, desperately trying to meet deadlines and find unpronounceable villages, they'll make you feel as though someone, somewhere, really cares. If things are going wrong, they can normally let you know if you're going to last the week or not.

The drivers are also an important link with readers, mainly because they're among the few people who actually bother to speak to them. They're the ones who respond to most of the phone calls from those who think they've found a new planet. When others call and offer long-winded explanations and intimate details about their serious health problems or difficulties with the TV repair man, it will be the newsdesk driver who's there to lend an ear. They're an oasis of humility and sensitivity in a desert of hard, back-biting professionalism.

By the time I got through to John, he wasted no time in telling me that The Editor was taking a particular interest in the amber ball. He said he had already administered a hat-trick of Big Bollockings. He suggested that all those involved in the story might not last the week. The top man had already likened one of his news editors to a vampire who only came out at night and who 'didn't have the charisma to motivate a sixer with an armful of cub scout initiative badges, let alone a team of reporters'. John urged me to get straight on to an executive editor. 'This is one for the big boys, mate,' he said in a low voice. 'The lads on this desk are havin' a laugh if they think they're up to it.'

I was passed on to one of the command bunkers where executive editors plan the futures of the national institutions which are our daily newspapers. By the time I got through, one of the great men inside had already been told by an excited assistant that the ball had been located and I was standing in a cellar waiting for instructions. He had been told that both the Sun and the German media had been given the slip, and that I was awaiting orders.

I could almost hear his great mind turning over, working out the next step in the masterplan to bring home a sporting icon. It's for this type of moment that editors are selected: moments when a wrong instruction or slip of the tongue can end in defeat, while a brilliant, inspired command can lead to utter and complete glory. Now was the moment for ice-cold nerve and inspirational command. The ball was in my hands, and I was ready for action.

'Can you steal it?' said the executive editor.

I looked at Haller and Riedel's expectant faces, which were about three inches away from my own. We were all pressed together in the tiny cellar, without even room for the Mirror photographer who was upstairs acting as a decoy for the Sun men.

The ladder leading up to the trapdoor exit was obscured by two big Germans. There were no windows. The mobile phone was pressed hard against my ear, but I would not have been in the least surprised if Riedel could hear every single word.

'Yes, I've found the ball and I think we're ready to do business with our great friends and allies from Germany,' I said, trying to sound as diplomatic and Germanically literal as possible. I continued: 'Our friends from Germany, including Herr Haller who is standing here next to me, less than three inches away from my face, is ready to do a deal with us. He and his friend, Herr Riedel, who speaks perfect English, can probably hear everything you're saying to me. They send their regards to you and hope to meet you one day.'

I smiled reassuringly at my new friends who were by now marking me even closer than Horst Hottges used to try and tail strikers like Geoff Hurst. There was a pause for a few seconds, and then a decision.

'Bring Haller and his friend to England. Tell them to bring the ball, too. We'll sort things out over here,' said the executive. His reasoning was simple: bring the opposition back to your own ground, and you're halfway to a home win.

'Herr Haller, will you come to England with me?' I asked, through Riedel.

He agreed. I told the executive to expect us back within a few hours.

'Vait,' said Riedel, before I hung up on London. 'Vee must work out exactly when zer ball comes into England. Vee vill not be taking it viz us.'

I kept the executive editor on the phone for another few minutes, as we improvised a plan. We hoped that it would be as effective as the masterplan which Alf Ramsey drew up to help his troops conquer the world in 1966.

We all agreed that route one – all travelling back to Britain on the same plane together with the ball – was far too dangerous. The German media and, far more worryingly, the Sun men, would be all over us and ready to kick us out of the game. It was already turning into a nasty, aggressive contest, and there were still plenty of options left open to the opposition, including theft.

Selling a dummy was a possibility, but again fraught with danger. We thought of announcing to the Sun team that Haller did not have the ball after all, and that we were going home. We would then spend a night at a motorway hotel before sneaking back to Neusass and whisking everyone back to Britain on a private jet. The trouble with that plan was that it would leave Haller and the ball unguarded. The Sun men would think nothing of keeping an overnight watch on his house and his restaurant. Our final plan needed to be bold and workable.

Haller, Riedel and I would leave the restaurant immediately and make for Munich. The Sun men were bound to follow and we would be back in London in time for first edition. We would then lose the opposition at Heathrow, stay overnight at a secret location in the Home Counties, and carry on our negotiations. Then, on the Friday, we would have the whole day to make sure the Germans got the money they wanted. When everybody was happy with the deal, we would go to another secret location and wait.

Meanwhile, Jurgen Haller, the photographer and, most important of all, the ball would remain at the Villa d'Este for an hour or two. When we were safely out of the way, pursued by the vast majority of the Sun contingent and probably the entire German media, our second team would make their way to Amsterdam. They would remain in Holland until they were entirely satisfied that our negotiations had been a success. When the money for the ball had been paid, they would fly into England and link up with the rest of us. Then we would be in a position to reunite Geoff Hurst with his long-lost ball.

From the German viewpoint the plan was acceptable because it meant the ball would not arrive in Britain until a price had been fixed, and the money paid over in cash. From our point of view it was acceptable because Haller would be with us at all times. His influence in making sure the operation went smoothly was crucial. The sinister Riedel would also be kept in sight, making sure he could not get up to anything sneaky.

The whole thing was simple; so, so simple. I shuddered at the simplicity of it all.

We emerged from the cellar at 4.10 p.m. local time. Operation Inflation was ready to be executed.

19 · Depth Charges

The price of the football had risen to £70,000. I often wonder whether a few more minutes underground might have led to the cost reaching six figures.

The historical significance of German hyper-inflation in the 1920s, when the price of a string of Kaiser sausages meant you had to take a wheelbarrow to the local butcher's instead of a wallet, seemed wildly over-played compared to the ever-rising price of Geoff Hurst's ball.

The Sun men, who miraculously had not found their way into the cellar, soon sensed there was something going on. They watched suspiciously as we all sat down in the restaurant's back yard, and began making telephone calls. Riedel and Haller were calling up overnight bags, in the way that all efficient Germans are prone to do. I expected that Riedel's bag would contain everything from dental floss to those irritating flip-flops which people wear in unfamiliar showers to make sure they don't get verrucas. He would also have a telescopic umbrella and a fold-away mac.

If anything, I felt more nervous than before Operation Inflation had been formulated. When we arrived so late at the restaurant I thought that the most I would end up with was indigestion. The discovery of the ball and the subsequent interest from senior executives on the paper had all come frighteningly quickly. We were no longer North Korea, willingly plodding along and having a good go at trying to keep up with the tournament favourites. We were the ones in control, the movers and shakers who had the path to glory beautifully mapped out in front of us.

We were now in a position where there could be no mistakes, where the senior editors were not hoping but *expecting* us to bring the ball back for Geoff Hurst and England. The pressure tempted me to ignore London and book a flight to anywhere in the world. Sadly this tactic has been tried by journalists in the past and failed miserably. (A reporter had located a missing English nanny on the Spanish island of Tenerife and, like us, was being pursued by a sizeable pack of rival journalists. His foreign desk agreed that the best thing for him to do would be to get the next available flight off the island so as to get away from them all and begin filing his copy in time for next edition. Twelve hours later, when the London-based executives had finally written off their exclusive and were beginning to worry about their man's safety – in that order – he finally called in. 'Where the hell are you, you worthless, useless, incompetent, rubbish, irrelevant piece of shit?' the incandescent foreign editor enquired.

'Rio,' came the reply.)

The Sun men did not look happy at all. They were tired, irritable and hungry. Now they also had a couple of subjects upon which they could aim their frustration and anger: Mike Moore and me.

I'd done a lot of things for newspapers in the past. I'd endured all kinds of hardships, but I still had a list of things I would not do for the sake of my journalism. These included dressing up in any kind of pantomime animal costume, taking part in contrived picture opportunities with B-list celebrities or initiating any kind of stunt outside a West End nightclub or 10 Downing Street. Top of the list, though, was anything which involved physical pain.

The Sun knew we were up to something. They began to gather round us, listening to my every word as I phoned the Mirror travel company. I ordered three places on the 7.30 p.m. Lufthansa flight to Heathrow from Munich. We would have around two hours to get to the airport, gain an hour in the air, and have plenty of time to file something for Friday's paper en route. Pictures could also be taken at the airport, so Moore had no problems about staying in mainland Europe.

The Sun also booked places on the Lufthansa flight and began organising their forces. Two of them kept a close guard on the Mirror photographer and Haller, while the rest of us were followed out on to the restaurant porch. There a minor panic set in when the German media desperately started firing questions at Haller. He looked at one stage as though he might be leaving us to take part in that evening's edition of Bavaria Tonight. Lead interviews on BBC World, Sky News and CNN did not appear out of the question, either.

Haller had been disconsolate after failing to win the World Cup in Chile in 1962, England in 1966 and Mexico in 1970. He felt the world's media had not given him a fair share of the limelight, especially considering his status as one of the finest midfield generals of his generation. He had slipped off to play his club football for Bologna and Juventus and, apart from the maniacal Italian press with their huge headlines and hysterical editorials, he had felt that not enough fuss had been made about his talent. Now he was back in the centre of things again. He might just be Helmut Haller of the Villa d'Este and the best sports shop in Augsburg, but he was relishing his new-found stardom.

'I am returning to England to take zer World Cup ball of 1966 home as a goodwill gesture,' said Haller, before launching into a detailed description of his Wembley opener.

At first we feared Haller was putting the whole of Operation Inflation in jeopardy. His goal-sized mouth would give the entire game away. Then it dawned on us that his bravado and showmanship were crucial to our plans. He was whipping up publicity which would spread all over the world. The ball was nowhere near him, so it could not be stolen.

Haller was the playmaker again – the sprightly terrier at the centre of the park through whom our entire game would be played. He would deal with the opposition, the crowds, the press interest. He would be our decoy and our finisher – our team-mate.

Haller's other spectacular contribution to the journey back to England came when I began loading the Opel Kadett which I presumed I would be driving back to Munich. As I fiddled hopelessly with something in the boot, one of the Sun men stuck his hand through the side driver's window of the car and stole the ignition keys. He then ran away.

Klaus, who was by now completely on our side and already looking forward to an inflated win bonus, immediately began bounding towards him. Other Germans rushed over from the Villa d'Este's porch trying to take pictures. The little group sprinted away down the alleyway at the side of the restaurant where we had spent so long locked in negotiations.

They ended up racing each other for around a quarter of a mile before the Sun photographer was brought down by a flying tackle. A scuffle ensued, so even if we had waited for the return of the keys, we would have still been standing pathetically on the porch for at least half an hour. We would have missed our flights and lost any hope of getting back in time for first edition. Eventually, I later learned, Klaus had got the keys back and gave them to Moore but the whole process had taken almost as long as it had to negotiate for the football.

Haller stared quizzically at the inactive Opel Kadett for a few seconds before picking up his mobile telephone. He called up two matt black and extremely sinister-looking Porsche sports cars. It really was an inspired move; the kind of thing you see in unlikely Hollywood blockbusters about Miami drugs barons, or filed as barely credible news-in-briefs by dubious foreign freelancers with names like Bruce or Giuseppe. I could almost picture the paragraph: 'A super-efficient German businessman came up with a perfect solution when a Hertz hire car was immobilised by a thuggish photographer who had stolen the keys. The Teutonic trouble-shooter picked up his mobile and dialled up a pair of Porsche 911 Turbos.'

The new cars were in front of us within a couple of minutes. Haller had executed his greatest move of the game so far with the same efficiency and calm with which he had scored his splendid opener in the '66 final. A little shimmy, a move to the left and the right, and then, *pow*, the killer strike, this time with his right hand and mobile telephone rather than his right boot.

Haller had phoned another ex-pro who had chosen a second career familiar to retired 1970s footballers: a dealership garage happy to supply sponsored cars to former team-mates. The garage also rustled up two expert drivers from their accounts department. They were not there just to make sure there were no delays at the airport; they were there to make sure the massively expensive cars got back to Neusass in perfect condition.

Haller and Riedel got one, while I was left with a supremely earnest chauffeur called Heinrich. He smiled enthusiastically as I plunged into the leather passenger seat next to him, flinging my overnight bag into the seat behind.

'English, English. *Ja*, English are my friends now,' he suddenly enthused, in such an exaggerated manner that I immediately felt uneasy.

Heinrich was probably about forty, with a Kaiser-sized moustache. Instead of the ubiquitous Henry Plantagenet hairstyle, he had more of a Libyan mature-maths-student light perm. He wore a sports casual driving kit, complete with black leather gloves and shades with irritating little designer labels on the reflective lenses.

Before jumping into the Porsche I telephoned Moore to make sure all was well. He said that Jurgen Haller was briefed and ready to go, and that they would not have too much trouble losing the *Sun* doorman and the photographer who had been left behind to tail them. All they were waiting for was the keys to their car, which were currently being fought over out of earshot in a back alleyway.

I spun round in my seat to make sure that Haller and Riedel were safely in the back of their Porsche. It was faintly amusing to watch the gangly goalkeeper crammed into the tiny space behind the two main seats. Flashguns were going off, and questions were still being screamed out in German as we made our way out on to the main Augsburg-to-Munich road.

A group of German TV people jumped into their outside broadcast van, which began following us. They put their foot down and appeared determined to tail us for as long as they could. In front of them was a large black Mercedes. It was full of journalists and photographers from the *Sun*.

Despite the opposition being in such close pursuit, Heinrich's driving was as deadly dull and oh-so-efficient as one might expect from a furrow-browed Bavarian with a Colonel Gadaffi hairdo who knew he could not put a single scratch on his boss's car. There were no handbrake turns, no wheel-spins, no obscene gestures to sales reps trying to overtake in the inside lane. No,

Heinrich just pulled up his black gloves, adjusted his driving fleece, lowered his dark glasses, put a German techno-pop cassette in the hi-fi and drove.

What we really needed were some exciting twists and turns but, being Germany, the roads were as bland as the local food. The main motorway from Augsburg to Munich is as straight as an arrow and enlivened only by the occasional service station selling environmentally friendly petrol and environmentally unfriendly sausages.

It was going to be a fraught journey but it would provide me with my first real chance of the day to get some copy over. Of course I was pleased that the real negotiations could now start, but realised only too well that it was not even half-time as far as the whole saga was concerned. I sat back in my seat and listened to the cassette. Like all techno-music it had a dull, monotonous beat and lyrics such as 'Boom, boom, boom' and 'Vee like to party'.

Heinrich tapped his fingers on the wheel and pointed his Porsche 911 in the direction of Munich.

20 · Unromantic Road

'Faster, faster,' I yelled at Heinrich, trying to bring out the Michael Schumacher in him. Unfortunately, 'faster' was one of many English words Heinrich could not understand, and one which few Germans can pronounce. 'Ja . . . vater, vater,' he grinned back at me. What did his father have to do with it all? 'Ja, my vater vud be proud of me,' Heinrich grinned, his Kaiser moustache showing a flicker of animation for the first time since we had met on the steps of the Villa d'Este. It was the only part of him to show any real animation for our entire two-hour drive together. 'I am helping my English friends. Vee are all brothers now,' Heinrich explained, rather melodramatically. 'Vat happened in zer past iz all in zer past now,' he continued, suddenly adopting a disturbingly literal tone of voice. 'Now, you talk about my vater . . .'

I sensed a confessional anecdote coming on. Heinrich's brow furrowed suddenly and he appeared ready to get something off his chest. My limited command of German was severely exposed by his rantings. As far as I could grasp, his father had either been a centre-forward involved in the controversial Berlin international of 1938 when England's players were forced to perform a fascist salute, or else he had been an Ossie double agent who had brought shame to the family's good name by betraying British intelligence at around the same time. Or both.

I told Heinrich that car conversations made me feel sick. He unfurrowed his brow and got back to his gear changes, and tapping his fingers to 'Let's go techno. Yeah, yeah, yeah. Boom, boom, boom. Vee like to party'.

Looking up into the vanity mirror at the back of the windscreen visor, I could see Haller's head bobbing up and down in the front seat of the Porsche behind us. He was grinning as the Sun men's Mercedes swerved and skidded in his car's slipstream.

One of the Sun reporters held up a sheet of paper and pretended to write on it using an imaginary pen. He looked like an awkward diner trying to get the bill from a haughty waiter. He occasionally pointed furiously at the side of the road. The reporter knew, of course, what Haller's reaction to our earlier sky scribblings had been, but saw no reason not to keep trying.

Haller began to pull quizzical faces, pretending he had no idea that he was being offered the chance to pull over on to the hard shoulder to sign a contract.

His face would become more and more serious and then, as the Sun car pulled alongside in the outside lane of the autobahn (we were travelling at around 100mph in the slow lane) he would burst out laughing.

Haller was enjoying the sport. In the same way that he had goaded and mimicked opposing footballers as a young man, he was revelling in the thrill of another chase. As a midfielder for West Germany and three club sides, his trademark mazy runs through the centre of the field almost always ended with a wide smile. Haller was naturally confrontational and saw ribald humour as the natural punishment for defeated opponents. Over the years he had also discovered that mimicry and cruel jibes about unfortunate personal features could be very effective. He was particularly taken by the FA Cup ears and buck teeth of one of the Sun journalists. As he laughed Haller put both his hands to the side of his head and wiggled them around in the style of a demented hare. You could see his lips mouthing a Germanic word beginning with 'c'.

Just as Jack Charlton had thrown his raised arms down in disgust at Haller's opening goal in the 1966 final, so the Sun men were becoming increasingly irritated by the German's baiting. They snarled and cursed. They were begin- ning to despise the 'little fat bastard' in the same way that England's defenders had disliked him so much 30 years before. As they stared out at him through two sets of side windows, they pulled faces and made hand gestures which had little to do with signing contracts. At 100mph on a grey German motorway they might as well have been smiling and clapping the comic brilliance of a midfield maestro. For the moment, I was glad Haller was on our side.

'I zink he iz happy,' said Heinrich, who had been watching the entertain- ment through his rearview mirror. 'Helmut laughs out loud, like he iz a young man again. He reminds me of my vater . . .'

I gave Heinrich a despairing stare before he twitched his moustache quizzically and returned to his driving duties.

Perfectly planned but featureless towns passed by as the rain-filled clouds above added to the depressingly functional feel of the main Augsburg-to- Munich road. It was a predominantly urban landscape punctuated by just a few pine forests and grain fields.

Our journey was developing into a flight of destiny and, although not expecting a sun-kissed Pacific Highway glowing in the purple sea haze, it would have been nice to have started out on a more atmospheric path to glory. The occasional green field would certainly have improved things.

We were not far from the Romantic Road, two hundred miles of Germany's finest architectural and rural heritage with highlights including the *residenz* of the prince bishops and the works of the woodcarver Tilman Riemenschneider in the Tauber Valley. Just as close were the fairytale castles of the mad King Ludwig II, and the historic towns of Heidelberg and Rothenburg ober der Tauber. All we got on our grim motorway were mind-numbing provincial towns like Neusass, concrete and tarmac, a token bit of uninspiring country-side and thousands of other cars.

When Heinrich put his foot down we would screech past numerous Volkswagen Beetles with stickers in the rear window saying: 'Learn to be the person your dog thinks you are.' There were also quite a lot of Trabants, some of the most embarrassing relics of East Germany's communist past. Made of glass-reinforced plastic, the cars are normally green or light blue and driven by lank-haired sociology students. They always pull out into an outside lane at 40mph, just when you're trying to speed up. They make a horrible rasping noise, have bumpers which hang precariously around an inch from the ground, and leave trails of thick black smoke. Their exhaust pipes are usually bouncing along the tarmac, causing more sparks than a metal shoe protector on Wembley Way. The 'Trabbies' have 'Berlin Wall – No Thanks' stickers in the rear window. Most were made well before November 1989 which, coincidentally, is normally around the time their drivers started their degree courses.

The Sun Mercedes overtaking us dangerously was about as uplifting as things got. Juggernauts speeding past at 130mph in no particular lane also helped to make the journey more unpleasant. They would creep up behind us and start flashing their massive headlights. If we ignored their signal they would pull into another lane and overtake anyway.

Those terrifying hulks pulsating along glistening tarmac, inches from Heinrich's moustache, left me in doubt that autobahns could only have been invented by a devil. The concept belongs on a 1930s general election manifesto under the Mass Destruction subheading.

Despite such close encounters, Heinrich, by now silent, appeared unflustered, if vaguely confused. While cruising past the first of many motor-way restaurants, he even suggested that he organise a pit stop so that we could stock up on takeaway sauerkraut and overdone Kaisers. I politely suggested that might be a worse idea than a confessional anecdote as far as his future prospects in life were concerned.

'I did not mean any offence,' he said.

'Don't worry, Heinrich,' I reassured him, before discussing my objectives out loud. The medium-term priority was to deliver Haller to London and the long-term priority was to secure the arrival of the ball. The short-term priority was to file some copy. Only eight hours in the country and I was already reasoning like a German.

I plugged my mobile telephone into Heinrich's unused cigarette lighter and began to file.

'Catchline: Ball. From Peter Allen in –' I shouted at a bemused copytaker sitting somewhere in east London. I paused to work out in which of the world's locations I was currently situated. '– In Neusass, Bavaria,' I offered, before quickly changing my mind. Neusass conjured up negative images. It sounded small, provincial, and obsessed with traffic-calming schemes. It made me think of Euro families wearing day-glo jackets and oblong helmets while negotiating traffic-calming measures on their matching bicycles.

'No – erase that,' I said. 'I'm actually in Munich.' The name of the German city sounded metropolitan and grand – sinister, even.

It was the copytaker's job to write down everything I said so that it could be passed on to my newsdesk and considered for publication.

Dictation on the telephone is called 'running copy'. It normally means journalists are sprinting out of a court building so as to be the first to tell the world that 'Arry the 'Atchet has drawn a 20 for chopping an associate to death in a Chingford health spa. Normally the words flow pretty smoothly and you're even allowed to use notes you made earlier. The dullest courtroom proceedings can accordingly be flamed up into something vaguely printable.

Hence a minor judgement by East Anglian magistrates – farmer fined £75 for shooting pigeon who was eating his seeds – becomes: 'The penalty for stealing seeds in south Norfolk is death, a court ruled yesterday. Killer farmer Terence Baldernose, 62, described the bird who was feeding off his produce as "miserable vermin". The court did not hear what the pigeon thought of Terence Baldernose.'

When you're being pursued by demonic lorry drivers, a German outside-broadcast van and Sun journalists along the autobahn to hell at 100mph somewhere between Augsburg and Munich, with no idea what you're meant to be writing about, the process becomes a little less straightforward.

'What am I supposed to be filing? What I didn't have for lunch – sauerkraut if anyone's interested,' I thought out loud.

'How do you spell "sauerkraut"?' asked the copytaker, using a copytaker's second-favourite expression. The first is 'Is there much more of this?' Other popular expressions frequently used by copytakers include 'Are you making this stuff up?' and 'What's this rubbish all about, then?'

I told her to erase everything I had said so far and composed my thoughts.

This was an important moment. I was on the way back to England having set eyes on the Holy Grail of our nation's sport. I was the first Englishman in 30 years to have touched the wondrous amber orb which symbolised everything that was great about our country. True, the ball might currently be in the hands of a dodgy German sports shop manager and a Formula One-obsessed photographer without a car, but I was still optimistic about its future. Surely this was something I could express with poetry and conviction. I braced myself and gripped the telephone tightly to my lips.

We were in a traffic jam around 15 minutes from Munich Airport. Heinrich began to pick his nose.

'The ball that soccer legend Geoff Hurst blasted to 1966 World Cup glory for England was yesterday back in British hands – mine,' I offered, not forgetting our Scottish, Welsh and Irish readers (I was certain they would be delighted by the whole story, especially the Scots).

That would do, I thought, adding for good measure: 'I tracked it down to the home of retired footballer Helmut Haller who played for losing finalists Germany in the historic 4–2 match.'

When a journalist gets a first and second line in, half the work's usually done. A couple more paragraphs and you can start to read out the big chunky quotes from your notebook so as to substantiate the introduction and pad out a decent thousand-word story. Then you can declare a relieved 'Ends' to the copytaker and head off to somewhere more pleasant than the soulless highways, windswept pavements and smoky workmen's cafés in which we spend so much of our time.

I rummaged through the pockets of my increasingly bedraggled blue suit and checked my notes. There were none. All the shorthand scribblings I had made were in the back of the Opel Kadett in Neusass. This was going to be a tricky thousands words.

Despite the obvious problems, I managed in the same way that I'd coped in 1994 without a floor pass to John Major's conference address. The event had been early proof that you don't need written documentation to report on anything. You just smile, look vaguely interested in proceedings, and wing it.

Anyway, this wasn't about Helmut Haller, or anything he might or might not have said. At this stage it was all about England. I needed to describe in graphic detail what it was like to find a sporting icon after it had been stolen and kept hidden for 30 years. I thought of the moment the ball first appeared, and what a subdued nation would think about it all. I began to file.

The copytaker started to sound marginally less bored than usual. Instead of stifled yawns and the munching of a feta-cheese-and-roast-vegetable sandwich (many copytakers have A-levels), I could just about hear a vaguely impressed mumble of 'mmm, mmm' after every sentence. True, she hadn't reacted with any particular excitement to my opening line, but there was nothing new in that. Copytakers are notorious for sounding bored and unemotional about every field of human activity. If you've ever tried using the only telephone line out of a desolate killing field to describe the horrific torture and murder of innocent people by gun-wielding maniacs, you'll know that a copytaker usually sounds as animated as a double-glazing salesman negotiating a new mortgage. Throw in a graphic description of pioneering micro-surgery and the discovery of Lord Lucan, and they'll sound as animated as the same salesman discussing index-linked equities with the actuary from two doors down.

Providing emotional support to distant journalists is something else copytakers fall short on. If there were a telephonic opposite of a Samaritan, it would be a copytaker. When you haven't eaten or washed for three days, haven't got a word in the paper for three weeks, and are calling from a place of indescribable grief in some inhospitable wilderness, you would understandably sound pretty low. Severely depressed might be an exaggeration, but when your photographer starts up about his new bathroom extension and Michael Schumacher's prospects in the Brazilian Grand Prix, you do start to wonder.

My lowest moment in journalism involving a copytaker came on the island of Sark, when I was pursuing a little-known arms-dealer across the Channel Islands with an ultra-keen photographer in tow. Our quarry had broken the United Nations weapons embargo to Rwanda by supplying shipments of AK-47 rifles, grenade launchers, rockets, mortar bombs, grenades and ammunition to the African state. He was not a man to cross, but it was an important doorstep. There are no cars on Sark, only sheep, so when we arrived we had to stand in the pouring rain as our luggage was unloaded on to the sodden quay. We placed what used to be two sturdy suitcases on an open cart and had to make our own way across two miles of countryside to our hotel.

After the hour-long boat trip I was feeling incredibly ill. It was as though my physical form and sense of direction in life had both been left behind in a Guernsey hotel room. I'd definitely left my breakfast behind – it was still smeared across the stern cabin waiting for the next 14-foot wave to wash it away on the return journey. By the time we completed the yomp to the hotel, my own sensible city kit was sopping wet. I felt lower than I'd ever done in my professional career.

The photographer, meanwhile, seemed alert and ready for anything that life could throw at him, even if it was a couple of mortar bombs and a few rounds from an AK47. He was one of those outdoor, physical photographers who carry camouflaged waterproof clothing and smear rabbit droppings across their faces to avoid detection as they skulk in heavy undergrowth. He probably

FALLING HERO

Geoff Hurst staggers backwards as, with trademark
puffed cheeks, he powers the amber ball past
Uwe Seeler to score England's controversial
third goal in the World Cup final of 1966.

BORDER DISPUTE

Roger Hunt, Bobby Charlton and Hurst turn away in celebration
as the furious West Germans claim that the ball did not cross
the goal line.

SAFETY AREA
Clutching the ball to his chest, England goalkeeper Gordon
Banks is surrounded by a wall of impenetrable defenders in his
penalty box.

FAMOUS FOURTH
Wolfgang Overath looks on quizzically as Hurst thrashes the ball
goalward to make it 4–2 to England in the most famous image
of the 1966 final.

BENCH MARK

West German manager Helmut Schoen (left) holds his hand to his forehead as most of England celebrates victory, Alf Ramsey (centre) remains seated while Harold 'Sit Down' Shepherdson leaps skyward. Jimmy Greaves (in suit, next to Royal Marine band leader) looks almost as disconsolate as he did when Roger Hunt took his place in the final team.

LAP OF DISHONOUR

Helmut Haller and his team mates celebrate coming second by parading the stolen ball towards the West German fans at Wembley.

GOLDEN DAZE

Elated yet clearly bemused, Nobby Stiles kisses the Jules Rimet trophy as his captain Bobby Moore (centre) and manager Ramsey congratulate each other.

BEATLES GAME

John, Paul, George, Ringo and Prime Minister Harold Wilson
help define the Swinging Sixties.

HEAD MEN
England managers Kevin Keegan and Tony Blair – two of the architects of 'footballing' Britain – show off their natural talent.

ALL TOGETHER NOW
Helmut Haller, author, and George Cohen let bygones be
bygones.

FINISHING TOUCH
Hurst finally lets Tilkowski get near the legendary ball.

had dental floss, a telescopic umbrella, flip-flops and a fold-away mac in his backpack too. He whistled 'Whistle While You Work' all the time and stopped every five minutes to answer calls on his mobile phone. The ringing tone was 'Whistle While You Work' too.

Things got worse. The arms-dealer, who seemed less of a priority by now than physical survival, had slipped off the island on his yacht. His secretary announced the news to us with a grin after we had waded across a couple of streams and negotiated at least two quagmires and four flocks of sheep to knock on the palatial farmhouse he called his office. It was also a fine family home, complete with swimming-pool and ornamental gardens. We could imagine the businessman – whose wares were regularly sold in lively South American hot-spots as well as wretched African states – staring across his grounds every morning when he was not on his yacht and thinking to himself: 'Death's been good to me.'

The next boat off the island was late the next morning and it was now barely lunchtime. Our tiny wooden hotel had just one heated room – the main lounge – and just one phone in the centre of it. The only other guest was a sweet old man recovering from a stroke. He'd spent his life working the nightshift at Ford Dagenham and wasn't the greatest conversationalist in the world, which was probably quite a good thing.

The photographer, meanwhile, had enjoyed a nip of whiskey (from his all-weather flask carried in his all-weather rucksack) and looked in his element as he rocked backwards and forwards on one of the three wooden rocking-chairs in the room.

'If you could pick your top ten of car braking systems from anywhere in the world, what would they be?' he asked.

'Copy, I've got to file copy,' I lied, crawling towards the telephone.

'You won't believe this,' I whispered at the copytaker. 'I'm incredibly ill, cold and wet and I'm just about to undergo mental torture. I've travelled miles to speak with someone who's not in, and the next ferry isn't until tomorrow. Do you think it will make a piece for the paper?'

'No,' came the reply.

'Oh,' I replied. 'But I'm on one of the smallest Channel Islands and –'

The phone went dead. Copytakers just never seem to listen.

Personal mutilation seemed a more attractive proposition than spending the next 24 hours in the company of a car-obsessed photographer and a silent invalid. We were also in the middle of a soulless, windswept mound of earth which Britain had been more than happy to leave to the Germans during the Second World War. Life did not get much worse.

The Porsche skidded to a halt outside one of the many terminals at Munich Airport and I jumped out, still clutching my mobile phone to my ear. Haller and Riedel zoomed up behind me. We left Heinrich to sort out the cars and strode purposefully towards a check-in desk.

As we were transported along the miles of moving conveyor belts and unhelpful signs which distinguish Munich Airport from all the other equally unattractive airports in the world, the copy began to flow like Bobby Charlton's tears. I even troubled Haller for a quote, to make my words sound more meaningful.

'Helmut, what does the ball mean to you?' I asked.

'Do you ever shut up about that blasted ball?' he replied.

'You'll have to do better than that, Helmut,' I insisted.

The sulky Riedel and Haller put their heads together and came up with a compromise. If I didn't mention the ball for the entire flight, Haller would come out with something really contrived and un-Germanically sentimental for me. We shook hands on the deal.

Haller said: 'The football means a great deal to me but I never realised it meant so much to the people of England. You're right to return it home.'

Corny, but he was getting into the spirit of things.

As I prepared to hang up on the copytaker, her voice sounded less like a bored drawl and more of a vaguely interested whine. And she only used the expression 'Is there much more of this?' twice.

By the time I said 'Ends', we were on first-name terms. 'Thank you for all your help, Brian,' I said, thinking to myself that Brian was a very odd name for a woman.

'Briony. Don't you ever listen, you bloody idiot,' Briony replied, before slamming the phone down.

21 · Air Play

The *Sun* Mercedes and the outside-broadcast vans had screeched up behind us. Flashguns and cameras were still going off with alarming regularity, and Haller was still being shouted at by the opposing journalists from both Britain and Germany. Reidel stood next to him, using his sinister glare to ward off trouble.

Munich Airport is noted for having one of the most complicated sets of departure lounges in Europe. For the next 20 minutes we were all able to forget our immediate problems in life on a troublesome quest to pick up our airline tickets, check in and get on our Lufthansa flight back to London. The *Sun* men had to put up with even more mobile phone calls from their editor as they tailed us around the interminable corridors and moving stairways.

'A14 or A50?' was our first problem as we tried to find the right desk. Before long, 'Where is A14 or A50?' became a more pertinent question as we found ourselves in the middle of a huge glass-and-polished-steel terminal which was not due to be officially opened until the new millennium.

Other passengers, mainly German businessmen in rimless glasses and check suits, stared in disbelief as they watched Haller, the football legend, being pursued by a mob of reporters and photographers. His extraordinary path round and round the departure halls and check-in desks of the vast airport appeared baffling to us, let alone the onlookers.

Throughout our journey Riedel had been clutching a large duffle-bag which could easily have been taken for a hiding place for the ball. It had a couple of big bumps in it and, considering Riedel was only expected to stay in England for a couple of days, they were unlikely to be his goalkeeper's gloves. A researcher working for one of the German TV companies targeted Riedel and tried to get him to open his bag. 'It iz your duty,' he whispered emphatically, as if both Riedel and Haller were letting the entire federal republic down by their treacherous flight to Britain.

When we stopped at a junction to consider the merits of taking escalator S4 to departure lounge A2/3, escalator S19 to departure lounge A4/12 or staircase N12 down to the gentlemen's toilets, the researcher – no more than six foot tall (which is pretty small in Germany) – pounced. He grabbed Riedel's bag and began tugging at the zip. Unlike many of the British journalists, this young German was motivated by heady idealism. The ball was nothing to do with money or circulation drives. It was to do with Germany's place in the world, and its bold progression into a bright new tomorrow (the lad was a big *Star Trek* fan).

Riedel was furious and started screaming at him. The two fell to the floor. The researcher was clearly shortsighted (the rimless lenses on his glasses were about two inches thick) but his features were those of a young fanatic. He looked in severe pain, both mental and physical, as he tussled with the lanky Riedel. The goalkeeper took every opportunity to grind his bony elbow into the researcher's ribs, a particularly unpleasant manoeuvre which he had frequently practised on fanatical strikers on the field of play.

'*Nein, nein.* Vee must have the ball for Germany,' shouted the TV man, who was called Wilhelm and wore a standard blond Henry Plantagenet hairdo along with a black polo-shirt, black jeans and black jacket.

He got the upper hand over Riedel and managed to reach inside the duffle-bag. Riedel had his arm around his neck and, even if the ball had been in the bag, would not have let it escape.

Wilhelm felt around for a few minutes before realising the bag contained little more than a pair of flip-flops, toiletries and fresh clothes. The bumps were caused by towels which all Germans carry on holidays with them for placing by the poolside in the morning to stop others from stealing the sunbeds. The old national character clichés are the best, I remembered thinking. Where Riedel was going, the towels would be about as useful as a pair of goalkeeper's gloves, but he still had them with him just in case.

The TV researcher was dragged away by two of his colleagues. He looked deeply ashamed of himself as he was told to return to head office for a severe telling off. He appeared to be on the verge of tears as he hobbled to a nearby coffee bar to sort out his bleeding nose – another result of Riedel's elbow manoeuvres. The watching businessmen moved their heads from side to side in horror. Wide-eyed fanaticism, even if it was based on feverish patriotism, had no part to play in the modern Germany. Any tactics aimed at acquisition needed to be moderate and non-committal. Heinrich, who had caught up with us after carefully parking the Porsches, consoled the researcher by buying him a cappuccino and shaking his own head furiously from side to side. 'Let me tell you vat my vater would think of all zis,' said Heinrich mournfully.

Wilhelm's eyes widened behind his milkbottle lenses as the two sat down to discuss the ethics of ball-stealing in the context of Anglo-German relations and Heinrich's father. It was all faintly touching.

I was still receiving calls from my desk, of course, but with a giant wedge of copy already filed and Operation Inflation well on course, I was in a far better position than the terrified rival journalists hanging around me. We finally managed to find our departure lounge and boarded the evening flight to Heathrow.

When we checked our seat numbers we realised that the travel company had pulled a master stroke. Aware that the team of Sun journalists, as well as half a dozen pathologically professional German TV people, were in hot pursuit, they decided to do all they could to throw them off the trail. In short, this meant booking Haller, Riedel and me into the economy-class seats at the back of the plane. They knew that the opposition would all be sipping champagne and nibbling salmon canapés beyond the curtain in business class. The travel people, who had been working for the Daily Mirror for years, were clearly well trained in helping to evade the enemy. They had probably attended management workshops on getting their clients out of difficult situations and spent hours in focus groups homing in on the hidden dangers of executive travel. Saving a notoriously tight-fisted newspaper group thousands of pounds by continually sticking its foot-soldiers in the goat section of the plane had nothing to do with it, of course.

As so often happens on overseas assignments, I had very little luggage with me. I've arrived with no more than a pen and notebook in baking deserts and on islands in the Far East with exotic-sounding names like Ping Pong. When you're told to be at the airport in half an hour you hardly have time to check your passport is in your top pocket, let alone get to your car to fetch your overnight bag. Instead, you have to dive straight into the nearest taxi and offer some extortionist at least £5 more than the usual £2-per-minute London cabbies charge for their expertise.

(Covering one of Sarah 'Fergie' Ferguson's skiing trips in 1996, most of us had been given at least an hour's notice of the trip, and were kitted out in passable ski kit. We had even been able to hire boots and goggles as we interviewed and took photographs of her at the top of the piste. Fergie had just announced her divorce from Prince Andrew and was contemplating a career as a high-profile fat girl for Weightwatchers, so was unsurprisingly co-operative. As we perched on the slopes scribbling down her rambling psychobabble about the mysteries of the mountains and how her spiritual journey in life involved being nice to everybody except Prince Philip, a broadsheet's chief reporter appeared off the chairlift. He was dressed in a pinstripe suit and brogues, and carried a small briefcase. His bald head and silk tie shone more brightly than the patches of ice in the end-of-season sunshine. 'Bloody hell,' exclaimed one of the photographers. 'It's the man from the Prudential.')

As well as the *Sun* journalists, the German TV crew were also sitting at the front of the Lufthansa flight in business class. Soon they wandered through the curtains and began to film at random. They filmed me trying to keep up a conversation with my German friends. They filmed other German passengers on the flight greeting the famous football legend Helmut Haller. They filmed the *Sun* reporters offering Haller £200,000 for the ball. One scribbled an IOU on a business-class napkin.

Bizarrely, the TV crew began to interview me at length. A golden rule of journalism is never allow other journalists anywhere near you. They always end up asking lots of embarrassing questions, leaving you feeling stupid and bemused. What's more, they're always pushy and aggressive, and will stop at nothing to get what they want.

TV journalists are by far the worst. Many promising Fleet Street careers have been brought to an abrupt halt by roving cameras. They normally start filming you when you've left a press conference at a crucial moment to have a smoke or chat up the pretty girl holding the portable microphone for the question-and-answer session at the end. Just when the chairman of a multinational corporation is being asked about what he was doing in a Rotherham steam-bath at four in the morning, your grinning face will be seen paying no attention whatsoever in the background.

The only reason I spoke to the Germans on the Lufthansa flight was because there wasn't a great deal else for me to do. I was trapped in a window seat by Haller – to whom I was not allowed to mention the ball – and Riedel, whom I did not really want to speak to anyway.

'Vhy do you do zis? Vat are your motives?' asked the earnest female German interviewer, complete with little round rimless glasses and a slightly ruffled Henry Plantagenet haircut. Unlike British TV girls, who are invariably young blondes with endearing smiles, she looked like a postgraduate Politics and Economics student. Instead of a pleasant, soft line of questioning about plans for the future and how I was feeling, propped up by a judicious use of my Christian name and lots of words like 'basically' and 'cheers', I was subjected to a harrowing 15-minute interrogation. The *fraulein's* questioning was cold and incisive, and sprinkled with words like 'socio-economic' and 'pan-nationalism'. She knew that with every air mile back to Britain the ball was slipping further and further from Germany's grasp. The only way she could get over her anger and frustration was to execute unpleasant, pernickety and vaguely academic interviews.

If there was a journalistic equivalent of scorched earth then this woman was its embodiment. She left no embarrassing question unasked, and did everything she could to destroy my confidence and line of reasoning: 'Come, come, Mr Allen, you don't expect me to accept that one,' she said, like some Teutonic Jeremy Paxman. 'I vant you to tell me straight. Vhy did you come to Germany to get ze ball?'

I explained that there was a desire to increase newspaper circulations involved, but the main aim was to bolster national pride by returning the most famous icon in our sporting heritage to the land where it rightly belonged. We had used the ball to conquer the world – including Germany – and we wanted it back.

She thought she was being particularly clever in suggesting that, to misquote the legendary Prussian general Clausewitz, we were using the excuse of football to continue a war against Germany by other means. I wasn't very impressed by this, and told her to refer that question to her colleague Wilhelm who would have finished his cappuccino by now and be on his way to his superiors to provide them with a statement about his violent conduct. My interviewer suddenly went very quiet and switched off the camera.

There was a period of relative quiet for an hour or so. The German TV crew were lost in thought at the front of the plane. The Sun men had given up their endeavours to bring Haller on to their side and were concentrating instead on making crude and predictable visual jokes with their business-class hot towels.

I stared out of the window, in the hope that nobody would try to interview me again. The coast of England started to appear 30,000 feet below. I'd been out of the country for less than 12 hours, but there was still something deeply reassuring about seeing home turf again.

22 · New Rivals

We touched down at Heathrow at 7.30 p.m. Everybody was cleared off the plane, including the Sun men and the German TV people. Thankfully they all went quietly.

Uniformed police officers were waiting to greet us. Haller's grin faded rapidly as soon as he saw them. For a few worried moments he was convinced they were the same officers he'd encountered at Wembley in 1966. They reminded him of the stoical British detectives who had set out to find Ronnie Biggs in the 1960s and Lord Lucan in the 1970s. This time, however, they'd got their man. 'Helmut, we meet again,' we half expected one to announce, in the relaxed, received pronunciation of Old Scotland Yard. 'We got the World Cup back in '66, I do hope we're on to the ball now,' another of the waiting policemen might have said.

Leonard Buggy of the Flying Squad had died in 1977 at the age of 61, but it could easily have been one of his assistants: 'Long time since you did that job up north. You've been sticking to your own manor, but we've been keeping a close eye on your old lock. Germany's a long way away, isn't it, Helmut. We haven't been impressed at all. Got something to tell us, Helmut?'

We thought Haller might shrug his shoulders, hold out his wrists to receive a pair of handcuffs, bow his head and reply: 'It iz ein fair cop. I vill come quietly.'

Instead he stood between Riedel and me and appeared to be on the verge of declaring himself diplomatically immune from prosecution, on the grounds that he came from a forward-thinking, non-committal federation.

'Are you in Mr Haller's party?' one of the policeman asked instead. The question prompted Haller's face to turn white and his hands to start shaking.

One of the policemen was from the anti-terrorist squad. He carried a Heckler & Koch machine pistol and wore a bulletproof jacket. 'Nothing to worry about,' he said, seeing Haller was in distress. 'We're just here to make sure nothing untoward happens to Herr Haller. He's got a big welcome party waiting for him.'

It was at that moment that we first realised how big the story had become. Until then, I was looking at it as a front-of-the-book-page lead – a happy, heart-warming story which did not mean a great deal in the scheme of things, apart from showing that touching nostalgia could still lift people out of their everyday lives. When the policemen explained there were around a hundred journalists and photographers waiting for us at Heathrow, and that the story was a lead item on almost every television and radio broadcast, I realised that my journey into Germany had whipped up the most extraordinary hysteria.

All those waiting at Heathrow had responded to a newsflash on the Press Association – the national wire service for Great Britain and Northern Ireland – which had announced: 'Former West German footballer Helmut Haller flies into Britain to return 1966 World Cup final ball to Geoff Hurst.'

The Lufthansa air-stewardesses smiled as we got off the plane and started walking up a short white corridor towards the main terminal building. All around us were airport personnel muttering into walkie-talkies. They were wearing those huge, officious security tags which huge, officious people always have to carry with them, especially in places with high-risk security ratings like Heathrow Terminal Two. A few of them stayed with us as we made our way forward, walking just behind the four police officers.

Four Heathrow-based photographers were allowed to take Haller's picture as we walked off the plane. Unlike the vast majority of photographers, airport photographers never travel anywhere. Considering where they work, this is particularly sad. Most of them have those tired, life-weary faces which are so commonplace in airports, many of which are among the most overcrowded and unwelcoming places in the world. These guys look like the plane-spotters you see standing on the observation gallery at Heathrow, writing down the number of the fifteenth 737 they've seen during the past hour. Their main job is to hose down celebrities as they fly in from glamorous places like Los Angeles. For the rest of the time the Heathrow-based cameramen have to fight their way through masses of tourists, looking for human-interest snaps illustrating stories about flight delays. The cameramen have a particular affinity with those who have been stranded and don't look as though they'll ever get the chance to go anywhere – the kind of people who lounge about in Departures for days on end with their trainers and socks off, moaning and eating junkfood in between numerous expeditions to the duty-free shops. An air-photographer whom I once worked with had been at Heathrow for 20 years. He was once asked if he could take a plane to Belgium, but said he didn't have a valid passport. He was never asked again.

The photographers followed us along the long corridors which all visitors to Heathrow, one of the biggest airports in the world, have to negotiate when they arrive in the country. Unlike Munich, there are few indecipherable signs and obscure maps, but the grey carpet leaves you feeling just as depressed.

They use the colour to cover up the stains produced by the unpleasant mass of trainer-footed humanity continually passing through the airport, but that doesn't make it any easier to cope with.

Our photographic escorts looked at our light luggage and were particularly interested in any obvious lumps which might signal the hiding place of a famous amber ball. Riedel, clearly upset by his brush with his fellow countryman back in Munich, was taking no chances and carried his duffle-bag wide open. He even let one of the photographers take a prod inside with one of his long lenses. Riedel had nothing to hide.

'Come on, Mr Haller. Give us a quick flash of the ball, sir,' shouted the Press Association photographer.

Haller refused but instead offered some light entertainment by back-heeling a Deutschmark into the air. On its way back down he caught it in his blazer pocket.

Haller continually indicated that he could not speak a word of English by replying 'Ja, ja' to everything anybody asked him, including 'How are you?' Even when a New York businessman who had no idea what was going on asked, 'Do you know where the gentlemen's bathroom is, please?' Haller replied 'Ja, ja.' The American appreciated Haller's upbeat *Can do!* attitude, but still had no idea where the toilet was. Riedel continued to look dull but excruciatingly efficient.

The grey carpet began to run out after what seemed like a couple of miles, and we finally got to passport control. The officials carried out their important duty which, as usual, amounted to little more than having a good laugh at the outdated photographs on show before waving the three of us through.

The policemen, photographers and assorted airport staff did not have to show anything, because they were all wearing those big security passes. The anti-terrorist squad officer just waved his machine pistol provocatively in the air and was let through immediately. I wondered if he ever pulled that kind of stunt outside West End clubs when the police social bar shut on a Friday night.

We had no luggage to collect, so ignored the weary-looking crowds flocking around the carousels. After so much aggravation the thought of scrumming down with a crowd of irritable jet-setters hoping against all the odds that their underwear had made it from Bangkok really didn't appeal . . .

As I stood at the sliding doors waiting for Haller, Riedel and our police escort to catch up, I knew that it was all about to go off. The journalists waiting in Terminal Two had been standing around for more than two hours and were ready for action. Even if Riedel wore his duffle-bag over his head, many would still think we had the ball in our luggage. It was the kind of confrontational situation which journalists thrive on.

We had done everything we could to diffuse the situation. We had told other desks that the ball would be arriving the next day, and that the only picture available was of a football has-been, who was a German to boot. There would be no interviews and Haller would be ghosted away as quickly as the way in which he used to spirit himself into opponents' penalty areas.

Nobody believed us, of course.

'Ready?' I said to Riedel. He curled his upper lip and furrowed his brow. Haller did a little shadow boxing and smiled. The sliding doors opened and we found ourselves at the beginning of the long, straight pen bordered by a metal security fence and cheap-suited car couriers carrying signs saying 'Mr Pong Ping from Ping Pong' or 'Crazy Luigi from Milan'.

'*Wo ist der Ball?*' everybody started shouting.

A couple of photographers darted over the fence and began taking action shots of Haller. They were kamikaze paps and even began trying to unzip Riedel's bag before being pushed away by one of our police escorts.

There was a roar of motor drives and the bright light of the terminal intensified with the scores of flashes going off all the time. More questions were screamed out in English and German.

'Don't say anything at all,' I yelled at Haller, above the noise.

'*Ja, ja!*' he shouted back at me.

Two of my *Mirror* colleagues rushed up the corridor and flanked Haller on each side. They both had something of the *Sun* doorman about them, combined with poor old Wilhelm's fanatical intensity and a bit of photographer. If questioners or lensmen got too close, they flicked them away with a well-placed elbow or mean-spirited personal comment.

A particularly unfortunate magazine journalist, more used to sitting in a cosy office and speaking to PRs called Gus or Sophie all day, was sent flying by one well-placed elbow, combined with a spare leg tapping his heels as he staggered backwards. He piled into two photographers who began swearing profusely at him. Fearing an imminent attack, the magazine journalist grabbed one of the lensmen's aluminium ladders and held it in front of him. This was a particularly unwise thing to do. 'You touch my ladder and I'll snap you in half, you weaselly little shit,' shouted one of the photographers.

The magazine journalist made straight for the London Underground where he composed his colour piece in a carriage on his way back to Notting Hill Gate. He hasn't been seen on the road since.

As one or two other journalists tried to get near the Germans, including *Sun* reinforcements (the ones on the plane had long since converted their Deutschmarks back into sterling and given up the chase), more Mirror minders banged into them. Fights started to break out as lensmen took swings at each other. Baggage trolleys were propelled backwards and forwards with accompanying shouts of pain as they ploughed into unprotected shins.

More 'How are you feeling?' clichés were shouted out, together with convoluted German interrogations sounding more like advanced economic treaties than snatched questions in Heathrow 'Terminal Two' on a Friday night.

I followed Haller and Riedel, who were being steered through the baying scrum to a waiting Jaguar. It was a mild April evening and there were even more people standing around the car waiting area. Baggage trolleys were still being hurtled about and at least one other magazine writer went the same way.

We jumped into the rear seat of the luxury car where a German interpreter was waiting, together with a Mirror lawyer. The driver, a south Londoner called Malcolm who appeared disturbingly enthusiastic about driving getaway cars, grinned as he watched our opponents struggling to stop us. 'You're having a laugh!' he shouted at the opposition, adding, 'Outrageous liberty!' as he asked the police to swat two photographers off his bonnet.

Malcolm revved up the engine, engaged the clutch and screeched away at a ridiculous speed which soon reached 70mph. 'Used to do this kind of work for me bruvver,' Malcolm enthused, without elaborating.

We were screaming into the tunnel which leads up to the M4 motorway when the lawyer suddenly said, 'Wait.' His incisive and alert brain had been working on the small print of intricate media documents all day, but he was still able to turn it to the specific problems of the situation in hand. 'We've got a problem,' he said, as if a judge had asked him why clause 11.2 of paragraph 10.16 in his High Court libel defence was incomplete. His usual mitigation was technical – namely that the office photocopier was malfunctioning. 'It's Haller,' the lawyer, an Arsenal season-ticket-holder, continued with insouciance. 'We've left him at the airport.'

Haller was still standing on the concourse fending off luggage trolleys, absurdly complicated questions delivered in his native tongue, airborne colour writers and dodgy minicab drivers who looked like Malcolm and offered to 'run you into town' for £150 cash. We were back outside Terminal Two within a couple of minutes and shoved Haller into the back of the car, together with Riedel.

The three of us were back together again, and this time on English soil.

23 · Home Toil

There were no motorbikes at the airport. The only way to be certain of a successful pursuit is to use oily louts on Hondas or Kawasakis. If one had begun tailing us as soon as we touched down from Germany, he could have followed our every move, right up to the arrival of the ball. Bikes can pursue a car driven by anyone, anywhere, even a top-of-the-range Jaguar driven by a top-of-the-range Cockney with a cuddly pound-sign on his rearview mirror and close links to south London's criminal fraternity.

That evening there was not a bike in sight. The only thing we managed to lose was a Ford Mondeo on the M4. Our driver executed a complicated manoeuvre on a slip road on to the M25 London orbital motorway. It seemed to involve crossing four lanes at once without indicating, crossing back again and then, at the last moment, braking hard, crossing back yet again and speeding down another slip road.

Why Malcolm did it we're still not sure. The Mondeo tailing us was doing no harm whatsoever and looked as though it was being driven by a perfectly respectable photocopier salesman. Malcolm's move certainly wasn't in the advanced driver's manual, and led to a cacophony of hooting by lorry drivers and mobile-phone sales executives alike.

Despite such idiosyncrasies, there were no complaints from any of the passengers in the Jaguar. After two hours on an autobahn, I certainly felt perfectly safe with the manic Malcolm in charge.

He executed similar manoeuvres throughout our journey, continually trying to lose people as we made our way anti-clockwise around the M25. The Mirror lawyer tried to explain that it was a perfectly legitimate occurrence to be followed by other cars on a motorway with anything between three and six lanes, but Malcolm was having none of it. The moment any car spent more than 30 seconds in his slipstream, which was often, he would put on his fog lights and speed up to around 90mph. Even if a car overtook him at 100mph he would start cursing, believing he was the subject of some over-complicated 'pincer movement'. After a couple of Audis scorched past, Malcolm pulled off at another exit and we sat in a lay-by for two minutes 'just to be on the safe side'. He even offered to get his 'bruvver's mob' to provide a few decoy cars. We all decided that might not be such a good idea.

We were making our way to a place where the Sun team would never think of looking for us: their heartland of the commuter sprawls stretching beyond the M25. It was somewhere we could all settle down for the night and in the morning carry on the negotiations to bring the ball back to Britain.

We stopped on the motorway for a further hour to take some photographs of Haller's arrival in the country. The German also wanted to get a feel for the place his old manager Helmut Schöen had taught him to respect and admire.

As he prepared to recapture the excitement he had felt on arriving in England in the summer of 1966, Haller proudly recalled his meeting with the Queen. He remembered the beautiful buildings he had seen in London, including the Palace of Westminster and the Albert Memorial, the Gothic shrine designed by Sir George Gilbert Scott in honour of Queen Victoria's prince and Coburg's most famous son.

Haller remembered some nice countryside around his team's training ground and the well-mannered, refined people who had given him such a great welcome. Now was a chance to reacquaint himself with the England of his youth.

We pulled into Clacket Lane service station between junctions 32 and 33 of the M25, near Westerham on the Kent/Surrey border. It could easily have been the same place that England players like Alan Ball and Nobby Stiles stopped off with their wives on the way back from the Eamonn Andrews TV special in 1966. Egg and chips and cups of tea were still on the menu, as well as numerous types of burger and hotdog.

Every year motorway service stations each serve an average of 450,000 portions of chips, 500,000 eggs and a million pots of tea. You can find anything you want there: 24-hour buffets, cash points, shops, nappy-changing facilities, £33-a-night motel rooms with no phones or views worth opening the stained curtains for. All are graded and given awards like 'Best Cuppa'. Annandale Water, on the A74, once won the double of Tea Council's 'Best Motorway Brew' competition and Scottish Tourist Board 'Loo of the Year'.

Like high-rise flats, office blocks and shopping centres, the stations are the embodiment of the utilitarian thinking of radical politicians like Harold Wilson. Together with vast road systems and new estates full of tiny-roomed houses, they are part of a grand, on-going plan which includes eradicating huge swathes of countryside.

Cities haven't fared much better. One of the architectural highlights of 1966 was plans for a 385ft-high, 34-floor monolith in London's West End. Where once we produced refined, stirring buildings like the Royal Albert Hall, we were by now among the world leaders in concrete sprawls or towers bearing crude, postmodernist names like Centre Point. They proliferated throughout the 1960s, '70s, and '80s as our country embraced every aspect of egg-and-chip culture, combining it unimaginatively with the hamburger ideology of an overweight America.

There were 60 service stations in Britain by 1996. Around a hundred will be dotted around the country by the early years of this millennium. Huge amounts of money are being spent. Watford Gap had a £5 million refurbishment paid for by its owners, Blue Boar, in 1997. The services are hugely profitable because millions of British people use them. They were, after all, designed for the classless masses to take a breather as they ferried the products from Britain's white-hot technological furnace around our tiny island. The amount of business interaction that goes on inside them is breathtaking. Bulk-buy deals on photocopiers and fridges are discussed all the time. That's why you see all those books in the newsagent's with titles like *Offensive Marketing* and *Everything Is Negotiable*.

As we wandered around, stretching our legs, it was disturbing to see Haller's eye caught by a book called *Even More Offensive Marketing*. We steered him away towards the egg and chips, easily recognisable as they sweated on a hot plate under a halogen light.

It's not just those, like Haller, who have something to sell who contribute to the success of service stations. Cars, the great modern leveller, are the only entry qualification to these concrete edifices, and anybody who has one can stop off. Those who have sat in their steel boxes for hours, despising the traffic jams and sheer bloody-mindedness of other drivers, can take a Welcome Break from the road rage and angst of the car culture in soulless home from home. Like cars, the Legoland service stations are a great common denominator of a new, mobile, aspirational Britain. Everybody – rich or poor, young or old – can learn to put up with the paint-like tea and the chef's daily special smothered in acidic tomato ketchup as they stop off from miles of alienation and tedium. Then, refreshed and revitalised by quality time spent with their fellow Britons, they can return to their cars and start hating everybody all over again . . .

You can't just blame it all on Harold Wilson either. The first service station, the Watford Gap on the M1 between junctions 16 and 17, was built in 1959 when Conservative Prime Minister Harold Macmillan was claiming we had never had it so good. He obviously hadn't tried the food, or sat in the yellow plastic seats bolted to the floor in case sales reps from Basingstoke tried to steal them, or a coachload of West Brom fans began throwing them at each other.

By 1991 service stations were even part of John Major's election strategy. He pledged that one day, if the Major masterplan came into being, there would be one every 15 miles. 'Every parent knows what I mean,' said Britain's last Tory Prime Minister. '"Next services 54 miles" when your child can't make ten.'

During his campaign Major called into a service station and was applauded by a canteen full of eager Britons stocking up on all-day breakfasts. Every class and shade of opinion were there, in a futureshock scene which would have concerned even the most forward-thinking 1960s radical.

There was a befuddled circuit judge, wrapped up in his Barbour jacket and on his way from his London townhouse to listen to yet another divorce hearing. He was irritated by the cheap suits and the constant use of the beery word 'cheers' being used by almost everybody, including the till girls with their Can't do! attitude to life. The blaring American rap music and constant ringing of mobile telephones also made him grimace.

Standing a few places behind the judge were two women wearing baggy leisure clothes. They were on their way to a gym. Both had part-time jobs in call centres, where their computers had been programmed to react to all kinds of enquiries from the public, while they themselves were only allowed to use stock phrases like 'Good afternoon and welcome to CompuBank. Michelle speaking. How may I help you?'

An information technology man, up for the Marketing Challenge, had just filled up his Suzuki jeep. With blond streaks, a gold earring and shoes so big and shiny that they could have been laid at the Harland & Wolff shipyard in Belfast, he had taken computers 'on board' and saw them as 'the way forward'. He said 'cheers' a lot to the checkout girls as he guzzled down a double cheeseburger and made sure his premium loyalty points were 'sorted'.

All were modern Britons: key players in the white-hot, technological, classless new country forged in a fiery furnace of post-war radicalism. Beneath the low ceilings of the service station and the lingering smell of heavy-duty disinfectant, they came together as a single people – united by safe, neutral ground and by a language reduced to reassuring conditioned reflexes.

In the middle of them all was the bespectacled, grey figure of John Major – classless, neutral, uninspiring and feeling completely at home. He waved and encouraged them all to vote for him so as to ensure the glorious advance of the British people through whatever history had to throw at them.

No wonder John Humphreys, presenter of the BBC Radio 4 Today programme, reacted to Major's stop at the service station by saying: 'Perhaps he gets clapped for eating the food.'

But there is a far more sinister side to the kind of service station we had taken Helmut Haller to on that Friday night. They are hotbeds of criminal activity.

Underworld bosses use them to organise armed raids and to fence stolen goods. 'Shooters' are exchanged along with insider information about bank security systems. Football fans meet at them to fight. The academics who study hooliganism would describe their attraction to service stations as being symptomatic of urban man's dependency on the drab, concrete, soulless sprawls in which they were brought up. In fact, like everybody else, they go to them because they're convenient, easy to find and you can fill up with petrol before making a few offensive wrist actions at rival supporters sitting on the coach from Birmingham. The football agents involved in all the 'bung' transfer deals which tarnished the game so much in the late 1980s also used to hand over their wedges of used notes at service stations.

In April 1996, when I arrived with Haller, I had a particular, very personal reason for disliking Clacket Lane intensely. Just two months before, a young man called Seamus McArdle had pulled up at its 'sister' service station, South Mimms, just a 30-minute drive round the M25 at the junction of the A1 (M). In his jeans and trainers, the 27-year-old McArdle did not look any different from the thousands of anonymous drivers who arrive every day. He said 'cheers' and 'sorted' a lot, and applied all the right conditioned reflexes to anybody he had to deal with.

It was Thursday, 8 February 1996, and McArdle had made a long business trip from Staffordshire before eating an award-winning breakfast and washing it down with a cup of award-winning orange tea. He checked his lorry and found a £33-a-night bed with no phone and views of the M25 behind its stained curtains. The next morning he rose early and drove to South Quay, in the London Docklands.

The business district, already a concrete-and-glass sprawl, was becoming more soulless and utilitarian by the day as it was forged into another testament to a new Britain populated by accountants and security guards. The latter's camera footage showed McArdle's lorry arriving soon after 5 p.m. and the driver getting out of his cab with an accomplice.

Two hours later, at 7.10 p.m., I was leaving the Mirror's newsroom high in Canary Wharf tower. It was a freezing night and I was keen to get away. The police had shut my carpark, however, because of a security scare. I stopped off at a pub for a half of Guinness.

As I put the drink to my lips there was a sudden shudder. I'd worked in Belfast before and knew exactly when to use the tired and predictable cliché 'I've worked in Belfast before, I know what that is'. All the pub's windows caved in. Accountants, computer people and security guards came running up the street screaming and covered in blood.

I picked up a telephone and told a copytaker: 'A massive blast in the centre of London's Docklands yesterday signalled the end of the IRA's seventeen-month ceasefire.'

The bomb had gone off under the Docklands Light Railway, killing two men and causing £150 million worth of damage.

Seamus McArdle, a member of the IRA's South Armagh Brigade who had appeared so at home in a concrete testament to modern British culture, had achieved his objective of causing as much damage as he could to another one.

24 · Sole Brothers

George Cohen, now 56, had agreed to meet Haller at Clacket Lane. The England right-back from the 1966 team lived just a few miles away in Kent with his wife, Daphne.

The two former internationals embraced like long-lost brothers. They linked hands by the mini-supermarket and exchanged reminiscences through our interpreter, who had arrived in another car. Despite their obvious happiness at the reunion, an odd, stilted conversation followed. It brought back memories of the time in 1966 when Alf Ramsey looked on enchanted as Alan Ball sat on Jack Charlton's knee and the pair put on a ventriloquist's dummy act.

'Helmut says it's great to see you,' said the interpreter.

'Great to see him too,' said Cohen.

'Helmut says, "How are you?"' said the interpreter.

'Fine. How is Helmut?' said Cohen.

'Fine,' replied the interpreter, without bothering to ask Haller how he felt. 'Helmut says you haven't changed,' he went on.

'Nor has he,' said Cohen.

The exchange continued in similar fashion for around three minutes, before Haller wandered off to see if there were any ballpoint pens and German crossword magazines on sale in the newsagent's.

'How much is he getting paid for this?' Cohen asked us.

'A lot more than you,' I replied.

The interpreter was quite high-powered and more used to carrying out simultaneous-translation duties in places like the European Parliament in Brussels. As far as the world of linguistics was concerned, his job at Clacket Lane was the equivalent of calling on Harold Pinter to knock out a few lines for an official team song before the Cup final, or even an obscene terrace chant. When the interpreter got together with his friends the following Saturday night he would probably have said that he got a huge amount of money for the easiest bit of translating he had ever done in his life. The words were so simple that Cohen could probably have translated the whole thing himself. He still wouldn't have ended up with as much money as Haller, though.

A photographer took a picture of Haller and me standing together. It was a triumphalist portrait of a great German hero slapping a British journalist and friend on the back. It was a pertinent symbol of how close our two countries had grown during the past three decades, and it was to adorn the front page of the *Daily Mirror* the next day. The picture was taken in the middle of a motorway service station on the M25, somewhere between the chewing-gum stand in the mini-market and not far from the Burger King restaurant and lavatories without locks on the doors. Truckers wearing acrylic football jerseys and still eating all-day breakfasts looked on.

Cohen and Haller eventually found a table near the lorry drivers and ordered some prize-winning tea. The rest of us, including lawyer, interpreter and another Mirror journalist, sat at another table keeping an eye on them both. Malcolm ordered a hamburger before returning to his Jaguar to rev up the engine a few times and practise his handbrake turns in the carpark.

It was around ten o'clock and I was just starting to figure out the kind of man Haller was. The sheer breadth of human life forms which journalists come into contact with each day sometimes makes it difficult for us to differentiate, but it's always important to try and assess the inner man or woman. Just because someone has three convictions for malicious wounding, for example, does not necessarily make him a bad person. Underneath that hard, criminal exterior is a heart and a soul. You need to think a little more deeply rather than building up a crass, one-dimensional profile of a complicated human being. You need to search for the real person; to look beyond the tattooed forehead and all-day-breakfast-stained fingernails. You need to look at a person's shoes.

In modern British society, a place where traditional differentials of class and accent have been completely distorted, footwear remains the best clue to a person's character. All kinds of people, from crusty old couples living in country houses to the acne-ridden louts who are paid the minimum wage to check McDonald's toilets every 20 minutes, go about their lives wearing myriad soles and uppers. These characters can come into a journalist's life for as little as two seconds before they slam the door in your face (or two days while they unburden their lives to you). Whatever the length of time, it's important to look at what lies below. It's unfair to generalise, of course. But as journalists, we have to. We would like to say that there are millions of vastly different characters in modern Britain, but because we need to keep life simple and uncluttered, all can be narrowed down to four: the Sturdies, the Comfies, the Trainers and the Barges.

The Sturdies are the ones in elegant women's shoes or brogues, like the judge at John Major's service station. When you see a pair clacking towards you, your assignment has a reasonable chance of being successful. Sturdies find journalism entertaining if, like journalists, a little odd and unwholesome. If you're sitting on a claret-stained sofa in the drawing-room of their rambling pile or Chelsea townhouse they might pull faces as if you're something which the King Charles spaniel found in the grounds, but they'll usually open a bottle of wine and tell you what you need to know. Members of the judiciary, antique-shop owners and cavalry officers usually have a raffish, devil-may-care side to their nature and see dealing with the press as an expression of it.

Comfies are far less obliging. These are middle-class *Guardian* readers who wear vegetarian shoes – often brown with synthetic soles and Cornish-pasty uppers. They despise anything to do with other newspapers, especially the small ones which they imagine to be full of naked women and guides to devil-worshipping. They normally work as counsellors or in the social services and have a snide, mind-your-own-business attitude towards anybody who interferes with their day-to-day lives, just like *Guardian* columnists themselves.

Even if they'd been kidnapped by laser-wielding spacemen and beamed up to a faraway planet, the Comfies would still remain tightlipped if you turned up to interview them. They'd act as if you were violating their right to personal self-determination, or some other vague philosophical concept they've touched upon in module one of their Open University psychology degrees. 'So what if there are lava grazes all over my body, three of my Cornish-pasty-wearing friends are currently being tortured and earlier yesterday I came close to having my head chopped off by a light ray. I don't think Joe Public has any right to know about my personal life, especially if it's going to be splashed all over the gutter press,' they would explain with haughty looks of indignation.

'Down to earth' and 'salt of the earth' are the kind of popular clichés applied to Trainers. Whatever they're doing they'll be wearing a pair of sports shoes, whether it's loafing around a shopping centre or doing something more formal, like appearing in front of a judge and jury. So what if they might be involved in some minor criminal activity? It doesn't mean they're not valid members of society, as entitled to dream holidays, financial products and luxury cars as anybody else. Unskilled manual workers who have developed a talent with sledgehammers and gaming machines often make excellent copy, and they'll usually give you the time of day on the way to their cells.

If there's a photographer present they'll normally break the ice with a heavyweight conversation about used Ford Sierras and the best route from Ilford to Chelmsford, avoiding the A12 and any police cars. Or, in the case of northerners, the best route from Bootle to Toxteth via a dozen dole offices, avoiding anybody in a suit. A particularly enlightening encounter with a Trainer came for me when I interviewed a Scouse phonebox thief called Bazza.

The interesting thing about Bazza was that he concentrated on phoneboxes which only took cards, which meant they had no money in them. He'd broken into 14 around Kilburn before he was arrested. A Trainer right down to his 1972-style Pumas, but nothing intrinsically wrong with him.

By far the worst are the Barges. Modern journalism is full of stories about the aspirational, and reporters are continually having to make their way through the security fencing and Rottweiler dogs surrounding the mock-Tudor mansions of Britain's new élite. They're called Barges because they wear chunky, black formal shoes. They splay out at the front, have huge heels, and are designed to be worn with shiny suits. The female equivalent are those shoes with massive heels which girl pop bands wear. As well as providing a few extra inches for short people, they're there to indicate a rise in status.

New Labour, whose inner sanctum contains a number of Barges, has by now embraced the lottery winners, pop stars and computer wholesalers who are the new millionaires, but getting the nod from the charismatic Tony Blair hasn't made them nicer people. If you get anywhere near their house, which is seldom, they'll immediately start to abuse you for causing an indent in the gravel on their drive with your car tyres. Heart-shaped swimming-pools and full-sized snooker tables abound in Barges' homes. Closed-circuit television cameras stand guard over their easily won material possessions, which also invariably include 48-inch wide-screen TVs and white leather sofas. Most Barges live on the belt of land straddling the M25 around Hertfordshire, Buckinghamshire and Essex.

We tried to work out which category Haller fell into. He certainly wasn't a Sturdy, because the German upper classes normally have duelling scars on their faces, spiked helmets and, at the very least, an oversized Kaiser moustache on the upper lip of their perpetually outraged, scarlet faces. Anyway, German toffs didn't spend their formative years playing football for Bologna and Juventus. And it would have been unfair to call Haller a Trainer because, despite the ball-stealing excesses of his early life, he did not have a criminal record.

He had the economic dynamic of a Barge. The ball was a finite asset and he was making sure that anybody who was going to relieve him of it paid top whack. In the days of trade unions and collective bargaining, negotiations over the ball's future would have been the simple matter of a few hours of Bavarian beers and sausage sandwiches in the Villa d'Este. There might even be a few long letters to the industrial arbitrators, ACAS. Haller's aspirational path through life as a former professional footballer with a restaurant and sports shop fitted him snugly into the Barge mould.

Haller also had a bit of the Comfy in him. The black leather brogue-style shoes with synthetic soles said it all. Certainly they looked sensible enough for the Comfy tag. We suspected he'd never been near a tabloid newspaper in his life, apart from appearing in them occasionally during his career. Haller was now working in a restaurant, which was fine. A lot of Comfies end up doling out quiche and wild-mushroom risotto in out-of-town bistros when they've retired from their administrative careers doling out poison-pen letters to innocent members of the public from London's New Labour boroughs.

Working in a town like Neusass proved Haller must be obsessed with traffic-calming measures and keeping dog mess off the streets. Like all Comfies, he was also continually asking questions and asserting his rights and expectations. He seemed to abide by the Comfy philosophy which, as for millions of Germans, could also be summarised by the maxim: 'I want to make this world a better place for me to live in.'

As we watched him sipping his coffee with his old sparring partner Cohen, I felt I was already getting to know Haller a lot better.

Around midnight our Jaguar pulled up into a top-secret location some-where in the countryside near Bishop's Stortford, Hertfordshire. It was one of those big, brash country-house hotels which you find all over an area favoured by affluent footballers and soap stars. It was the kind of place they took their families to for dinner at the weekend and their lovers during the week. We were deep in Barge country.

25 · Uphall Struggle

The Uphall Hotel is 60 miles from Heathrow and just nine miles from Stansted Airport, so it only gets to call itself a Country Inn-'style' hotel. This is the equivalent of a hostel in Snowdonia calling itself an Alpine Resort-'style' hotel, or a motel in Chingford describing itself as a Central London-'style' hotel. On the plus side, though, its hundred rooms are clean and presentable. Its staff can satisfy a variety of requests. It has an unheated indoor swimming-pool, and small dogs are made to feel very welcome. The Uphall brochure does not give a definition of what counts as a 'small' dog which, I suppose, could create problems for some, but it does describe itself as 'a first-class country facility' and goes on: 'It is a spectacular, Old English-style manor set in sculp-tured gardens and over one hundred acres of woodland park. Gastronomic English fayre and informal dining is combined with croquet and Pimms on the lawn to create an unforgettable experience.'

We parked on the shingle drive, taking care not to cause any obvious dents, and made our way to the reception. Haller and Riedel looked vaguely impressed, but only because almost anything would be vaguely impressive after the kind of places we'd just come from.

A pimply youth with an already bald head, ill-fitting black suit, black tie and white shirt was standing at reception ready to greet us. He was the night porter and looked as though he might be studying for a BA in Undertaking at one of the local universities. 'Welcome to Uphall,' he said with all the feeling of someone reading out the back of a packet of salt-and-vinegar crisps. 'My name is Dean. How may I help you?'

'We're here on a company booking,' said one of the Mirror executives. The newspaper had booked us in under false names.

'Who are yer?' asked Dean.

'Grimm,' the executive replied, without flinching. 'Seven in the name of Grimm.'

Dean didn't flinch either. I doubt he would have flinched if Snow White, the Seven Dwarfs and Hans Christian Andersen had all turned up for an Easy Break weekend.

Three more Mirror executives were waiting for us in the English Country-'style' lounge. We all shook hands and sat down in the hotel's plush armchairs.

After the M25 service stations it was nice to be in a place with proper carpets, a roaring fire, paintings on the wall and some vaguely civilised people. It was also good to know you could make your way to the toilet without fearing you would be beaten senseless by an overweight trucker with ketchup stains down his acrylic football shirt and 'Kick to Kill' tattoos across his arms.

We asked Dean to rustle up a few trays of 'gastronomic English fayre'. He returned just over an hour later with three plates of tuna-and-sweetcorn sandwiches and a dozen warm bottles of beer.

'Just like Number 10 when the unions ran the country,' one of the more senior executives offered, attempting to break the ice with Riedel.

The German appeared to have taken an instant dislike to the Mirror man. Riedel appeared to take an instant dislike to everyone. The problem was that his instant dislike turned into a dislike which lasted considerably longer than an instant – it probably lasted for ever, in fact.

The beer-and-sandwiches joke was a pretty weak one anyway. The executive had meant it innocently enough, but we were still negotiating to get the ball into Britain. We were hoping half an hour in front of the Uphall fireplace would end with a slick deal ensuring the swift return of the ball. The infamous beer-and-sandwich negotiations between the government and the union barons in the 1970s had ended with almost a decade of power cuts, Leicester Square being renamed Fester Square because of the piles of rubbish on the streets, and England failing to appear in the finals of the World Cup for twelve years. It was a time when schoolboys like me had no exciting internationals to look forward to, let alone foreign holidays. Forget sun-drenched weeks on the Costa del Sol – quite often we didn't even have any lights in the house. We had to look elsewhere for stimulation. I found mine through innocent childhood pursuits like lighting candles and failing desperately to build scale models of Messerschmitt 109s. I often had to try and stick my Airfix kits together in the dark, so instead of small wartime fighters I ended up with tiny replicas of the kind of buildings Sir Norman Foster keeps churning out in cities like London and Berlin today.

One of the executives used a gold-plated remote control to turn on the enormous television above the mock-Tudor fireplace. He flicked through the vast array of satellite channels, to the BBC News on the hour. The 1 a.m. head-lines were being announced, the most prominent of which was news from Germany that Helmut Haller, the legendary footballer, had decided to return the 1966 World Cup football to England. More than that, he had agreed to work with the Daily Mirror to ensure the ball's safe return to Geoff Hurst. Even better, the ball would be paid for by Richard Branson, the multi-millionaire boss of the Virgin business empire. 'So Branson's an Acrylic as well,' I remember thinking to myself.

'How much did you say you wanted for the ball?' I asked Haller.

He chuckled. Riedel, however, looked far from amused. The German keeper was refusing to enjoy the hotel's hospitality and was still obsessed with the price of the ball. He started tedious negotiations, mainly with our lawyer, which went on for around two hours. Occasionally he would scream out, 'Nein, nein! That iz not enough,' which we all considered a bit over-emotional, especially for a New German. At one stage he threatened to walk out. We advised him that he had no idea where he was and that the hotel was surrounded by a hundred acres of parkland, with stark new towns and motorways beyond. He decided to stay put.

Eventually, at about 4 a.m., we thought we had reached some kind of agreement which would ensure Operation Inflation remained on course. The next morning we would travel to London to collect £70,000 in used bank-notes. Once Riedel had counted it – 'Every single note,' he assured us helpfully – Jurgen Haller would be given the green light over in Holland. There were eight flights he could take from Amsterdam to Stansted and the whole trans-action would be co-ordinated to make sure he was on one of them. The ball would land and security guards would take it to a 'safe zone' (jargon was already evolving around the operation) somewhere in southern England where it could be debriefed and reinstated into public life after its 30-year exile.

After a day of thinking of nothing but the ball, we had turned it into a little English character on his way back to Blighty after three decades in an alien land. Its transition to respectability would not be an easy one.

'We'll give the little fellow a wash and brush up and put him up for membership at the Garrick,' said the executive who had made the beer-and-sandwiches joke.

We all agreed it was time to go to bed.

26 · Glow Slow

As I settled down in room 52 of the Uphall Hotel at four o'clock in the morning of Friday, 26 April 1996, I knew that we were on the verge of a heroic moment. It was time to relax for a few hours and consider what had been achieved so far.

The ball had been found in less than one day. Six *Sun* reporters and over 30 foreign journalists had been neutralised. Helmut Haller and his sidekick, Thorsten Riedel, had been persuaded to come to England with us, and with any luck were sleeping peacefully next door. The whole of England was talking about our mission. Jurgen Haller and Mike Moore were in Amsterdam. The amber ball was with them. The Germans were happy with our final plan to get it back to Britain.

Hundreds of thousands of editions of that day's *Daily Mirror* were, at that very moment, coming off the presses. Every edition, available all over Britain, Europe and parts of the USA and Australasia, would be dominated by the successful mission to return the 1966 World Cup ball to Geoff Hurst and the English people.

It was time to take Malcolm's trainer off the Jaguar's accelerator and enjoy the moment. My air-conditioning system had been turned off to stop the irritating drone. I'd knocked back an entire bottle of £2 carbonated English spring mineral water (the spring was north of Harlow, I think). There was only the very distant rumble of the M11 motorway to accompany my joyful descent into an untroubled and contented sleep.

I felt nauseous, frightened and clammy all at the same time, which isn't bad going, even if I was in Hertfordshire.

I thought of Geoff Hurst on the night before the 1966 final, when he too had been unable to sleep a wink in the Hendon Hall Hotel. Alf Ramsey had told his striker and the rest of his team: 'It's going to be the biggest day of your lives and you will win. Goodnight, gentlemen.'

Nobody in a position of power had said anything like that to me. Instead of friendly congratulations for my part in Operation Inflation so far, I'd simply been given a stern pep talk from some overworked executive. Cutting out all the pleasant bits, it was something along the lines of: 'If this doesn't work, you're out.'

Despite glamorous overseas assignments, journalism can be a terrifying experience. Reporters are at the sharp, backstabbing end of the trade. People expect you to turn ideas into reality and you're only ever as good as your last exposé of aristocrats who spend their summer vacations clubbing ducks. Editors and all those other executives who inhabit newspaper offices hire you because they think you're up to the job, and that you'll make them look good when your stories contribute to a product which is lively, informative and full of well-researched animal-cruelty exclusives.

You're expected to initiate and make a difference. When things stop working and you stop producing, the options are pretty clear. It's no good executing complicated coffee orders in between rewriting stories from the Press Association to try and make up for your shortcomings. You have to go. If you don't, executives will act swiftly. In these days of industrial tribunals and huge compensation payouts, they won't grab you by the scruff of your neck, sweep everything off your desk into sinister black bin-liners and walk you out of the building, though. They'll get security guards to do it for them. Competition in journalism is intense as hundreds of media outlets compete for the best story, and hundreds of would-be staff journalists compete for the few jobs available. Stress, insecurity and unadulterated fear are as much a part of the job as free air miles and service-station loyalty points.

The story I was working on that day was so huge and important to so many people that there was no alternative for me but to get it right. It was all or nothing. I could easily have thrown in the towel at the Villa d'Este. I could even have borrowed a couple of Thorsten Riedel's towels at Munich Airport and taken the next flight to Tenerife. Instead, I had the courage to tell my desk that we had the ball and it was on its way back to Britain. They had shown a worrying amount of faith in me, and not just the kind of faith which involves a gentle, if slightly patronising wink, followed by the words 'Thanks, mate, well done'. It was the kind of faith which caused them to splash my ill-informed ramblings all over the front page of a massive-selling newspaper read by around ten million people a day, including a number of ABC1 readers with large disposable incomes and the potential to become future employers of mine.

It was the equivalent of running a front page on Friday, 29 July 1966, announcing 'England win the World Cup – full story inside. More tomorrow'.

I telephoned my night desk for reassurance but they had all gone home. The only editorial person left in the entire Canary Wharf office was the night duty copytaker. I decided to try and get some sleep instead.

In journalist terms, the return of Geoff Hurst's ball was an immense, historic, awe-inspiring story. Most of the millions of words churned out for printing and broadcasting every day are about the dark side of human existence. They recount the squalidness, the misery and the sheer, unadulterated horror of life in the modern world, notably in places like the Balkans, Africa and Clacket Lane. There are so many obviously terrifying things which happen in society. We need objective information about them, but that does not mean they don't ultimately leave us feeling sad and depressed. Every day of the week, a small, affluent little island like Britain yields up the most gruesome tales imaginable.

There are the stories about double murders in isolated villages, where a retarded gardener mistakes his next-door neighbour for a burglar and spears him with a pitchfork. The neighbour's wife then appears and he spears her too – not because he mistook her for a burglar but because he's retarded.

There are the stories of groundbreaking open brain surgery operations where a hapless Ukrainian nursing assistant finds he's mislaid one of the scalpels. He finally remembers where he left it after the surgeon has sewn up the patient's head.

There are the dire industrial tribunals involving pettiness and hate between workmates who've fallen out over where the photocopied body-part portraits popped up after the office party.

There are the bitter divorces in which men and women are reduced to snarling grown-up children fighting over real children and the Internet-guided toasted-sandwich-maker they got for Christmas.

There are the features about life in soulless, concrete council estates where you have to have some experience of burglary and mugging if you want to have any hope of making something of your life.

Other perennially sad stories include the ones about hospital waiting lists the size of New Year sales queues, and the sacking of illegal immigrants from the Ukraine whose only crime was that they wanted to build a better life for their loved ones (six further counts of falsifying medical qualifications and sneaking into operating theatres are normally taken into account with this kind of story).

All are tales about real life, of course; because real life is cruel, depressing, squalid, uninspiring and often deadly for millions. When people complain about journalists only ever being interested in bad news, they should spend a little time thinking about the world in which they live. Our planet gets the newspapers it deserves.

The twentieth century was the most violent and destructive to date. There were two terrifying world wars – a nuclear explosion which wiped out two entire cities and their inhabitants was used to end the second. There were revolutions, counter-revolutions and post-counter-revolutions. Across whole continents like Africa there were civil wars and bloody conflicts fought with guns supplied by the kind of men who hang around on bleak, inhospitable islands full of sheep. There were famines, and football-hating dictators luxuriating in regal splendour while everyone else lived a Médecins sans Frontières jab or UN bread roll away from disease and starvation.

The worst man-made problems are, of course, often caused by the same, petty tribal quarrels which have set neighbours at each others' throats for years. Whether you are talking about vengeful Catholics and Protestants in the six counties of Northern Ireland, desperate Serbs and Kosovans in the Balkans, or a street of rival households in Clapham, south London, bickering over parking places, the resulting hatreds are not that different.

Journalists have to deal with every manifestation of human angst. Even without the wars and domestic murders which happen with terrifying regularity, we also have to be briefed daily on all the other developments of life in a technological age which, for the vast majority of people, is at best stupendously bland and conformist, and at worse lethal.

Every day millions of us have to make tedious journeys to work, mixing with the very people who are about to make the rest of our day so miserable. We have to sit in overheated, open-plan offices working long, tedious hours on beeping computers just to keep up the mortgage payments on houses we will never really own. We have to put up with ill-mannered, sullen colleagues for up to 14 hours a day, only to discover that the daughters for whom we started sacrificing all our money when they were babies have done something really stupid, like taking up horse-riding.

We have to visit vast, impersonal supermarkets to wheel trolleys around with all those other glum, robotic shoppers standing gormlessly at the checkouts, or stocking up on processed food and lavatory paper.

Throughout all this we have to try and keep up trite conversations with the person we find ourselves next to in our drab offices, service stations or DIY centres; people with whom we often have very little in common apart from mutual distrust. This situation is depressing enough when we come face to face with a potential pitchfork murderer when our train or Mondeo grinds to a halt outside Norwich. It becomes intolerable when the other person involved is someone with whom we were once particularly close, like a spouse or offspring.

Real life involves being filmed almost 24 hours a day by CCTV cameras recording every insignificant movement of a mistrusted population. Our grainy images are kept for posterity by local councils, security firms and the

Home Office in the hope that they may one day be used in evidence against us.

In turn we have to watch increasingly squalid and unpleasant television shows, full of interviews with off-beat 'personalities' gibbering hysterically about their personal philosophies and sex lives. As well as real soap operas, we have to sit through documentary soap operas showing exactly what it's like to be an estate agent in Dundee or photocopier salesman in Dartford. If we don't, we will have absolutely nothing to talk about when we make our two-hour journey to the office the next morning.

The amber ball was nothing to do with that side of life. It was about the almost indescribable heroic moments which lift us out of the bland and the mundane – moments which you can't have routinely and which you can't share with like-minded people at out-of-town shopping complexes. They are times which can't be index-linked or put in savings accounts or reduced to sleazy confessions on daytime TV shows. The ball symbolised those single, never-to-be repeated chapters in eternity which leave us dizzy, confused and longing for more. It's like the beat of your heart when you fall deeply and hopelessly in love with someone. It's like listening to the united beat of a thousand tiny hammers bringing down an iron curtain. It's like a lone human being making a tiny step out on to an inhuman, lunar landscape.

These are moments which it is impossible to be cynical about, because they lift us towards the stars and help us soar above the tacky, utterly predictable world in which we've found ourselves beyond the year 2000.

They're nothing to do with petty office rivalries, messy and unfulfilling domestic situations, forced meetings with people we don't like very much, supermarkets, dream holidays or financial transactions. You can't make cheap, offensive jokes about them or rubbish them in any way. They're a million years away from a selfish, mean-spirited age full of people obsessed with virtual reality and wholly dismissive of their country's heritage. They're about having a vague idea about the sweep of history and our place as individuals in the movement of peoples through time and space.

Most of us should have at least one moment like this in life (although I sometimes wonder about people who work in banks), while those who try really hard might have a few more. Once you stop looking for the heroic and concentrate solely on the mundane tasks of keeping a home together, earning a living and making tired relationships work, life really does become a lot worse than ordinary.

Of course, the modern world has given us plenty of help to see us through. We have TV companies opening their satellite and terrestrial bilge tanks 24 hours a day; ever-louder home stereos and lawn-mowers with which to persecute our neighbours who park so selfishly; exotic holiday resorts echoing to the sound of British regional accents; gyms oozing with neurotic sweat; Internet-guided kitchen gadgets which we get for Christmas and use only once; and the chance to establish our reputation as cheerless half-wits by appearing on daytime television discussion shows presented by cheery half-wits.

All were designed as the props for lives lived by generally blameless and fundamentally decent people – people longing to be imaginative and passionate and to strive for something out of the ordinary which will allow them to soar above their day-to-day routines.

For football supporters in England, 5.15 p.m. on Saturday, 30 July 1966, was a time when none of the mind-numbing normality of ordinary life mattered. It was nothing to do with predictable hobbies, neighbourly disputes, quivering lips, tutting, notes in windscreens, disapproving shakes of the head or any other mannerisms of so many twenty-first-century Little Britons. It was a moment when tears flowed freely, when total strangers hugged each other, when England was united in an outpouring of air-punching ecstasy and screams of 'Yesss!'

Our victory in the final of the greatest sporting competition in the world was gut-wrenchingly exciting. It led to feelings of overwhelming happiness – of unadulterated joy.

Watch a recording of the game and concentrate on the faces of those 11 young men in blood-red shirts, strutting and swearing in the July sunshine. You can see the crowd on the verge of tears, their quivering bodies a reminder of faded optimism and excitement. They represent a feeling that life isn't solely about virtual reality or kitchen extensions or reprimanding each other for not using our indicators.

Behind the material props and the disasters and the suffering and the vindictiveness and the base inhumanity which people are capable of inflicting on each another, there is something that no one will ever be able to take away from us.

What happened on that rainy summer's day was proof that the best of life is about having a passion. England winning the cup was life at its unquestionable best. It was a moment which might never be repeated, but which all of us have as part of our legacy.

The ball was the embodiment of that feeling. It made us soar above and beyond. It was an amber glow to lift us out of our mediocrity.

27 · Alarm Call

I woke at around 7 a.m. This isn't strictly true, because there was very little for me to wake up from. I'd hardly slept at all. I'd sort of lain down with my eyes shut and spent most of the night dreaming lightly about sudden ends to glorious, romantic chapters in life – the sort of thing you do when you've split up with your girlfriend, or eaten a lot of cheese. Except this was nothing to do with romance. This wasn't even anything to do with a few late-night slices of Brie. This was the down side of reality: I really was on the verge of being publicly humiliated and losing my job.

The giant TV set at the bottom of my hotel bed had erupted into life with the BBC's *Breakfast News*. The lead item on that morning's review of the papers was the World Cup ball. It was delivered by a man with a bow-tie and a good suit. He was a respectable-looking character who took life seriously and undoubtedly had an index-linked pension. He appeared nonchalantly authoritative as he held up the front page of the *Daily Mirror* for Friday, 26 April 1996. He said something along the lines of: 'And there's journalist Peter Allen arriving back at Heathrow with German footballer Helmut Haller. Today Mr Allen will be unveiling the 1966 World Cup ball itself.'

His claims weren't strictly true, of course. First of all we weren't at London's biggest airport. The picture was of me and Haller standing in a motorway service station surrounded by menacing truckers wearing acrylic jerseys and eating all-day breakfasts in between ferrying their potentially lethal loads across the country. The man in the bow-tie, and our millions of readers, did not know that because the front-page photograph had been cropped to get rid of the unsavoury bits. Their place was taken by a large headline – one of the largest I'd ever seen, which is saying something considering all the Italian football papers I've skimmed through. It announced that *Daily Mirror* man Peter Allen had found England's lost ball.

A small picture of Geoff Hurst in his red 1966 England shirt was also on the page, just in case younger readers did not know what he looked like. It had been taken from a larger picture of the entire World Cup squad, which included a former squad member who had recently been declared bankrupt at Portsmouth Crown Court. Again, the sub-editors had decided to crop out the unsavoury bits.

The man in the bow-tie also held up a copy of the *Sun*. He said something like: 'Mr Allen is going to be a pretty unpopular person with the *Sun* today, because he's got the ball and they haven't.'

The *Sun* had their own huge headline. It referred to Helmut Haller and accused him and his son Jurgen of wanting too much money for the ball. An editorial complained about all the time *Sun* journalists had wasted trying to negotiate with Haller in the Villa d'Este, and said that the football was Geoff Hurst's anyway and that the Germans should not be allowed to make any money out of it.

Other papers likened the contest for the ball to the Blackie the Donkey saga of the 1980s. A number of newspapers had set off to a Spanish village in the mountains around 60 miles from Madrid to rescue the animal. It was being tortured as part of the community's annual festivities which included an old custom whereby the fattest villager sat on the donkey, usually until it collapsed and died. Again, the *Sun* had been favourites to rescue Blackie and bring it back to Britain. Its reporter got to the donkey first but slipped off for a few rounds of San Miguel, intending to buy the animal off its Spanish owner a few hours later. Don McKay, a veteran Scottish journalist then working for the *Daily Star*, tracked the donkey down to the sun-dried field where the *Sun* men had left it. He impressed its owner with his impressive command of the language (his Spanish accent was far better than his English accent), exchanged legally binding contracts and returned the animal to England and safety. A *Star* horse-racing cover was placed on top of the donkey and the fledgling newspaper's circulation surged forward like a 9–4 favourite at Ascot.

Kelvin MacKenzie, the editor of the *Sun*, was incandescent with rage. The reporter who had let Blackie out of his sight tried to attack McKay at Dover, but by then it was too late. Blackie ended up enjoying a long and happy retirement in a donkey sanctuary in the West Country, far from his foreign tormentors.

It was a bright, sunny morning and, when I went down to the dining-room for breakfast, I started to feel a bit happier. There would be problems ahead, but this was all or nothing. If I failed I might have to consider spending the next few years of my life plugging PR drivel under the watchful eye of characterless managers called Gus or Sophie. If I succeeded, however, I might get to keep my job for a few more months.

The photographers nibbled bananas while the rest of us pondered the day ahead with cups of 'Real Coffee' and 'French-style Croissants' smothered with 'Traditional Marmalade'. Debbie, the girl serving us, was a vast improvement on Dean of the night before. This wasn't difficult, of course. To be better than Dean you just had to be able to fetch coffee in less than an hour, and not approach every routine task as if you'd been asked to split an atom in four.

Debbie had greeted us with words to the effect of: 'Good morning. Welcome to the Uphall breakfast experience. How may I help you?' She had her conditioned reflexes down to a T but, as I was to discover, she found it hard to think beyond the sentences she had been taught during her training. Debbie was like the vast majority of people working in British service industries, be they call centres or cafés.

We sat about reading through the newspapers and talking. Riedel was still vaguely negotiating, which is what he seemed to enjoy doing most. At about 9.30 I wandered out of the breakfast lounge for five minutes to pick up my mobile phone from my room to be ready for a quick departure. When I got back the quick departure had already taken place. The entire breakfast room was empty, with just a few banana skins and bits of croissant lying around.

Debbie rushed in from the kitchen. 'Good morning. Welcome to the Uphall breakfast experience. How may I help you?' she said.

'I've already experienced it,' I said, my voice sounding tense. 'Where have all my friends gone?'

'What, you mean the brothers Grimm?' she replied.

It turned out that a freelance photographer working for another newspaper had been spotted lurking in the hotel grounds. A gardener had became suspicious when the cameraman began to climb a tree and point a long lens towards an upstairs window. When he struck up a conversation about Formula One, the gardener called the police.

Worse than that, there was an entire German TV production team camped outside the main gate. They had done extremely well to find us, especially since they were working in a foreign country. They were brilliantly equipped with little tents and binoculars, as well as dental floss and telescopic umbrellas. As is typical of foreign journalists, however, they had been reluctant to give the story the final push. If they had turned up for an Uphall breakfast experience, they may well have got another interview with Haller and the rest of us.

'What do I do now?' I asked Debbie in desperation.

Sadly, her conditioned reflexes did not extend to getting people out of tabloid fixes. 'We have traditional English breakfast tea, we have traditional English breakfasts,' she said.

I ran into the Great Hall and asked the receptionist where everybody had gone. The Grimms – Haller, Riedel, the lawyers, my journalistic colleagues and Malcolm the driver – had all dived out of a window and escaped down a gravel path at the rear of the hotel before jumping into the Jaguar and a Mercedes. Malcolm had executed three SAS-style rolls before driving his car through an open window and shouting, 'Go, go, go!'

I started to gibber at the receptionist. 'This is serious. Very, very serious. I have to find my brothers. I mean, I have to find my business associates. You have to help me. Please, please help me,' I begged.

The receptionist stared at me with a mixture of pity and incomprehension, rather like traffic wardens do when you ask them for a couple of minutes to move your car as they place notice of a £60 fine in your windscreen. Except the receptionist did not look at me as if I was something from outer space. She looked at me as if I was the Creature from the Black Lagoon.

I was starting to feel deeply unhappy. I was completely isolated in a wilderness of Old English hospitality where those around me could offer nothing but vacant stares and traditional or continental breakfast.

I felt almost as lonely as I had done on my first shift on Fleet Street. Then I had been placed on the reporters' desk as far from the newsdesk as it was possible to get, which was quite a long way considering the vastness of the old *Mirror* offices at Holborn Circus in central London. (The newsroom was like an elongated football field. Despite its clamour and noise, journalists could easily find a quiet, isolated corner to sleep off their hangovers at any time of the day or night.) I was at the desk for around seven hours before the monotony was broken by my telephone ringing. My hands started to sweat as I looked around for support. Apart from other casual staff fresh from the provinces, the only other people sitting at my desk were old staffers who used to leave a jacket on the back of their chair and a cigarette smouldering in an ashtray before 'nipping out for a quick livener' – sometimes for days at a time. I feebly picked up the receiver before stumbling out the words 'D...D...D...Daily Mirror'.

'I know it's the effing *Daily Mirror*,' replied a gruff voice. 'This is an internal line and I'm the effing news editor. Now take this call. Some old granny's discovered another planet.'

I didn't get anything in the next day.

As I contemplated a premature and inglorious end to my role in Operation Inflation, I recognised an undercover *Mirror* staff photographer pulling up in his Ford Mondeo. He jumped out and began to fiddle with the equipment in his boot. He was tall and stocky and dressed in a black biker's jacket, jeans and heavy trekking boots. There were newspapers, sticky fast-food containers, plastic coffee cups and piles of photographic equipment on his back seat, as well as an old copy of *Playboy*. He was an undercover press photographer who looked just like a press photographer.

'Oi!' he yelled though the front doors of the hotel. 'On the back seat. Now!'

I nodded at the receptionists, who immediately started off on another of their conditioned verbal reflexes. Something along the lines of 'We hope you enjoyed your stay with us, Mr Grimm. Was everything all right?' This is normally a guest's signal to start droning on about the inability of the trouser press in their room to execute even the most simple of tasks, like pressing trousers. Or to start moaning about the night porter's habit of leaving cigarette ash on the tray in which he was serving rounds of tuna-and-sweetcorn sandwiches which, now that you ask, were also full of ash . . . On this occasion, I thought it best to make a swift exit.

I flung myself onto the rear passenger seat of the Mondeo. The photographer threw a rug over me which covered my head and entire body.

'It's just in case the Germans at the main gate see you,' he said, evoking images of Stalag Luft III. We moved forward and I could hear raised Teutonic voices. Most notable among them was the woman who had interviewed me on the plane over. She still sounded as though she was working on a doctoral thesis as she discussed her documentary with her superiors in Munich. She was also barking out orders at her camera team, all of whom were engrossed in telephone conversations of their own. I resisted the temptation to hurl a half-eaten French-style croissant in their general direction.

We sped through the semi-rural, semi-suburban lanes around the hotel and, within 20 minutes, had linked up with the rest of the team at a lay-by.

The executives had all long since returned to their high-backed chairs at Canary Wharf, but our band had been swelled by a veteran on-the-road reporter whose massive experience was to prove invaluable over the next few hours – not so much his experience of journalism, but his experience of dealing with cantankerous, difficult foreigners who did not see much point in anything in life apart from furrowing their brows a lot and making life as difficult as possible for others. Don McKay, the man who had brought Blackie the Donkey back to Britain from a Spanish hell in the 1980s, was on our side.

'I think we've lost the bastards. Let's move out,' said the Scotsman, who had lost none of his passion for the job.

McKay was wearing black cowboy boots and felt certain he could inject a little of the John Wayne into proceedings on that bright April morning. Despite his clear lack of interest in the 1966 World Cup final, he was ready to use all his Scottish canniness to make the job work. His intense enthusiasm for the nitty gritty of Operation Inflation was matched by nobody, except perhaps Malcolm the driver.

We drove on towards central London in silence. We'd missed the worst part of the morning rush hour and Malcolm seemed a lot calmer during daylight hours. Instead of snarling and grunting at every other car on the road, he contented himself with the odd flicked V-sign at anyone he spotted in a Suzuki jeep. Riedel had pledged to say nothing until the money was firmly in his hands.

Everything seemed relatively calm, when Haller suddenly felt queasy and wanted to stop somewhere. We'd got rid of the Sun. We'd got rid of the German TV crew. We'd negotiated the delivery of the ball after hours of angst. Now Herr Haller was feeling car sick.

We were forced to pull in at another motorway service station. It was probably the one we'd been to the night before, but we were past caring by now. Haller got out of the Jaguar and made his way to the canteen for a sit-down. He put his elbow on his knees and began to wipe his brow with a handkerchief. '*Nein, nein,*' we could hear him saying to Riedel, who remained disturbingly calm and efficient. Everyone else in the café looked like a reporter, a photographer or a German cameraman. Everyone from the baseball-capped truants playing the video games in the corner to the sales reps negotiating bulk photocopier orders over endless cups of orange paint tea. Everytime one of them looked up from their dubious activities we began to get twitchy. Discussing photocopier prices is not the most stimulating thing in the world. Shooting virtual aliens does not hold the attention for long either, especially if your formal education ended as recently as last Tuesday. Accordingly, we were twitchy for most of the stop.

Then Riedel started up again. 'I am not happy with zer negotiations,' he said. 'I vant more of a guarantee that vee vill be getting our money on time.'

It was time for Don McKay's years of experience in dealing with all forms of human life to come into their own. The Scotsman's command of the situation was intense and powerful. He was like a grand master who had abandoned wooden pieces on a chess board to concentrate on guiding players with hearts and souls. He knew all about body language, the subtleties of voice tone, leg-crossing and hair arrangement which differentiate us all from the inanimate. He could read people like a weekend colour supplement. He could move them as if he was a mystical soothsayer from the windswept Highlands of his native land.

McKay's sturdy heels moved towards Riedel. They stopped inches away from the German's sensible black slip-on loafers. The Scotman's knowing eyes stared deep and hard into the cold, unflinching Germanic forehead, two feet above him.

Time appeared to stand still. It may have been two minutes, it may have been two hours, but there was not a word said and neither of them blinked. That same impenetrable, ever-wise stare which had tamed a peasant farmer in old Castille was as steely and true as it had ever been.

Riedel went completely quiet.

Haller stood up and said: 'It iz time to go and get zer ball.'

McKay paced back towards me. 'If that Riddle pipes up again I'll make sure I really do effing well chin him,' he said.

Haller had used his sick break to call Jurgen. He and Mike Moore were ready to fly back from Amsterdam but, as agreed, there would be no movement until the money was in the hands of the Germans. Still staring at the odd mix of humanity clustered around the service station, we got back in the cars and resumed our journey.

We reached Lloyd's Holborn branch at noon. We were all still dressed in crumpled suits and, mainly due to lack of sleep and long conversations with Riedel, were looking the worse for wear. Malcolm's driving, which got friskier as the morning progressed, had not helped either. As soon as we left the motorway and entered the London suburbs he'd begun trying to force bad drivers off the road. His definition of bad were those drivers who tried to keep up with him. He also seemed to have something against non-car drivers as well, especially anyone on a motorbike. Bikers on big Suzukis or Kawasakis over 750cc did not have much trouble but those on pedal cycles or, even worse, those delivering pizzas on mopeds did not stand a chance. Malcolm also got irate about any pedestrians who interfered with his driving by carrying out irritating, selfish acts like trying to cross the road.

The bank was opposite the old Mirror building and on the same street as its veterans' local pub. (It had earned the nickname 'The Stab' in honour of all those journalists who had been called over to its saloon bar for a 'quiet chat' with a senior executive before finding out that there was no way back into the building.) We thought of nipping in for a livener but decided that might not be such a good idea. Most of us, especially McKay and Malcolm, did not need livening.

Bank workers, whose daily excitement usually extended to their journey to work or the coffee run, nudged each other and began to whisper as we were led to a 'secure room' at the back of the building by the manager. Our progress was still being broadcast on radios and TVs all over Britain so they knew exactly who we were.

Two official Mirror Group bodyguards joined us in the bank's back room. I recognised them as the rather sad-looking men you see lounging about in front of closed-circuit TV screens in office blocks all over Britain, normally reading copies of *Playboy* hidden under their reception desks. They were the men who frequently wouldn't allow me into Canary Wharf tower without the correct paperwork. I'd always thought this odd, as you normally need the correct paperwork from your doctor to stay off work. Once they had given me a cleaner's pass to hang around my neck for the day, and I failed to return it at the end of my shift. I got a severe reprimand next time I saw them. They threatened to ban me from going to work for life. Worse than that, they said there was a woman who polished the computer screens on the 23rd floor who had missed a day's pay because of me.

As every single note of the £70,000 was counted out before the eyes of Riedel and Haller, the security guards stared around the room in the style of those Stasi agents who used to run behind the East German leader's Trabant Deluxe. They even went so far as to hold their right hands in their inside breast pockets, trying to make out they had guns down there, instead of packets of chewing gum and leaky biros. With their dark glasses and furrowed brows, they looked deadly serious. Sadly their potato sack uniforms – complete with oversize red badges advertising their company name – spoiled the effect, as did their frequent habit of slobbering their tongues outside one side of their mouths and occasionally scratching their genitals inside their trousers.

With the money in order, we raced back into bustling Holborn.

The Germans used a mobile phone to call Jurgen Haller and Moore. There was a flight in 15 minutes' time and they were booked on it. Operation Inflation was bang on course. The amber ball was on its way home.

'Put your trainer down, Malc,' shouted McKay. 'I'll ride shotgun,' the Scotsman bellowed, letting out a long, throaty laugh which almost drowned out the Jaguar's engine propelling the car forward at 70 miles an hour.

Ten minutes later we drove back to collect Haller and Riedel.

28 · Danger Roam

Jurgen Haller and Mike Moore had a mysterious journey from Augsburg to Amsterdam. It wasn't mysterious in the sense that other people weren't exactly sure which route they took. It was mysterious in the sense that they themselves weren't exactly sure which route they took.

Their part in Operation Inflation was a lot more delicate than ours. They had the amber cargo with them throughout, and knew that the slightest slip would be disastrous.

After retrieving the keys to the Opel Kadett, Moore had slipped off to an autobahn service station for a few hours before returning to the Villa d'Este under the cover of darkness. The Sun men who stayed to watch him had assumed we had taken the ball along with Helmut Haller and Thorsten Riedel on the flight back to Heathrow. Our opponents soon grew tired of watching the Mirror photographer sipping mugs of orange-coloured tea while prodding a plate of particularly repugnant-looking pickled cabbage which had spent most of the day sweating under the bright lights of the service-station restaurant. Moore also found time to adjust his shutter speeds as he stared out of a greasy window on to the main Augsburg-to-Munich road. For some, fiddling with camera lenses is one of the most tedious activities on earth, but photographers can absorb themselves in it for hours. The Sun men assumed Moore would eventually be flying out of Germany via Munich as well, so set off to doorstep the airport there.

Instead, Moore drove to Haller's house and found Jurgen packed and ready to roam. The ball was placed in a white plastic supermarket bag, wrapped in a black polo-neck jumper and a check jacket, and then put inside a brown hold-all. Haller kept a tight hold of it. Then the pair set off in the opposite direction to Munich, to the first airport they could find.

A wily German freelancer, who was especially keen to persuade Jurgen Haller to keep the ball he had legitimately been given as a birthday present, tipped off local police that there was a car travelling along the autobahn with two men and 'an illegal hidden object' on board. This terrified traffic officers. (Only a couple of years before, detectives had to deal with two Russian dissidents with a lead container full of enriched uranium hidden in the boot of their Mercedes. The men, a 36-year-old nuclear scientist and a 42-year-old

169

unemployed fruit-and-vegetable merchant, were eventually trapped when they stopped off, predictably enough, at a service station near Augsburg. They had been hoping to sell their deadly cargo for £400,000 a kilo. Thankfully, secret agents had been tailing them for two weeks so that while they were preparing to enjoy a Chef's Special of sauerkraut and sausage in the German equivalent of Clacket Lane, they came across a welcoming committee. Twenty officers of the élite Sonder Einsatz Kommando jumped out on them, pointing machine-guns and a Geiger counter at the boot of their Mercedes.)

Haller and the photographer might not have passed themselves off as nuclear scientists but they certainly had the look of unemployed fruit-and-vegetable sellers about them. They did not expect anything similar to happen to them but still kept a steady eye on all uniformed officers who approached. Jurgen said that Augsburg had a perfectly respectable airport and seemed an ideal place to wait for the green light to fly into London. They could book into a hotel in the city, have a meal and prepare for their flight of destiny, ready to be greeted with open arms in England.

Haller had, of course, forgotten that Rudolf Hess had thought much the same thing when he set off from Augsburg Airport on 10 May 1941. Full of supposedly idealistic thoughts and good intentions, he had climbed into a Messerschmitt – one of local-boy Willy's creations – and headed for Britain. He left a farewell note for his superiors claiming he was off 'to risk my life to make peace and end the bloodshed'. Hess parachuted out at Eaglesham, near Glasgow, claiming he wanted to meet the Duke of Hamilton and sue for peace. For all his efforts Hess was awarded a lifetime sentence in Spandau Prison after the Nuremberg trials. (Hess's real motives are still among the greatest mysteries in the history of the world, along with the identity of Jack the Ripper, the truth about the *Marie Celeste* and, of course, whether Hurst's second World Cup final goal was in or out.)

Moore said he would be happier to take the bus. The pair could grab a couple of rucksacks and pretend to be over-age students 'finding themselves' on the road, just like the American beatniks. They had the black polonecks and stubble already. Jurgen said they were more likely to find themselves at the wrong end of a Sun man's fist, and started dropping hints about wanting to pack the whole thing in and stay at home.

The compromise was to take a short flight to Amsterdam and wait there. The Dutch city is the perfect place to waste a few hours, especially if you're into mind-altering chemicals or women with flexible morals.

As Haller and the photographer drove around looking for the small airfield, they passed Landsberg Prison, where Hitler was incarcerated for a pitifully short nine months after his ill-fated *Putsch* in 1923. As is typical of Germans, he didn't waste his time inside on rehabilitation courses learning how to change spark plugs or get a Grade C media studies GCSE. Instead, he churned out the massive *Mein Kampf*, one of the most self-indulgent, tedious books ever written, but one which directly led to the worst war in the history of mankind. The idealistic Jurgen Haller, a committed New German, felt certain that his own flight of destiny would help to overcome such bitter memories.

The pair did not see much of Amsterdam. They booked into a hotel at Schipol Airport and waited for the green light. Most of the other guests were the airborne equivalent of the sales reps you see driving Ford Mondeos on the M25. The only real difference was that instead of discussing the best route to Luton avoiding the M1, they discussed the best route to passport control avoiding the grey carpet at Heathrow. They weren't the best company. Apart from a half-hour chat at the bar, when they discussed their movements, the custodians of the amber ball spent most of the time alone in their rooms. They watched features about home banking on Sky TV and tried to get their trouser-presses to press their by now extremely crumpled trousers.

When the call came from Helmut Haller they had already exchanged the oppressive, uninspiring walls of their hotel for the oppressive, uninspiring walls of a departure lounge at Schipol. They had booked two places on every flight to Stansted that day, just to be on the safe side, and were airborne within 15 minutes. On board they felt confident enough to take the ball out of its hiding place for the first time and take some photographs of it. It was not a very busy flight, so they put the ball in its own seat and even put a safety belt round it. Some of the stewardesses giggled at the sweetness of it all. A passenger sitting directly behind them – whose huge moustache and jet-black hair made him look a little like Saddam Hussein – thought that the pair should be locked up.

At 1.30 p.m. the plane started its descent into Stansted. The two passengers on board who were playing such an integral part in Operation Inflation began to feel extremely excited. Whatever happened next, it was going to be an eventful landing.

Another plane was coming in at Stansted at exactly the same time. On board was a bald *Sun* reporter who looked like a pub bouncer and a photographer who looked like a savage tight-head prop who had absconded from a rugby scrum. After overnighting in Munich they had got to the city's airport early on Friday morning. The *Sun* newsdesk told them that the ball was almost certainly still in Germany.

Sun readers at motorway service stations all over south-east England had seen Haller, another odd-looking German and a load of geeks from the Mirror, but none appeared to have the ball. The Mirror's triumphalist front page had been a dummy, and they were still very much in the game.

The bald Sun man snarled and stared at the crowds milling around him. Somewhere there was a Mirror photographer and a German with Geoff Hurst's football. He reasoned there was a very good chance that they would not be leaving the European mainland via Munich, so set about finding out exactly which airport they would be using. He and his colleague began checking all the flights returning to mainland Europe. It was a difficult, exacting job which loosely involved telephoning as many check-in desks as possible and asking if passengers Haller and Moore were planning to go anywhere.

After their first call to Lufthansa at Geneva, the Sun men thought it was time for a quick livener. They reckoned they could manage a couple of sly swifties before carrying on with their task. At one of the numerous bars at Munich Airport the reporters ordered a couple of 'little beers'. Sadly, there is no such thing as a 'little beer' in Munich. The only ones available are huge, frothing beers from the numerous breweries all over southern Germany. They were handed a couple of measures which looked like the barrel Herr Burgermeister taps at the end of each September to signal the start of the Oktoberfest when five million litres of lager from six Munch breweries are made available to lager louts of every shape and size from all over Europe, including a massive and particularly enthusiastic contingent from England.

The Sun men knocked them back and decided they were quite good . . . Then they knocked a couple more back. By the time they'd finished drinking they could not have cared less if there was a German citizen Haller and a United Kingdom citizen Moore booked on the 2.30 NASA space shuttle to Mars. As the afternoon slipped by, their troublesome trip to Germany began to pass in a joyous haze.

Other members of the Sun's foreign legion eventually worked out which flight Haller and Moore plus football would be on. Another Sun reader selling photocopiers in the Low Countries had checked in at a dreary hotel at Schipol and seen two men and an odd-shaped package sitting at the bar. The men were sipping espressos. He had vaguely heard them mentioning the World Cup ball. Knowing the paper was on the trail of the amber relic, he had telephoned the newsdesk on the freephone number made available to foreign tipsters.

A Sun freelancer, one who normally covered the Amsterdam flexible morals beat for the newspaper, began working on the tip-off. It did not take him long to discover which flight Haller and Moore would be on. The pair had annoyed a number of flight staff already by cancelling seats on planes. It was clear they were trying to get in by early afternoon. It was just a question of waiting until the last moment before every flight closed and taking it from there.

When there was no cancellation for the lunchtime fight out of Schipol, the Sun knew they had their men.

29 · In-flight Deal

Nineteen *Sun* reporters and photographers were ordered to Stansted Airport. They were accompanied by seven nightclub bouncers who had been hired by the newspaper to 'keep order' when the ball finally arrived. All were fully qualified doormen, hugely experienced in violent confrontations. They knew how to snarl up their faces horribly while adding to any kind of mayhem which might be going on in their immediate vicinity.

The bouncers' other main brief at the airport was to wrestle any 'trouble-makers' to the ground, relieve them of their 'stolen property' and finally to toss the 1966 World Cup ball through the sunroof of a *Sun* staff car waiting outside the main terminal building with its engine running.

The two *Sun* men in Germany, meanwhile, were ordered to make their way straight on to the next plane to Stansted. Through a twist of ill-fate, there was a charter flight leaving half an hour later. It was full of English tourists, most of whom appeared to be on their way back from a warm-up for that year's Oktoberfest. The *Sun* team paid the equivalent of £200 cash – all in used Deutschmarks – for the two remaining seats.

'That's cheap,' said one as he handed over his money. 'Can't we upgrade to business?'

It was impossible. There was no business class – only goat.

As the *Sun* reporter squeezed into his tiny seat with his knees almost touching his chin, alcohol-induced euphoria turned to anger. He stared back at the neat rows of oddly-shaped faces and acrylic football shirts which made up the majority of the flight. They appeared to leer back at him.

'Where did you get this lot from?' he snarled at one of the stewardesses.

'Just relax, we'll be off now, sir,' she smiled back. The flight attendant was used to dealing with all kinds of difficult passengers: children whose ears were liable to pop, old ladies with a fear of flying, seething tabloid newspaper journalists ...

Pacified for the moment, the *Sun* man quickly grew bored. He looked out of the window but saw nothing but cloud cover. He fiddled aimlessly with the ventilator knob above his head and the dry, shapeless meal on the tray in front of him. He belched a couple of times as his fumes intermingled with the mass of other noxious gases being emitted by the Acrylics around him. They were handing out bottles of German lager and some were singing beery football chants. A number of them had tattoos and ear studs. All wore training shoes.

The Sun man started to feel more at home. He grabbed a lager from one of his fellow passengers, and began holding forth. 'Lads, I've got something to tell you all,' he said.

The Acrylics listened intently as they were told why two Sun staffmen were on their flight. The reporter told them the story of a wicked, fat little German who had stolen the most famous ball in English sporting history and kept it hidden for 30 years. He had thought nothing of depriving Geoff Hurst, the man who won the World Cup for us in 1966, of the most important thing in his whole life. What was more, the stinking German's son would be waiting for them all at the airport to take the piss. He would have the stolen ball with him and would be ready to mock any English people he could find on their home soil.

Curses and shouts began to fill the plane. 'Bastard. Let's have 'im,' was the most common cry.

'I'll do a deal with you, lads,' said the Sun man. 'I'll point him out. You duff him up.'

The Acrylics began chanting patriotic songs. The Sun men got up and began conducting the airborne choir. They sang 'We'll never be mastered, by those foreign bastards' to the tune of 'The Red Flag'. They sang 'Rule Britannia' and 'God Save the Queen'. They sang 'The Theme from Rocky' without knowing the words, but they were enjoying themselves.

The few hairs on the Sun reporter's head began to bristle with pride. He could feel the sweat pouring off his back and seeping into the beer stains on his shirt.

The passengers gave off an odour which historically has always been linked with English fortitude. It was the smell that had seeped out of the ale-houses of Portsmouth from where Royal Marines had selected the beer-swilling thugs who would seal England's glory at the Battle of Trafalgar. It was the smell of the London drinking-dens where guardsmen had downed their last jars of brandy before mustering under their Iron Duke to stain two square miles of soil with the blood of Napoleon's invincible Old Guard. It was the smell of the working-men's clubs – just like the one at Trimdon – from where labourers had, twice in the last century, left to suffer unimaginable horrors in their quest for peace on a Western Front.

These lads might be drunk, they might have bad teeth, menacing leers and necks considerably wider than their heads were long, but they were British. They were the salt-of-the-earth sons of the forgotten empire whose grit and determination on foreign fields had ensured our finest hours. Theirs was the martial spirit which had made Britain great. Theirs was not a smell to be hidden by overpriced cosmetics from effete, decadent nations like Italy and France. It was the earthy reek of the ancient soil of England.

'We will shortly be touching down at Stansted Airport,' came the announcement over the tannoy.

Emotional tears were pouring down the Sun man's face as he was led away from one of the exits. 'We have to land before you can get out,' said one of the stewardesses, ever helpful and understanding. She buckled him into his seat as the rest of the plane carried on chanting 'Ingerland, Ingerland, Ingerland' to the tune of 'Beer we go, Beer we go, Beer we go'.

The 19 Sun staffmen and seven nightclub bouncers arrived at Stansted a few minutes before Jurgen Haller and Mike Moore. The Sun cohorts were as intimidating as the mercenary doormen standing next to them. Some looked like all-in wrestlers while the smaller ones had that oddly cross-eyed, psychotic look which you normally associate with knife-wielding delinquents from broken homes. They formed a line across the airport's departure gate, folding their arms in a menacing show of strength.

The Mirror had sent two staff journalists to meet the plane. One was its Birmingham correspondent. He was white-haired and in his fifties and was probably the most inoffensive thing to come out of the city's journalism since the Birmingham Post last produced a knitting supplement. The other was the paper's consumer correspondent. She was a Bristol University graduate who was so mild-mannered and unthreatening that the Sunday Telegraph had once tried to headhunt her.

The utterly unevenly matched forces stared at each other on either side of the arrivals channel. Thankfully, the Mirror force would not be alone. An anonymous call to the Essex Constabulary had warned that there might be 'a row going off' at Stansted that afternoon.

Policemen in the Stansted area spend most of their time stopping people for speeding on the M11, so when it was announced that there was trouble brewing at the airport, half the force volunteered to attend. When it was announced that there might be a chance to wear riot gear and beat up tabloid journalists, the other half volunteered as well.

The feeling of anticipation was enormous as word came that the passengers on both planes had disembarked. Haller and Moore, who had expected to be met by nothing more threatening than a surly baggage-handler, began to make their way to arrivals.

A maniacal scream rang out to the airport's rooftops: 'Come on, lads. This is our land!' shouted the bald Sun reporter as he bounded across the terminal building followed by fifty Acrylics still shouting, 'Ingerland, Ingerland, Ingerland!'

They were spitting venom and snarling their faces up like irate bulldogs. Shiny fibres strained across their beer bellies as they thundered forward. Their huge trainers squeaked on the well-polished floors. Inside their stained jeans and cheap leather jackets, they were bracing themselves for a hard, violent confrontation.

The Sun reporter was the first to go in. He flung himself in the air like a devoted doorman who had spotted a surly student making obscene hand gestures outside a city-centre pub. Instead of just administering an educative slap, however, he grabbed hold of Haller's torso and pulled him to the ground. The German screamed in horror as he prepared himself for a stream of blows.

Arcylics began hurling themselves at anybody they could see, which was mainly each other. Moore, more than six foot tall and with an imposing wing-commander moustache and a heavy tripod in his hands 'looked a bit tasty', according to one of the Acrylics.

By now the Sun men on the other side of the airport could just about make out what was going on. They began to shout and scream and cheer their colleagues on.

Everywhere Jurgen looked from his position below the Sun reporter there were threats of violence. He was quivering and speaking in German, which only made matters worse.

'Where is it?' shouted the Sun man. 'Give us our ball back. Give us our ball back now, or you're going to get a serving!'

Young Haller began to look more and more like Jacky Simon. He rolled his eyes and held his hands in the air, as numerous nationalities had been prone to do during centuries of altercations with the British. The manoeuvre was a difficult one, bearing in mind he had a Sun reporter on top of him, but he was trying his best to come over as alone and non-committal as a surrendering Frenchman.

As Haller's protests increased, he was allowed to sit up and explain, in perfect English, that he did not have the ball on him. Both Sun men started to shake him violently. Jurgen burst out crying. He collapsed in a heap with his head in his hands.

At that moment 20 policemen came charging in to break up the distur-bance. The Sun men were led away, one grimacing madly with his legs shaking in the air like an upturned goat. As his suit trousers were pulled down slightly below his beer gut, you could just about see a pair of Union Jack boxer shorts.

The official police incident report read: 'Attendance in force at Standsted Airport. Two men detained following a bit of an upheaval. One German slightly hurt.' The note did not quite convey the full drama of the incident, but its real message was clear: at least two *Sun* staffmen had played their last part in Operation Inflation.

A senior policeman stuck out his hand towards Haller and announced: 'Good afternoon, Mr Haller. Welcome to Stansted Airport. I hope you enjoy your stay.'

(The scene was very similar to the one at Glasgow Airport in the late 1960s when England arrived for an international against Scotland. A reporter had stuck out the hand of friendship to the visiting national manager and said: 'Welcome to Scotland, Sir Alf.'

Ramsey replied: 'You must be effing joking.')

A few of the *Sun* reporters on the other side of customs began shouting questions. Moore told Haller to ignore them all. He adopted the Franz Beckenbauer approach to pre-match interviews, which essentially involves adopting an inscrutable stare and saying 'Nein' a lot.

(Alf Ramsey had been pretty good at that too. Before a match against Poland in Katowice in 1966 he had been asked about the surprise inclusion of Martin Peters in his team, especially so close to the World Cup finals. Asked if he could explain Peters' new role, Ramsey replied: 'No.')

Jurgen brushed himself down as Moore guided him away from the Acrylics who were beginning to disperse. Moore gripped the brown holdall slung across his right shoulder even harder, and the pair were escorted by the police back out to the runway.

The worst was over, Haller was assured. All the aggravation and nastiness could be forgotten. He would not have to deal with the pack of hate preparing to take him apart on the other side of the sliding doors. He would not even have to go through the ignominy of having his bag searched in the customs area by a surly creep with an ill-fitting suit and the manners of an orang-utan. Instead, he could relax and enjoy the last ten minutes of his epic journey in style and comfort. We had chartered a helicopter. We had spent thousands of pounds on ensuring that our very own aircraft would lift us above all our enemies and propel us to our meeting with destiny. We had thought the whole thing out, smartly and efficiently. We had prepared well.

So had the *Sun*.

Their helicopter was parked directly behind ours. You could tell which was ours because it was empty apart from a grinning pilot called Nigel wearing a white shirt and epaulettes. You could tell which one was theirs because it was crammed full of long lenses and threatening Sun men with scowling, determined looks on their faces. They were pointing at us as if to say, 'That's it. You've gone far enough this time.'

Jurgen Haller began to consult his Lufthansa timetable for the next available flight back to Munich. He tried to phone his dad on his mobile phone but there was no signal. The only signals available on the tarmac were from a maddened Sun team, and they weren't the kind that you can talk about in polite company. Jurgen Haller began to cry again.

It was left to Moore to provide further proof of his worthiness in the field. He ran towards the pilot of the rear helicopter and asked if he could have a quick word with him somewhere quiet. On any runway 'somewhere quiet' means somewhere not on the runway. The pair disappeared back inside the terminal for a few minutes.

Once he had taken his headphones and cap off, the helicopter pilot, called Julian, was surprisingly eager to accept some serious aeronautical advice from the Mirror photographer. He brought up the subject of crosswinds, aggressive cloud formations . . . and £500 cash. The pilot – who was going through an expensive divorce at the time in which 'nerdy first-name' had been cited as the main grounds for his wife's petition – had accepted all Moore's advice.

A few minutes later the Mirror helicopter took off, with nothing following apart from a pair of curious seagulls.

We had pulled into a hotel carpark on the north London/Hertfordshire border, at about the same time that the amber ball took off in the helicopter. Malcolm had got 'a bit lost' on the way from Holborn up the A10, but a motor-bike despatch rider had escorted us for the last 15 miles.

There were plenty more stops. At lay-bys. At service stations. Outside public toilets. The desk wanted to be absolutely certain that nobody knew where we were. We were not even told the name of the hotel, such was the secrecy with which the whole operation was now being handled.

We parked next to some other cars and waited. Looking around, the grounds of the hotel were not dissimilar to the Guided Weapons Division sports ground which Haller had trained on with his German team-mates in Hertfordshire before the final in 1966. We all wondered what was going to happen next.

Then there was the sound of rotor blades. The buzz made us feel that this might finally be the big one. Geoff Hurst appeared from out of the back of one of the other parked cars. He was wearing his original red England shirt from 1966. Helmut Haller jumped out of the Jaguar for a friendly spar with his old adversary. The two exchanged pleasantries, as Riedel translated.

Then the helicopter landed. Jurgen Haller could be seen smiling behind the perspex window. He was still visibly shaken by what had happened at Stansted, but he knew that what was about to happen had nothing to do with his own personal well-being. It was all about the pride and joy of an expectant nation.

30 · Word Wars

Justification is one of the most important words in a journalist's vocabulary. Formally, it's the best defence against libel. When a London barrister on the kind of win bonus that will allow him to afford an Arsenal season-ticket stands up in the High Court to fight an accusation that his client's work is defamatory, he will not only have to prove that it was true, but that it was justified.

In his refined North Bank tones the erudite lawyer will announce that it was entirely in the public interest to produce a two-page spread on a New Labour minister's 'lost Saturday afternoon' with a South American full-back. Charges that it was defamatory to link the poor form of Atlético Montevideo with the leisure activities of one of the Prime Minister's closest allies will also be heavily refuted. During the protracted legal battle, the barrister will need to prove that every word in the article, even the four paragraphs about the ball-juggling llamas, were entirely justified.

Outside the civil justice system, justification is just as relevant to the journalist's daily routine. It underpins all those 'What does it all mean?' or 'Why bother?' questions concerning drives round the M25, early-morning doorsteps in Ilford, or any stories involving the bar staff from *Eastenders*.

As we all stood on a patch of grass somewhere in Hertfordshire waiting for a leather ball to arrive at a cost of thousands of pounds and massive disruption to numerous lives, such questions were paramount. We wore the looks of pallid, unhealthy menials who had been surviving on tinned fish sandwiches and lukewarm beer. Our clothes were dirty and dishevelled. The family and friends closest to us had remained excluded from our fights, our foul-mouthed verbal exchanges and our chases through some of the most uninspiring places in the civilised world.

Alan Clark, the former cabinet minister and historian, encapsulated our mood when he described reporters as 'fellows with, in the main, squalid and unfulfilling lives, insecure in their private lives, insecure in their careers, and suffering a considerable degree of dependence on alcohol and narcotics'.

But it's not just the personal insults and base prejudice of a statesman of letters which we have to put up with (albeit one who enjoyed a colourful and unpredictable life of his own, full of controversy and squalid sex). Already there were far lesser commentators trying to undermine what we had achieved. We expected criticism from other newspapers, because one of all journalists' principal roles in life is to rubbish the best work of their peers. When Blackie the Donkey was rescued, the rest of the press did not portray him as a loveable animal hero symbolising the great British public's affinity with persecuted mules worldwide. They said he was miserable and disease-ridden vermin whose proposed immigration to Britain was a national disgrace.

Similarly, our own efforts were being derided as a farcical and expensive publicity stunt. It was inevitable that such comment came from newspapers, which are seldom adventurous enough to send their reporters out of east London, let alone to an international departure lounge. In the face of such petty jealousy, we felt no need to justify ourselves to anyone.

The views of academics specialising in anything vaguely related to football are worth countering, however. This is not just because any plimsolled sociologists who while away their days using words like 'fundamentally' all the time are an easy target, but because it's important to prove that many of their theories have as much relevance to the advancement of human know-ledge as the cups of insipid instant coffee which act as the major stimulant to their under-active brains. The University of Stafford, for example, runs a course in the Manchester United and England midfielder David Beckham.

Leicester University's Scarman Centre is an honourable exception. 'Occasional Paper Number Seven' of its Crime, Order and Policing series has much to say about the return of England's 1966 World Cup ball. Its poignant references to George Orwell, Henry Newbolt and the Daily Mirror suggest that the underfunded department can at least afford some books and a pile of daily newspapers to go with its termly batch of wholesale Nescafé.

The academic study is officially called 'War Minus the Shooting?', in deference to Orwell's observation that international sport can be dangerous because of the unhealthy nationalism it arouses. 'Jingoism, the English Press and Euro'96' completes the title. The paper points out that dictators and propagandists are ideally placed to distract people from their true democratic goals by playing out pugilistic fantasies in the relative safety of a packed stadium. The 11 England players who, on the advice of the British ambassador, were forced to give a Nazi salute before their game in the Olympic Stadium in Berlin in 1938 would certainly have agreed, especially after they trounced Germany 6–3.

Newbolt's stirring advice to Victorian and Edwardian public schoolboys to 'play up, play up and play the game' was, the Leicester academics note, a maxim just as relevant to the colonial soldiers of the period who relied on discipline and teamwork to build an empire. The rhetoric of warfare had slipped on to the school playing-field. By the 1990s things had got even worse.

Sport had become the main outlet for countries' petty squabbling over the contentious issues which divided them.

Popular newspapers encouraged this xenophobia with their unhealthy obsession with recent British history, says the paper, especially when the country's population had to put up with something really militaristic, like winning. Football was all about power and prestige, goals previously only attainable through open warfare.

So the paper reads: 'The *Daily Mirror* claiming victory in the race to recover the ball recreated Geoff Hurst's last goal in the 1966 final. Nostalgia for England's only tournament victory was a recurrent theme throughout the next month, reflecting a desperate desire for sporting success. Football would appear to have been a way of demonstrating that England was still a significant player on the world stage. This working back to a more glorious era of national success was echoed in the tournament's slogan "Football's Coming Home".'

There is particularly strong criticism aimed at the *Daily Mirror's* 1996 '*Achtung!* Surrender' front page, which portrayed our footballing battles with Germany as a re-enactment of the century's bitter world wars. *Mirror* editor Piers Morgan argued that Basil Fawlty had got away with such excesses on *Fawlty Towers* (the 'Don't Mention the War' episode of the comedy came 11th in the *Observer's* 100 greatest TV moments of the twentieth century, on a list which also included Neil Armstrong's first Moon steps, the release of Nelson Mandela and the fall of the Berlin Wall). But the academic paper concurs with a National Heritage Select Committee report which condemned newspaper coverage of Euro '96 as 'xenophobic, chauvinistic and jingoistic gutter journalism'.

The political correctness which we have dragged with us into the twenty-first century does not consider a sense of humour an appropriate defence for such excesses. Thus the Leicester sociologists state: 'This kind of defence is misplaced. It is based on a mistaken assumption that humour somehow exists in a separate cultural sphere – divorced from its social context.'

Even if the readers of Britain's most liberal Sunday newspaper do find the sight of a goose-stepping Basil Fawlty imploring his tearful German guests to have a drink 'before the war' to be one of the most amusing sights of the last millennium, the Scarman Centre does not.

We were not the only ones considered guilty of inappropriate nationalistic feelings. The Germans sensed that the entire population was as fixated with our '39–'45 triumph as our '66 victory. So German culture minister Michael Naumann said in February 1999: 'Britain is obsessed with the war. It is the only nation in the world that has decided to make the Second World War a sort of spiritual core of its national self, understanding and pride.'

Accordingly, like our learned friends, we must justify the return of the World Cup ball and all it represents by once again casting our eyes a few years back into the past.

At the end of what would have been the 1944–45 season, the young Princess Elizabeth had stood in front of another huge, triumphant crowd, far larger than the one she was part of at Wembley just 21 years later. It was Tuesday, 8 May 1945, and she was on the balcony of Buckingham Palace. The men and women thronging the London parks as far away as Kensington Palace looked almost exactly the same as those who would turn up to cheer on England in 1966. They used words like 'blimey' and 'wotcha'. They wore dark suits, duffle-coats and headscarves. Their metal shoe-protectors kicked up sparks all along The Mall. Thousands of children were dressed in their school uniforms.

The Prime Minister, Winston Churchill, stood a few feet to the Princess's left, just as Harold Wilson was to keep a respectful distance at Wembley. King George and Queen Elizabeth held their right hands high above their heads and punched the air regally. The British people chanted hysterically as they waved Union Jacks and red-white-and-blue banners. Tears flooded down ration-thinned faces as total strangers hugged one another in a mass outpouring of emotion, mixed with relief that they would no longer have to get by on one egg, a box of tea and a pot of jam per week.

Over 21 years the Princess's face, as well as her hairstyle, would remain exactly the same; she was as refined and pretty as the image engraved on the country's currency. The only difference in 1945 was that Elizabeth was dressed in a military uniform, complete with pips on her shoulders, rather than a yellow dress from a summer collection created by an upmarket designer from Gloucestershire.

The royal party was celebrating Victory in Europe day, when we really had reaffirmed our status as a world-class nation. Although complete underdogs at the outbreak of war, our armies had finally crushed the mighty *Wehrmacht* and the fanatical Nazi divisions which fought alongside it. The unstoppable fascist war machine, tragically manned by the same kind of talented and decent young men who represented their country at Wembley in 1966, had been destroyed. It did not matter that it had been the Russians who suffered most, nor that the Americans had paid for it all. Europe was liberated and our servicemen and women would be represented at every former battleground in the world where our enemies offered their surrender.

Almost all the players in the 1966 England squad were born during the Second World War. Jimmy Greaves recalled the Essex of the 1940s with the words: 'My first memory is sleeping in the Anderson shelter in Dagenham ...

We slept in the shelter most nights and adults were always going on about Hitler and the bloody Germans.'

The feeling of euphoria carried on into the next decade. We had been materially bankrupted by the war, but our indomitable spirit was made manifest in the 1951 Festival of Britain, held exactly one hundred years after the Victorians' Great Exhibition. Organised by Clement Attlee, the Labour prime minister, and Herbert Morrison, it was based on 30 acres of bomb-damaged and derelict riverfront opposite London's Charing Cross Station. The festival was ostensibly a £12 million vision of a 'bright, light-filled future in contrast to the grim days that had passed so recently', but at its heart was a celebration of the achievements and products of empire, including a steam train from India and paintings of Queen Victoria surrounded by supremely loyal turbaned guards. Louis Mountbatten had disengaged us from the Raj in 1948, but there was no question of disowning our imperial past and pretending that it had never happened.

Attlee and Morrison knew that the exhibition would 'give the people a lift', which is just as well since their blighted experiment with nationalisation was, economically, still keeping us firmly on our knees . . .

By the time Princess Elizabeth was crowned in Westminster Abbey on a cold, wet and miserable 2 June 1953, her proclamation had already made her the first queen to be known as 'Head of the Commonwealth' instead of the Empire. She, more than any British monarch in history, knew exactly what it felt like to reign over a country sliding into mediocrity. Her subjects were being forced to endure the mind-numbing influence of TV and the rampant commercialisation of every sphere of national life. Ordinary men and women whose heroism had once flourished in extraordinary circumstances were being forced to act like vacuous and materialistic nonentities, utterly divorced from any sense of history.

Nowadays, against the background of the kind of political correctness being expounded by Midlands sociologists, the Queen is constantly being asked to apologise for our country's legacy. In 1999, during a state visit to Africa, she was forced to admit that the Boer War had been 'a tragedy'. The excesses of Nelson, Wellington, Wolfe, Clive, Gordon and Lawrence of Arabia have also all been marked down for a regal 'sorry'. The stirring works of Kipling, Elgar and Newbolt are also on a yellow card. Before this century is out, it would come as no surprise if Sir Alf Ramsey's victories against 'foreign partners' did not receive the royal seal of disapproval too.

Even Tony Blair, a man who grew up polishing army boots as well as listening to The Beatles, used his keynote speech at the Labour Party conference in Bournemouth in 1999 to tear into our past. With evangelical zeal he promised to 'set our people free' from their traditional conservative values, blaming them for the incarceration of Nelson Mandela and the assassination of Martin Luther King. The racist murder of black teenager Stephen Lawrence at a bus stop in south London was another horror related to all that had gone before.

In another speech later that year, the Prime Minister likened the legacy of empire to an unpleasant disease: 'We have got over our imperial past – and the withdrawal symptoms. No longer do we want to be taken seriously just for our history but for what we are and what we will become.' English, the language of Shakespeare and Kipling, was no longer an artistic device which could stir the country's passions towards great, heroic feats but, said Mr Blair, 'the language of the new technology'. His vision of the new Britain is of one made virtually real by the infra-red beam of new technology, playing a role 'not as a super-power, but as a pivotal power'.

Like Chairman Mao in 1966, New Labour politicians believe in a 'year zero' where centuries of history are wiped out as easily as Clause 4 was from their manifesto. They believe that all the struggles and triumphs of our forebears can be obliterated by no more than a well-chosen soundbite. It is a view which has no respect for the march of history. Instead of seeing us all as individuals united in our respect for common values and institutions as we advance through time and space, it reduces us to dull consumerists, too uninspired to forge the world by ourselves without the aid of a remote control or computer mouse.

A pivotal power is one which applies its finest minds to uncontroversial activities like web design and accountancy; where a stultified workforce spends ever longer hours trading in virtual reality; where the pursuit of human happiness is measured in pension-plan contributions and 'dream holiday' brochures; where there is no interest in national character or personalities or ideas or feats of daring; where we have no significant influence on the future of the world other than that due to our pivotal position on the map of Europe.

Of course there have been numerous blemishes on every expression of British nationalism, be they as disastrously significant as Churchill's Gallipoli campaign or as trivial as the steel helmets which Piers Morgan had super-imposed on the heads of two England midfielders for his 'Achtung! Surrender!' front page. Of course we didn't always get it right in the past, but harking back to a time of greatness cannot be rubbished as being intellectually or politically incorrect.

What the return of the World Cup ball represented was a brief reminder of

English glory. Its tiny presence hinted at a time when the monarch and her people had a conception of their proud history; an era when they were going forward together, ready to face the challenges of the future with as much courage and determination as they had dealt with challenges in the past.

For that reason alone, ensuring the return of the 1966 World Cup ball to this island was entirely justified.

31 · Man Reunited

Jurgen Haller jumped out of the helicopter, landed on the Hertfordshire field and kicked the bright orange ball high in the air. It was caught by the wind and drifted a few hundred yards towards the country lane we had driven up to get to the hotel. Geoff Hurst and the rest of us stared towards it as it finally came to rest on top of a hedge.

There was a huge grin on the young German's face. The ball he had kicked so ferociously was a 'leisure ball' he had picked up before boarding the plane at Schipol. He laughed: 'Funny, *ja?*'

No one replied. Haller returned sheepishly to the helicopter, ducking his head below the still-revolving rotor blades, and pulled out a brown holdall. He rummaged around inside and removed a pair of trousers and some old newspapers. Then he held up another ball.

Geoff Hurst strode towards him. Haller rolled the England World Cup football gently towards him. For the first time in 30 years the amber orb was back at his feet. It lay on the soft, slightly boggy ground. Its panels were dulled and scuffed in places, but its glow was unmistakable. It caught the light of the same milky sun which had lit up Wembley on that greatest of English summer days in July 1966.

Hurst thought about the damage he had once inflicted on the soft, sturdy leather; how he had connected with maximum effectiveness three times – once with his head and twice with his feet. He recalled how Hans Tilkowski, his dark-blue jersey covered in white chalk dust, had been left immobile or sprawling helplessly. Hurst was longing to hold the ball in his hands and inspect it for the first time in his life as the holder of a World Cup winner's medal.

The rest of us stood around in a huddle. We were remembering Hurst's masterful third goal, the one that sealed an unbeaten World Cup final hat-trick and a bitter German defeat. We could picture Bobby Moore sending the long ball forward which Hurst had cantered on to with a gusto matched only by the jubilant spectators already running on to the pitch. We thought of the blond England captain hugging his West Ham team-mate in a display of unparalleled joy. We thought of a day when the two men, not yet 30, really had reached the stars.

Although Bobby Moore had never been far from his mind during the past three decades, Hurst was thinking more about his second goal, the disputed one. He thought about how it had cannoned so teasingly against the crossbar, and then back towards the chalky goal-line a millisecond later. The ball's extraordinary flight had caused a footballing war between two mighty nations which, even now, remained unresolved. 'The Thirty Years War' was how *The Times* had described it. The newspaper leader writers were keen to see it brought to an end. One of the shorter chapters in the saga was still being played out, but an armistice was in sight.

The ball – the symbol of that bitter contest – was back in Hurst's field of vision. It was back in its rightful place, on a simple strip of English soil, nestled neatly on a clump of grass. It would not have mattered whether the grass was being trampled by millionaire professionals or a group of Saturday-morning park players enjoying a kickabout. It certainly did not matter that the ball was now surrounded by a group of tired journalists rather than a screaming crowd of almost 100,000 supporters. The talisman was in England, where it belonged.

Hurst began to walk towards his ball.

Inevitably, there was still a German standing above it. Inevitably, he was called Haller.

'Vy do you think you should have my ball back, Herr Hurst?' asked Jurgen, grimacing inscrutably in a way only Germans seem able to do. His eyes were still misty, following the problems in the arrivals hall at Stansted, and the fact that nobody had laughed at his leisure ball joke. 'My vater gave it to me,' he said.

The words caused Hurst to stop suddenly.

'It vas a present on my fifth birthday. It means so much to me and my family. And to German football. And to my country. Vee are the vinners now and I can still keep zer ball.'

It may have been that Jurgen Haller was still joking, but it is always very difficult to tell when a German is trying to be funny. Humour has never been high on the curriculum in *Gymnasiums*. It's doubtful that those swordsmen who sliced each others' faces up at universities like Heidelberg and Göttingen were completing PhDs in Being Funny either. Germans have always been far better suited to heavy industry and sticking the prefix *Doktor Doktor* before their names, which you have to suppose is vaguely funny, although the Germans themselves wouldn't know it.

There were around 20 of us watching as Hurst considered the significance of the occasion. Thirty years earlier he had seen 11 Germans beaten into the ground as the amber ball helped seal his reputation as the supreme master of the game. He had run triumphant rings around men with names like Wolfgang, Franz and Horst. Alf had got it perfectly right when he said the Germans were 'finished' by the end of normal time.

Now Jurgen Haller was trying to outwit him in the same way that his father Helmut had done under Wembley's Twin Towers 30 years before. He was standing in front of the son of the father; the father who had stolen his trophy and never shown even the slightest hint of remorse.

Hurst thought fleetingly about executing the most crunching tackle of his career. He thought about unleashing the same kind of kick which had reduced the amber ball to its present, slightly distressed condition. The English lion even thought about unleashing a Scottish warrior called McKay on the last obstacle between him and the ball.

Then he remembered he was a senior partner in a respectable Home Counties insurance firm. 'Come on, Jurgen, hand it over,' he said diplomatically. With the manners of the perfect English gentleman, he shook hands with the German and bent down to pick up his ball.

Helmut Haller was nowhere to be seen. In the same way that he had sloped back to the dressing-room 30 years ago, he had now slunk back to the hotel bar for a thoughtful whisky. He knew this was a moment he had denied Hurst all those years ago and felt he had no real part to play in the final reunion.

For at least 30 seconds everything was quiet. We all stopped chatting among ourselves. The helicopter's rotor blades had finally come to a standstill.

Hurst picked the ball up and placed it against his lips. He closed his eyes and, in a moment of quiet reverence, kissed its amber panels.

A cheer went up. As the photographers' flashlights exploded and their shutters whirred, all felt supremely satisfied. The picture – Hurst in his famous red jersey kissing his famous orange ball – would appear in the next day's Daily Mirror under the headline 'They think it's all over – It's his now'.

The introduction to the story read: 'It's the moment all England has been waiting for – soccer legend Geoff Hurst reunited with his World Cup hat-trick ball,' followed by Hurst saying: 'It's a piece of our history. I never thought I'd see it again.'

The 1966 World Cup ball was back home.

32 · Goal Rush

It was only 3 p.m., at least six hours before first-edition deadlines. There was still plenty of time for the opposition to equalise.

To fulfil the terms of our contract with Richard Branson (who together with Eurostar was putting up the money) we had to get the ball, Hurst and Helmut Haller to Waterloo Station in central London as quickly as possible. Publicity photographs were to be taken of the three of them standing on the platform of the Eurostar terminal where hundreds of thousands of football fans would be arriving a few weeks later for the start of the Euro '96 championships.

The ball, watched 24 hours a day by security guards, was to be placed in a bulletproof glass case so that as many people as possible would be able to see it. Our immediate goal was to get the ball to Waterloo as quickly as we could.

We were in tense mood as we raced down the A10 in the Jaguar back into central London. We'd stopped talking about the dash from Munich to London, and the fight at Stansted. There were more hazards to come.

Following royal guidelines, our three most important players were travelling in three separate cars, just in case anything happened to any of them. We had Haller in our car, while Hurst and the ball followed behind in convoy. The amber leather, under lock and key in a sturdy container, was strapped into the boot, along with a security guard. (Actually, that's not quite true. By now we'd given all the danger-aversion and counter-threat specialists their tube fares home.)

There was the sound of rotor blades up above. We assumed it was our own helicopter returning to Stansted, but Malcolm pointed upwards and, through the sunroof, we immediately saw it was the Sun's. It didn't have sinister markings, like a skull-and-crossbones or a clenched fist, but the number of long lenses protruding from its windows left us in no doubt as to whose side it belonged to. We could almost feel the hot, clammy breath of the journalists on board, muttering and cursing as they played catch-up.

'Let's split up,' the senior journalist in Hurst's car suggested over the mobile telephone.

'No, too risky,' someone else replied, concerned that the Sun would still stoop to ball-napping, or even Haller- or Hurst-napping.

The Sun were particularly annoyed that Hurst had jumped ship to the Daily Mirror after learning that we'd got the ball. He had reneged on a contract with them and joined the winning side. As in the football market, there is little loyalty on Fleet Street.

We passed Canary Wharf tower, the nerve centre of the entire Mirror operation. In the middle of all the frantic activity was Eugene Duffy, a gritty Celtic supporter who had picked up a dour, Black Country sense of humour and Mexican moustache during his local newspaper days. Beside him was Andy Lines, a fanatical Chelsea fan prone to burst out into unedited renditions of 'One Man Went to Mow' when things weren't going his way.

Their newsdesk had been turned into an operations table-top resembling a command centre last seen at Biggin Hill during the Battle of Britain. The positions of rival newspapers and Germans were being monitored non-stop on large-scale situation maps. Telephones rang continually. Often it would be a Sun journalist – or reader – trying to find out where we were. The desk had received at least 20 calls from bogus Peter Allens. More sadly, Don McKay had made a genuine call when I went missing at the Uphall Hotel, and was told to 'eff off and grow up'. It was now four o'clock and one of the largest, slickest operations in recent Mirror history was being executed to perfection.

By far the worst job in the newsroom that day was, as usual, the celebrity ring-round. Those involved sat like oppressed Mexican peasants, with the Zorro-like figure of Duffy watching their every move. As a task, the celebrity ring-round ranks alongside checking the toilets in McDonald's every 20 minutes, or working as a shoe attendant in a bowling alley. Perhaps the only people who fare worse in life than celebrity ringers are those Disneyland functionaries who have to dress up as cuddly cartoon characters and scoop up the excrement deposited by the live animals in the homestead farmyard.

That Friday the six reporters assigned the task of calling the big names of the moment to find out what their reaction was to the big issue of the day were facing the usual difficulties. Big names are invariably out and, even if they are contactable through their agents, seldom have a reaction to anything unconnected with themselves, least of all the big issue of the day.

Accordingly, journalists are reduced to calling the small names of the moment, who are always in and happy to make a comment about anything you care to mention, even if it is as irrelevant and uninteresting in the scheme of things as their own modest careers. It is because of this that there is an unofficial blacklist of exceptionally minor celebrities whose knowledgeable words drawn from a lifetime's experience in soap-opera walk-on parts and gameshows are barred from the pages of every national newspaper. Their exclusion makes the celebrity ring-round even more difficult.

So it was that on the day when the World Cup ball was finally returned to Britain, desperate celebrity ringers sought the views of the Prime Minister's brother, Terry Major-Ball; Richard Briers, star of a 1970s ecological sitcom set in Surbiton; GMTV breakfast presenter Eamonn Holmes; film-maker and restaurant reviewer Michael Winner; and England rugby player Victor Ubogu.

Some of the comments were roughly expressed but to the point. Vinnie Jones, the footballer who was later to become a film actor noted for his violent performances involving car doors, said: 'This bloke Helmut Haller obviously still had the hump and was trying to level things up. It's great that the ball's back with Hursty.'

Others were more conciliatory. Barbara 'Babs' Windsor said: 'I was in a matinée at the time of the final and kept running off stage to listen. It's lovely to get the ball back. You have to feel a little bit sorry for the poor fella who has to hand it back, though.'

English football officials, however, still had nothing but stern words for Haller, without even the lyricism of a Tofik Bakhramov to lift their comments above the prosaic. FIFA's director of communications, Keith Cooper, said: 'Legally the ball belongs to us, but spiritually it belongs to Geoff. As a gesture of fair play, Haller should have handed him the ball. We supplied the balls for the World Cup and if it was returned to us we would have made sure Geoff got it at a special presentation.'

Ken Aston, senior referee in the 1966 competition, said the ball should have been handed to the organising committee, but added: 'I wouldn't have done that – I would have given it straight to Geoff Hurst.'

Best of all, though, were the comments of the Golden Boys of 1966, all of whom expressed their delight at the return of the ball.

'I assumed Geoff had it,' said Bobby Charlton. 'It is traditional for a player who scores a hat-trick to keep the ball and I'd no idea he didn't. I'm delighted the ball is coming back to England. It's great news.'

Nobby Stiles said: 'I had no idea it was missing until a fortnight ago. Winning the World Cup was more important at the time, but it's great that it's back.'

'That ball is part of Geoff,' Alan Ball said. 'People who score hat-tricks should get the ball. England should have the ball.'

Riedel appeared a lot more relaxed. He turned towards the journalists sitting around him in the car and said: 'So, I suppose you vill be writing about all zis one day. It would make a good story, ja?'

We stared incredulously at the lanky figure lounging in his leather seat. Did he think we'd gone through the last 24 hours because we had nothing better to do? Did he think we'd travelled halfway across mainland Europe with hardly any food or drink because we had not been away for a while? Did he think the bunch of devil journalists circling overhead were there because they felt like a Friday-afternoon helicopter ride down the Thames?

The stupidity of Riedel's question almost provoked McKay into shouting 'Emergency exit!' at Malcolm. It was one of the manoeuvres the pair had discussed during one of our frequent motorway services pit-stops and would have resulted in the driver stopping suddenly, and hurling everybody with a German passport out onto the tarmac. Anyone who had also admitted to the profession of 'goalkeeper' on the document would have gone first.

McKay instead tried to be as diplomatic as Geoff Hurst. 'Thorsten, it's our job to write about this kind of thing. That's what they pay us for,' he said.

In many ways it was quite a good thing that neither Riedel nor the Hallers had seen a copy of that day's *Daily Mirror*. It's quite common for journalists to keep their work away from their subjects. It avoids the unseemly complaints which sometimes stem from even the most well-researched and informative articles. When a government minister resigned after being held up at knifepoint by a drug-dealer he had met at a notorious homosexual pick-up spot, he paid little attention to the sordid details of the ensuing publicity, so his overall reaction was one of silence. When, however, he was later spotted with a woman friend enjoying a quiet weekend break by the sea, he read every word of the allegations. The minister described the reports as 'poisonous, vindictive, utter lies', adding, 'There is not a shred of truth, they produced not one shred of evidence.'

Presentation can also be a problem. When I went to a party in east London to 'celebrate' the lives of the Kray twins, I assured its organisers that I was after a 'few choice lines to pay tribute to the boys'. I promised that my readers saw them as a pair of loveable Cockney rogues rather than the gangsters jailed for the murders of George Cornell and Jack 'The Hat' McVitie. My article, published the next day, sadly made them sound like the double killers of popular imagination. One of the Krays had telephoned the party from his prison and announced: 'When I get out we'll have the biggest party in the world,' before bursting into tears. His friends on the outside said I deserved to be knee-capped for my 'unsympathetic' interpretation of the evening. If I was going to end up with a couple of perforations in my knees, I decided the headline writer deserved one in the head at the very least. Above my article he had written in big letters: 'It's my party and I'll Kray if I want to.'

It was probably just as well that the Hallers were not in a position to give us their reaction to the headline on the front page of that day's Sun: 'The Greediest Krauts on Earth'.

As we approached central London there was a concerned call from Andy Lines. He said: 'Careful. I think the Sun know where you're going. Just be careful, and don't panic. There's nothing to worry about.' Just before Lines hung up we heard him singing 'One man went to mow ...'

For weeks, staff at the Mirror had been certain that there was a News International mole passing on information to Wapping whenever anything vaguely interesting was happening. This might range from an embarrassing spat between colleagues to the next day's 'World Exclusive' front page.

Hence the Sun had heard all when the toilets became blocked in the Mirror newsroom and a sign went up saying: 'I am sick and tired of people dropping bits of toilet paper in the urinals. It blocks up the sanitation system and takes a lot of time and effort to remove. Please stop it.' Within hours the note was the talk of the Sun newsroom, with the added twist that it had been signed 'David Montgomery, Chief Executive'.

It was sweet revenge for the time that Sun editor Kelvin MacKenzie had to appear before a Commons Select Committee to answer questions about why he had published a news item about a short-sighted man mistaking a tube of superglue for haemorrhoid cream and glueing up his buttocks. MacKenzie had run the piece under the headline 'John's Gone Potty and Glued up his Botty'.

More worryingly, a senior Mirror reporter had arranged to meet a photographer at an east London police station earlier that April to witness a high-ranking criminal being bailed. Because of the exclusivity of the tip-off, the station was cryptically referred to as 'Bobby Moore's nick'. Sure enough, when the newsmen arrived under the blue lamp at West Ham, the Sun were there in force.

We parked next to the Eurostar station at 5.15 p.m. We were just a few hundred yards from the site of the Festival of Britain of 1951, when the symbols of imperial might had been displayed in all their glory. We were looking forward to seeing an even greater symbol of English greatness placed in the station itself.

A white anorak was put over Haller's head. We then began shuffling towards the entrance of the station, causing far more attention to be paid to us than if we had just walked in. Tourists and down-and-outs began nudging each other and pointing at the odd sight. Geoff Hurst received the same treatment, and the ball was dropped in through another entrance.

Eurostar security staff were waiting for us. Most were in uniform, but one was dressed in civilian clothes and looked marginally less dim than the rest of them. We suspected he might work for the *Sun*. We kept a close eye on him, as he took us through a security scan and led us up a ramp to the main waiting area for the Eurostar trains.

Calls began to flood in on our mobiles. There were at least five *Sun* reporters and photographers in the vicinity of Waterloo. All had been primed to locate, photograph and preferably steal the ball as soon as possible. Richard Branson, wearing his usual polite grin, looked oblivious to what was going on. 'Hello, nice to meet you,' he ventured, with the refined, unflustered charm of a public-schoolmaster. 'Hello, Geoff, lovely to see you. And you, Helmut. Nice to see you back in the country after all these years. So you're the people who got the ball back. Do come upstairs.'

We looked left and right and crowded around the footballers. This was an exceedingly dramatic and potentially dangerous situation. Richard Branson was acting as if it was sports day at Stowe.

A camera crew from Live TV, the Mirror Group's fledgling TV channel, filmed us, and two official photographers were also in action, one working for the *Daily Mirror* and the other for Richard Branson. The vast, opaque plastic dome covering the Eurostar terminal appeared relatively camera-proof, but we still felt uneasy. We were dealing with enemy photographers who could hose down a celebrity in the millisecond it takes to throw a cigarette butt out of a half-inch gap in a limousine's jet-black windows – men like Daniel Angeli, the hitman's hitman, who had pinpointed financial advisor John Bryan sucking the chubby toes of his client, Sarah Ferguson, from deep within thick green undergrowth in southern France.

As we walked along the platform – Branson strolling nonchalantly, the rest of us marching to order like a platoon of Grenadier guards – the security man in civilian clothes reached for his top pocket. 'Go, go, go!' screamed Malcolm, as McKay went flying towards him.

The Scotsman had been on edge ever since Hurst considered unleashing him on Jurgen Haller when he got out of the helicopter. When he was on a big one, an hour and a half was a long time for McKay to go without a dramatic incident. This was the same journalist who, during the war in Kosovo a few years later, was to receive a reprimand from the military chiefs in the Balkans who claimed he was too forceful and aggressive in his questioning at NATO press conferences. This was while their warplanes were pouring thousands of missiles and bombs on Serbia, and élite regiments were preparing for a ground invasion of occupied Kosovo.

McKay, who like the rest of us had seen the sudden movement, thought there might be a sure-shot camera in the man's pocket. Even a fuzzy snap of the newly discovered ball on a throwaway camera would be worth £20,000 to anybody who sold it to the *Sun*. In spite of the £30,000-odd of equipment which photographers carry with them, it is almost inevitably the shaky, barely discernable snap which makes it on to the front page and to the title of Picture of the Year.

33 · Lost Labourers

McKay grabbed the security man by the shoulder. He reached inside the man's top pocket and pulled out . . . a chewing-gum wrapper and a leaky biro.

'It's for my youngest, Mr Hurst,' the security man ventured politely, thrusting his improvised autograph pad forward. Hurst scribbled the words 'To Kylie [she was an '80s child], Regards, Geoff Hurst'.

'No more sudden movements,' cautioned the Scotsman, as we all continued our menacing Stasi routines.

The terminal hadn't yet been opened to the public at the time, and the only people around were workmen putting the finishing touches to the multi-million-pound station. They loafed about in the manner of typical British builders – applying a light dusting of chocolate to their freshly brewed cappuccinos, making sure their bacon sandwiches were neatly filled and had just the right amount of ketchup, and smearing their white vans with dirt so they could then write cheeky messages on them.

'Orwite, Hursty?' one shouted, performing a two-handed thumbs up. 'Larvely goals, mate,' he added, as if it was still 1966 and Hurst had just emerged from the Wembley baths.

'Happens all the time,' said Hurst, in the clipped tones of certainty so befitting a single-minded striker. 'Everyone thinks I only ever played in one match. To them nothing I've ever done since is important. Everyone who comes up to me in the street wants to discuss my second or third goal. It never stops.'

Other workmen, wearing bright yellow hard-hats, began to congregate around us. Waterloo Station – the scene of many a fight before and after football matches in the capital – is often full of boisterous supporters, and the workmen on duty that day felt perfectly entitled to join in with a bit of rowdiness. They cheered Hurst and jeered Haller.

'Hursty, Hursty, show us your ball, show us your ball,' sang one, showing off some impressive topicality.

Another, whose neck was considerably wider than his head was long, grunted: 'We are Millwall, We are Millwall, No one likes us, We don't care.'

We greeted his irrelevant rendition of an outdated terrace chant with silence. Even the builder's mates stared at him incredulously as he brought his recital to an embarrassed close. (He reminded me of the Portsmouth skinhead I once saw chanting 'You're so thick it's unbelievable' at a group of fellow Pompey skins because he thought they were following Chelsea away. 'But you were dressed in blue,' he explained apologetically after realising his mistake and abandoning any thoughts of a ruck before three o'clock. 'Anyway, how was I meant to know where you came from?' he added. All were too polite to point out the Star and Moon – Portsmouth's badge – shaved into his fellow fans' crewcuts.)

The workmen, all 30 of them, began to circle us and now appeared more than slightly menacing. 'It's the little fat German,' shouted one. We thought he might have added a word of Germanic origin beginning with C, but the roar of one of the new Eurostar engines drowned him out. As the train drew level with the platform, the builders reached for their mobile phones.

By now we were at the far, uncovered end of the platform at Waterloo. 'Bandits at Waterloo roundabout,' came a warning over our own telephones.

Andy Lines had received new intelligence from a Millwall supporter called Dale at the station. He said he had telephoned the Mirror because 'Me mate Daryl is on to the Sun, and I want a slice of the cake. They told him they had a couple of people at Waterloo roundabout, so that's why I'm telling you. How much do I get?'

We knew that he would immediately tell his mate Daryl that we knew that the Sun had people at Waterloo. Then Daryl would phone the Sun newsdesk to say that we knew that they had people at Waterloo, producing the situation whereby the Sun knew that we knew that they had people at Waterloo Station, and that we knew that they knew.

The workmen – all aspiring towards German sports cars, designer watches, white leather sofas and all the other status symbols coveted by aspirational men with oversize necks – would be passing round information between themselves and the two national newspaper desks all evening, with only a few breaks for their Italian coffees and bacon sandwiches. The circular conversations would go on until first-edition time, if not longer.

Once somebody becomes a tipster for a national newspaper they often feel that anything they hear or see can never be deemed unimportant again. If they witness so much as a pensioner tripping up on a cracked paving stone, let alone a celebrity blowing their nose, they'll be on to a newspaper quicker than a less conventional desk-botherer can tell you about the new planet he's discovered.

The secret is to make it as hard as possible for them to contact you, hence another golden rule of journalism: never give anyone your personal telephone number.

Our immediate attention was focused on the female *Sun* journalist and photographer who had been spotted wandering around the ugly concrete traffic marker between Waterloo and Westminster Bridge. We looked to our right, but could see only disused station buildings and a couple of fire escapes.

Branson was still being charming, although the expression on his face had changed from mildly interested to slightly concerned – rather like a businessman staring down the platform of a provincial station waiting for the 7.15 to Waterloo. He knew the ball was about to be uncovered by security guards. If a photographer was hanging off one of the fire escapes or circling the Waterloo roundabout in an unmarked Ford Mondeo then this was the moment it was all going to go off. Apocryphal tales of photographers putting on white coats to get into hospitals are certainly untrue, but their ingenuity can never be underestimated.

Both Haller and Hurst had replaced their off-duty golfer kit – polo-shirts, casual jackets, flannels and comfy shoes – with something a bit more formal. Haller wore a blue striped shirt and a dark-blue suit. Hurst looked like a suburban insurance broker in a Prince of Wales check suit, blue button-down shirt and yellow tie. The footballers were polite and respectful towards each other.

Even Richard Branson had made an effort. Instead of his usual jeans and jumper, he was wearing a light-grey suit and blue shirt. For many of his publicity photographs the Virgin boss appears in underpants, or even in drag, so he was obviously taking us seriously. With more furtive looks to left and right, two of the security men took out a leather holdall, complete with steel padlock, and began to open it.

'Steady, steady,' said McKay, trying to infuse the occasion with more melodramatic spin than was necessary. We were thankful that Malcolm had returned to the Jaguar to play with his cuddly pound sign.

The ball was popped out and placed between the two former internationals. Branson stuck his grinning face between them, and the formal pictures were taken, ready to be placed in those tacky PR documents produced by companies like Eurostar. The captions would be so predictable – something like: 'A smiling Geoff Hurst and Helmut Haller embrace in the spirit of European unity epitomised by our bright new service.'

There was a sudden and only vaguely discernible flash of bright white light in the distance, which had nothing to do with the tame photographers who were hosing down the three celebrities on the platform.

'Go, go, go!' screamed the Scotsman, flinging himself towards the ball. He landed on top of it as the rest of us gathered round in a circle.

Haller and Hurst were wide-eyed with panic, like manic defenders pleading offside after a South American forward's spectacular opening strike. Branson looked quizzical but largely unperturbed, as did Thorsten Riedel.

We shepherded Haller and Hurst back down the platform towards the cover of the opaque roof. Another coat was thrown over Haller's head. We also threw one over Riedel's head – not because we were trying to disguise him, but because it was a good way of annoying him.

I remained behind for a few moments and stared out in the direction of the flash of light. I could see nothing except a blacked-out window at the back of a derelict Victorian tenement block. One of the window panes had been pushed out but there was just darkness beyond. The building was clearly disused, but I could not help feeling that there was a photographer inside who had got a shot off.

I later learned that a wily freelancer had indeed made his way up to the eighth floor, pushed out a pane of glass and lain in wait for the first picture of the ball. He had managed to take just one shot, and its focal point had been an orange object neatly placed between Geoff Hurst and Helmut Haller. The pin-sharp photograph of Richard Branson's beard – one of the most over-exposed images in modern Britain – was never used.

With our publicity shots in the bag, we were able to split up. Hurst went off to 'somewhere in Essex' without the ball. It was put back under lock and key and escorted to a bank vault in a secure van.

Hurst was due to deliver a speech that night but was under contract to say nothing about the ball until the next day, by which time we would have gone to press. We piled Haller back into the Jaguar and drove him the few minutes to the Imperial Hotel, off Trafalgar Square. It was to be our safe house for the evening.

'Time for a quiet night,' we suggested to Haller with a smile.

'Nein,' he replied with an equally cheery grin.

Haller's wish to enjoy a night out in London made us extremely worried. Although pictures and copy were complete, the German could still be of great use to rival newspapers or other media organisations. If he was going to spend a night out on the tiles in central London, we would need to stay with him. The thought of the German getting drunk and spilling his heart out to somebody about how he never wanted to take the ball in the first place was too much to contemplate. He might say that someone in authority, like Helmut Schöen or Ludwig Erhard, had forced him to take the ball.

We were extremely keen to hide Haller away in one of those shoebox rooms which London hotels dish out at £200 a throw. He would have a multitude of satellite TV stations to entertain him and could order as many mangy club sandwiches on room service as he wanted. So what if *Eurovamp II* – 'She's back and she's angry' – appeared on the hotel bill? Our VIP would be rested and ready to return to Germany. By the time the early-morning voices of Filipino cleaners were floating around the corridors of the Imperial, the story would be in the paper and we would all be able to relax.

Apart from celebrity ring-rounds, 'minding' is the most soulless and demoralising job in journalism. It's usually practised by Sunday-newspaper journalists who have to sit on their sources for up to six days before going to press. Often those being minded lack a rudimentary knowledge of how to form the most simple personal relationships. Their grasp of personal hygiene can be even more basic. All journalistic subjects constantly ask questions about the story, and demand that you buy them things because it's all 'on expenses'. In the same way that people vomit on your carpet and snog your girlfriend 'because it's their birthday', so people feel they can order six bottles of vintage champagne before vomiting on your carpet and snogging your girlfriend because it's 'on expenses'. They laugh loudly and tell unfunny jokes before shouting: 'Oh, come on. Where's your sense of humour. After all – it's on expenses.'

You have to keep reminding them that expenses are a fair reimbursement provided by newspaper companies for money spent out of your own pocket in the line of company duty. This normally means a bottle of wine with a contact followed by a quiet, inexpensive meal. They are not intended to cover alcohol-fuelled rampages through late-night strip joints followed by four-in-a-bed orgies.

The trouble with Haller was that he was easily recognisable and spoke German. Half the tipsters in Britain were by now looking for balls first and German footballers second. It was going to be a trying night, made worse by the fact that McKay was choosing the restaurant.

We checked into the Imperial and, after a few minutes in our shoeboxes, met in the foyer. We were still all looking shifty and dishevelled. Thankfully, most of the people hanging about in the foyer were tourists from America who had never been near a football stadium in their lives.

There were also quite a lot of people who looked like pimps and prostitutes. Instead of decent, honest people who might make a few hundred pounds by reporting us to a rival newsdesk, they were shifty and dishevelled characters just like us. That gave us a warm feeling inside.

34 • Party Peace

We made our way to La Barca. If you're looking for an intimate little bistro to have a quiet, undisturbed meal in select company, it's an excellent choice. It's situated discreetly near the Old Vic Theatre in south London, well away from the more glamorous restaurants on the other side of the Thames. You occasionally get a few thespians appearing in *A Midsummer Night's Dream* in for a late-night parmesan-and-onion pizza, but apart from that the bulk of the clientele are tourists who've got lost trying to find Waterloo Station on their way back from the Imperial War Museum.

Those with malnourished friends who play Bottom for a living, or people who enjoy the company of foreigners with bright carry-macs and nylon backpacks full of maps and water bottles, might bump into someone they know. Otherwise, the place is a watchword in quiet anonymity.

When we arrived we asked for a particularly isolated table in the corner. McKay was a regular and had tipped off the management that we were coming, without explaining who our VIP guest from overseas was. A waiter in black tie evening dress escorted our party in. He appeared calm and completely in command of the situation. He assured us that our visit would yield nothing but peace, tranquillity and the finest Parma ham outside of Parma.

Then he recognised Haller.

La Barca is an Italian restaurant. It is run by native Italians from places like Parma, Bologna and Turin. Many of its waiters, particularly the younger and more boisterous ones, know everything there is to know about Italian football.

'Helmut of Juve!' screamed the black-suited head waiter.

At first we pretended not to notice, and tiptoed towards our badly lit table at the back of the dining-room.

All the other waiters started shouting and cheering. Chianti corks popped. Loud, pumping music began to blare out of speakers which had earlier been playing soft, operatic arias. The music was allegedly from the foothills of Tuscany, although it sounded more like an intensely loud and emotional Italian folk singer practising his rustic chants to the backing of one of the German techno-pop cassettes from the floor of Heinrich's Porsche 911 Turbo.

The waiters started performing odd, ritualistic movements with their huge pepper grinders – many were swinging them around their heads.

We were steered to the main guest-of-honour table right in the middle of the room. Instead of being illuminated by candlelight, it was underneath two enormous spotlights which beamed down from the ceiling like giant Stasi Ossie-detectors.

'For the hero of Turin and Bologna,' shouted a waiter, as he force-fed Haller a dozen slices of Parma ham. He then poured what looked like half a bottle of Chianti down his throat.

Instead of appearing embarrassed and concerned like the rest of us, Haller looked in his element. He asked for some more ham and began dipping his ciabatta in olive oil. It was as if he'd never tasted good Italian food before. As proprietor of the Villa d'Este, he probably hadn't.

The music was turned up even louder. We were urged to stand on our seats and start dancing. The Italians started singing even more loudly, as a dozen more Chianti bottles were opened.

'This is all very kind,' I said to Renzo, the head waiter.

'No, no. It's the least we can do when we have an Italian hero here,' said Renzo. 'When we have a football hero here it is time for lights, good food, wine and music and the best of everything. It is time for a celebration. Anyway,' he added, 'you're the one who's paying. I heard it was all on expenses.'

It was barely seven o'clock and we hadn't even ordered our starters.

Haller started speaking in Italian, revelling in describing killer midfield touches against Inter and goals scored against AC Milan. Some of the waiters at La Barca actually came from Milan, but didn't seem to mind too much.

Chefs began to appear from the kitchen as our table became a throb of fiery Italians all talking about football. Renzo got on the telephone and called a few more members of his family along. He said he was a distant relative of Paolo Rossi, the striker whose goals won the World Cup for Italy in 1982. His team had beaten West Germany in the final in Madrid.

A rotund man in a baseball cap with a big camera appeared at the front door. We could see the headline already: 'Haller's Shame – German football legend's Chianti binge using ill-gotten money made from Hurst's ball' (the late-night sub-editors on Sunday newspapers are seldom up to much).

McKay flung himself towards the front door and grabbed the unfortunate visitor by the scruff of the neck. It turned out he was from Arkansas and was trying to find his way to Victoria Station. 'Ach, you're the wrong side of the river. Come on in and pull up a chair,' said the Scotsman.

An Englishman arrived next, also carrying a camera. McKay grabbed him by the scruff of the neck too. It turned out that the new arrival had been at a christening at nearby Southwark Cathedral and was looking for a lavatory before taking the train back to Surbiton. McKay fixed him with one of his impenetrable stares, trying to establish whether he had the look of a freelance press photographer about him. The man apologised profusely for being a complete stranger who had wandered into a restaurant inadvertently after attending a celebratory service in a place of God. He promised he would never do it again.

From then on, everybody who entered the restaurant, whether they were carrying cameras, handbags or umbrellas, were set upon by the supremely dedicated Scotsman. He frisked everyone and, if they were allowed in, ordered them to sit at a table where he could keep an eye on them. McKay also insisted they concentrate on their drinking – even if they didn't want a drink.

A down-and-out who had been forced out of his cardboard box by the construction of a new multiplex cinema near Waterloo Bridge wandered past. He had a long beard, clothes which appeared decades old and a plastic supermarket bag which carried all his worldly belongings – it was empty. The tramp's name was Wilf. He said he had been one of the labourers who helped set up the Festival of Britain close to Waterloo Station on the South Bank in the early 1950s. He'd not been able to get a job since, although he did not explain why.

Wilf could have been a victim of James Callaghan, Margaret Thatcher or even the trade unions. We did not push him on the subject, especially when he began to allude towards a special sitting of Horseferry Road Magistrates Court in November 1952. At that stage we weren't interested in his past. Wilf was embraced like an old friend and invited into the restaurant for a cheering cup of goodwill. It wasn't a night for standing on cold street corners in the wind and rain or sleeping in makeshift shelters. It was a night for joining in a united celebration. After some food, Wilf ended up slipping off with the American tourist's camera and six bottles of Chianti.

'To Herr Haller,' said McKay, lifting his glass.

The Italians were delighted by the presence of their guest of honour from Germany. They raised their glasses. They clapped and cheered. They danced and sang. The English diners all had a pretty clear idea who Haller was. They exchanged toasts with everybody, smiling uncomfortably and keeping an eye on the nearest exit just in case things got out of hand. A table of Irish people did not have a clue who Haller was. They got completely drunk and invited us all over to Dublin for the millennium celebrations.

Haller grabbed another bottle of Chianti and began recounting more anecdotes from his professional career. Many would lose a great deal in translation, but the best was an explanation of why he would never apologise for taking Hurst's ball. 'Never apologise,' boomed Haller.

He described how Nobby Stiles had made a half-hearted attempt at saying sorry for his tackle on Jacky Simon during England's 1966 match against France. Many years after the championships, the defender approached the Frenchman on a reunion boat trip up the Thames. Stiles, dewy-eyed and sincere, explained how he had never had the chance to apologise before, even though he had always wanted to.

Jimmy Greaves, watching the encounter from across the deck, told Simon: 'Don't listen to the dirty little bastard.'

Even Thorsten Riedel smiled at that story. He was slightly more relaxed by now, and looked as though he might even be on the verge of enjoying himself.

'Everything all right with you, big man?' asked McKay.

'Ja, I think this iz zer best party in London tonight,' Riedel replied.

The German goalkeeper was uncharacteristically wrong. There was another great party in London that night. It was taking place less than five miles from the unglamorous area of the city where we were eating cold Italian starters and drinking bottles of Chianti. Despite the short distance, it was happening a world away – in the royal borough of Kensington and Chelsea, a place where the rich and famous buy homes and where international footballers stay in five-star hotels.

Across Westminster Bridge and Parliament Square, down Victoria Street, through the squares and stucco-fronted mansions of Belgravia, past the parks, and on to the edge of Kensington Square, the *Sun* had booked the entire Roof Gardens. It was a club at the top of the old Derry and Toms building which, during the early 1970s, became the final home of the Biba fashion empire. Its six floors were celebrated as a 400,000-square-foot memorial to Swinging Sixties chic, with platform shoes and flared trousers being sold by the thousand. The British soldier's scarlet jacket, a revered symbol of the British Empire, had also been sold as a fashion item, and the Union Jack, the most emotive icon of imperial majesty, had appeared on everything from underwear to headscarves.

The club had always kept up with the times. It was built in the late 1930s when its Tudor arches, Moorish courtyard and sunset-pink flamingos became the last word in post-war metropolitan decadence. The eternally modern Richard Branson himself bought it in 1992 and, after giving it a £500,000 facelift, re-established it as one of the most fashionable places in London. By 1996 the club was, like Branson, a glittery and hugely successful testament to the financial confidence of Britain's new hierarchy. On either side of the gardens there were famous landmarks: St Mary Abbots Church, Kensington Gardens, Earl's Court and the Natural History Museum. Landmarks of the old empire, like the Royal Albert Hall, also stretched for miles around on every side – many could be seen from the vantage-point of the opulent nightclub full of Armani-clad entrepreneurs whose own empires embraced film and pop music companies, computer firms and model agencies.

A few months before the Sun party, the club had been hired out to the movie star Brad Pitt for the launch of his latest film. He had posed for pictures in its lush gardens, surrounded by novel and expensive attractions, including the flock of eternally youthful pink flamingos. One of the birds, it was said, had appeared in Miami Vice.

At the well-publicised party held at the Roof Gardens on Friday, 24 April 1996, there were no deranged Juventus fans swinging pepper grinders around their heads. There were no dysfunctional diners with the London A to Z-reading abilities of Calabrian hill farmers. There were no hangover-inducing bottles of very ordinary Italian wine which cost about 9p each when brought into Britain along with a batch of £5-a-dozen shepherd-funk techno imports from Milan.

Stuart Higgins's fiftieth birthday party was just like all the others held at the Roof Gardens: it was slick and upbeat. Media stars and starlets stood around in small groups with representatives of almost every other field of British life, including Labour politicians, international sportsmen and showbusiness people who'd had more than a walk-on part in EastEnders.

The designer suits worn by male guests were slick and shiny. They went perfectly with their barge-fronted formal shoes. Women wore low-cut black mini-dresses and huge heels.

Understated disco melodies wafted around the room from hidden audio speakers. Lighting was low and atmospheric. Champagne cocktails and bottles of ice-cold beer were expertly delivered by sophisticated waiters dressed entirely in black. It was a picture of metropolitan sophistication; the last word in Cool Britannia.

At around 11 p.m. Piers Morgan, editor of the Mirror, arrived to join the celebrations. He had been generously invited despite being the figurehead of the Sun's greatest rival. He smiled and waved at the other guests, many of whom he knew well. Few were saying much, though. There appeared to be something not quite right. Stuart Higgins was especially quiet and withdrawn.

Morgan thought the party needed livening up. He disappeared down into Derry Street, Kensington, and collected a pile of newspapers which his driver had picked up at Victoria Station.

The front page of Morgan's paper for Saturday, 27 April 1996, was upbeat and exciting, just like Stuart Higgins's party should have been. It showed a full-page picture of Geoff Hurst planting a kiss on England's World Cup football. It was an image which would bring joy to millions, including all those at the party upstairs.

Morgan returned to the birthday celebration and began handing out copies of his newspaper to everybody, including Higgins.

It really was the very best party in London that night.

35 · Semi-final

We took Haller on a long walk around London the next day. He had a very good reason to spend a few hours visiting places of architectural and historical interest. A pilgrimage to shrines of British inventiveness and culture through the fresh, sparkling air of a London spring morning would do a lot for him – like help get rid of the horrendóus thumping headache he had picked up south of the river the night before. Haller was impressed by the royal parks, but Trafalgar Square, the Mall and Buckingham Palace made him feel queasy. It was something to do with the legions of tourists wearing bright carry-macs and little rucksacks full of maps and bottled water. They reminded him of his dining companions at La Barca and made him feel even more ill.

In Hyde Park we stopped off in front of the Household Cavalry barracks, where a group of my friends were playing football. We had been meeting in the same place most Saturday mornings for around three years. It was not uncommon for us to bring along new players, but they were normally solid midfielders from the *Independent* or industrious right-wingers from the *Daily Mail* newsdesk. When I turned up with a former international footballer who had scored an opening goal in a World Cup final, most were pretty impressed.

We thought of joining in the match. It might just have been a park kickabout but my friends prided themselves on the high standard of intricate, controlled football we were all capable of. When we arrived the score was 16 to the team mainly dressed in white, compared to 24 for the team mainly dressed in any other colour apart from white. Haller said he was still feeling a bit under the weather and would rather watch.

Early in the afternoon we drove him and Riedel to Heathrow where they caught a flight back to Munich. The newsagent's in Terminal Two had sold out of the *Mirror* by then, but there were still piles of untouched *Suns* lying about. In their late editions they had managed to get a fuzzy, out-of-focus picture snatched from Live TV of Hurst brandishing the ball at the Eurostar station, but apart from that their coverage of the historic reunion was distinctly non-league.

Haller and Riedel did not show a great deal of emotion at passport control. We had been through a lot together over the past two days, but there was no tearful hugging or frantic shaking of upper torsos. There wasn't even any shadow sparring or 'we'll meet again'-type monologues interspersed with tearful sighs. But there was nothing rude about Haller's typically German lack of emotion. He knew that despite the fights, the drunken revelry, the motorway chases and the sheer frenzy of the past two days, what he had been involved in was important and real. His return to England had been nothing to do with trite gestures. He had been part of something which had stirred a great old nation. He had delivered a football which, to the English people, was as important as those which he had presented to strikers with unerring accuracy during his professional heyday.

Haller took my hand in a tight grip and squeezed it as he had squeezed the hand of a British monarch 30 years before. 'Peter. It vas a pleasure,' he exclaimed before disappearing through passport control.

Riedel followed, looking distinctly non-committal.

The next day we arranged for Hans Tilkowski to take Haller's place. Geoff Hurst wanted to relive three of his greatest moments with his ball, and the humiliated German goalkeeper from the 1966 final was the man to help him. They had first met in 1965 when Tilkowski's club side, Borussia Dortmund, defeated West Ham twice in the European Cup-Winners' Cup.

We took the pair to a municipal playing-field in a commuter sprawl in southern Essex. It was the kind of settlement which would once have called itself a hamlet or village, but an influx of white-collar workers from the financial-services sector, many wearing huge shoes and shiny suits, had removed any hint of rural charm.

Most of its larger houses had mock-Tudor façades with car ports, immaculately gravelled drives and dogs standing guard. CCTV cameras also kept an eye on the clean 4x4 jeeps parked everywhere, as Sunday-morning car-washers, all wearing casual sports tops and tracksuit bottoms, scrubbed them even more.

The ground itself, the choice of a Mirror photographer who lived locally, was full of young boys with designer crewcuts and diamond earrings. Piles of Doberman Pinscher and Rottweiler turds had also been scattered around the field as impediments to a successful photo shoot.

Hurst and Tilkowski changed into their original 1966 shirts in a small wooden hut covered in graffiti. When they emerged, a maniacal Sun photographer came running across the pitch towards us.

The boys playing on the recreation ground had been well brought up. They knew how to wear threatening baseball caps and hoods to disguise their threatening haircuts, how to mope menacingly around shopping centres, and when to telephone the *Sun*'s newsdesk to try and scupper a rival's Day Two exclusive.

Hurst, who had so far enjoyed the easy bit of Operation Inflation, suddenly learned what it was like at the painful end. He was pushed into a getaway car driven by Malcolm and rushed away at breakneck speed. Steaming along the A12, and then along the M11 motorway, he was squeezed in beside me and a *Mirror* photographer. It was a very odd experience for him, but I was quite used to such antics by now. I calmly began interviewing Hurst about his memories of the 1966 World Cup final.

As Malcolm negotiated the difficulties of a completely flat, empty motorway on a quiet, sunny Sunday morning, Hurst told me about his greatest sporting moment. I was oblivious to Malcolm's shouts and screams, his handbrake turns and his sudden exits on to slip roads. Even his curses wafted gently over my head. All I was interested in for the next half an hour was a compelling and vivid description of the greatest football match of all time.

We even managed a few minutes at a Little Chef near Bishops Stortford. Hurst ordered tea. There were, of course, plenty of dubious characters still paying an unhealthy amount of interest in us. Helmut Haller in a casual jacket had caused enough of a stir, but Geoff Hurst wearing his bright red number 10 shirt, white shorts, red socks and football boots caused even more of a commotion. Even those less bright youths who were struggling to get the cosmic interceptor to work on their video games and had missed Hurst, might have been interested by the person sitting next to him. Hans Tilkowski, complete with his dark-blue shirt and cap, was sipping a cup of milky coffee.

By this stage, though, none of us were bothered by any of the attention. Hurst's glorious reminiscences made all the hardships worth while.

At 20 minutes' notice Andy Lines had arranged for Hurst to play on a 'safe pitch' where he lived. It was the home ground of Hatfield Heath FC, and was surrounded by agricultural land and high hedgerows. Lines was certain that it was *Sun*-photographer-proof. His brother Richard unlocked the gates for us. Margaret, their mother, laid on some more tea for Hurst. Andy ran around asking Geoff if there was anything else any of them could do for him. The Lines family had always been big fans.

We did not, of course, kick the original ball around too much. It was far too precious. The thought of it surviving for 30 years before disintegrating in a Hertfordshire field following a miskick from some mule who'd only ever played park football was too much to contemplate. One of the bulls in an adjoining field also appeared attracted by the deep amber glow, so we took no chances.

Instead, we took some photographs of the ball to make it look as though it was in action. This mainly entailed me holding it up in the air, Hurst putting his foot next to it, then me running away at the last moment so that I would be out of the shot.

(It took me back to my days of work experience on a local paper when I had to blow bubbles behind the new Pears Soap Girl of the Year. The photographer, Murray Sanders, made me blow soapsuds through a small plastic loop behind the young woman's beautiful auburn hair and just below her panting breast. Again, just as the camera was about to click, I had to scurry off to some hole nearby. I did not reach similar depths of humiliation until my first celebrity ring-round, although the pictures turned out superbly.)

Hurst's 19th-minute equaliser in the first half of the 1966 final was not too difficult to recreate. I stood in front of the striker, lightly tossed the ball up in the air for him to head it down, and fell backwards into the sodden ground as the lens clicked. I gave Tilkowski a good shove, too, making sure that he ended up in a sprawl miles from the ball. (Tilkowski had in fact stood motionless when Hurst scored with a header in 1966, but I still enjoyed having a go at a German goalkeeper after all those hours with Thorsten Riedel.)

The 'Was it or Wasn't it?' goal in the 12th minute of extra time was even easier. This time I just had to place the ball close to the goal-line as Hurst stood a few feet away with his cheeks puffed out. I made sure the ball was a full inch on the inside of the goal and then gave Tilkowski another hard push. As Hurst ran away with his hands in the air, I also offered my services as a Roger Hunt. Me with my hands up in the air, so certain of a goal that I couldn't be bothered tapping it in for good measure, would add to the excitement of the photograph, I thought. I was later cropped out.

Then there was the final goal – the goal of all goals. Hurst leapt up in the air, in that wonderfully athletic, hurdler-stye pose which had become one of the most recognisable symbols of the '66 championships and which he was still capable of. He puffed his cheeks out to bursting point and narrowed his eyes like an Olympic marksman.

I stood around two feet away from him and, again, tossed the ball lightly in the air before ducking out of sight of the camera lens. I made an athletic leap almost as impressive as Hurst's, flinging myself to the muddy ground as the camera whirred. Tilkowski did not need a shove this time. He just stood rooted to the spot, as immobile and hopelessly beaten as all the Germans had been 30 years before.

The return of the ball undoubtedly had an effect on England's European Championships of 1996. It was a magical competition and the whole country was moved by it. From the opening game at Wembley, when we beat Switzerland, through to the semi-final itself, the nation was enthralled. Millions of people up and down the country huddled around televisions at home or huge screens in pubs. Others went to all the games live. People were smiling and happy. They were singing the anthem 'Football's Coming Home' by Frank Skinner and David Baddiel, and the one with the goatee from The Lightning Seeds whose name nobody ever remembers.

The lyrics of the song said everything. They told of 30 years of hurt, of Jules Rimet still gleaming, of that tackle by Bobby Moore, of Bobby Charlton belting the ball, of Nobby Stiles dancing, of how none of us had ever stopped believing that it might all happen again. The song concentrated on the good memories. No mention was made of the later devastating defeats to Germany and Argentina, the draws against Poland, the hat-trick of failed World Cup qualifying rounds, the shame of Norway, the hooliganism and the despondency.

Wembley, the towering edifice constructed in the 1920s as a spiritual boost for a nation shattered by the First World War and wallowing in a world trade slump, became the centre of our culture again. We thought of the thousands of soldiers who had helped construct it as a centrepiece of the British Empire Exhibition of 1924. They had sliced the top off Wembley Hill and removed 150,000 tons of clay. The stadium cost £350,000 and fundraising had been launched by the Prince of Wales at Mansion House in time for the Bolton against West Ham Cup final in 1923.

As I sat through five England games and the Euro '96 final I stared around Wembley's interior, imagining all that had gone before. Its opening match had seen 200,000 turning up for the FA Cup final, instead of the expected 125,000. Billy, a legendary white horse, had held the crowds back. During the FA Cup final of 1930 the Graf Zeppelin had flown overhead, distracting thousands who had been engrossed in another Arsenal win.

The scene of the 1948 Olympics and 1966 World Cup final was once more the ferro-concrete focal point of the public imagination – the manifestation of a nation's obsession.

We were singing in one voice once again; all classes, all shoe styles, proud and united.

The World Cup ball took pride of place in the celebrations. Before the opening match against Switzerland, the spoon-bending psychic Uri Geller said the amber colour was one of immense power. Just in case its banks had run down a bit over the past 30 years, though, he 'energised' it with even more supernatural ability. The entire England squad preparing for the 1996 championships also touched the ball.

'I have filled the ball with my positive energy,' said Geller. 'Touch and rub the football and concentrate for two minutes on England winning ... You can bend the ball towards the goal if you try hard enough.'

Thousands of amateur strikers and midfielders tried doing the same thing with their own match balls before Sunday-morning league matches the next day .

We beat Scotland with an outstanding goal from Paul Gascoigne. The bagpipes and kilted clansmen singing 'Flower of Scotland' and making crude jokes about Jimmy Hill were silenced.

We demolished Holland, the masters of Total Football, with our finest performance in years. Their glowing orange shirts appeared as lacklustre and dull as a departure lounge at Schipol.

We were lucky to beat Spain on penalties, but that was all part of our summer. For years we had always been the ones who suffered from dodgy offside and penalty decisions. This time we had that little extra bit of luck, and really felt like winners.

Even in the semi-final against Germany on Wednesday, 26 June, it appeared that everything was going right. We played like lions. Our immaculate first goal looked as though it might be enough, before another lucky equaliser. There was Gascoigne's one-in-ten chance to finish the Germans off in extra time. The game seemed to go into slow motion as he stuck his leg out, and micro-inched towards connection with the ball coming in from the right wing. Somehow, inexplicably, it managed to evade him and rolled harmlessly away.

Then there were the penalties. There always seemed to be penalties against the Germans. Sitting behind the royal box in the Empire Stadium, I wanted to jump down on to the pitch and play my own part in the game. I wanted to place the ball at the feet of an England player, and then an inch behind the German goal-line. I wanted to give the German goalkeeper a good shove, so that he ended up miles from the ball. I wanted to see him looking as dejected and unhappy as Hans Tilkowski had looked between the same posts 30 years before.

I thought hard and long about the amber ball. It was nothing to do with Uri Geller, the man of mystery, who said he had invoked its mystic powers by getting readers of the Mirror and viewers of GMTV to rub its printed image. It was nothing to do with the superstitions. It was just that the greatest symbol of our finest two hours was an appropriate thing to be contemplating as we faced up to another great battle against Teutonic guile and efficiency. I thought of our proud victories during 31 years of English dominance before the 1966 World

Cup final. I thought of Stanley Matthews scoring in the 6−3 victory in Berlin on 14 May 1938, and again in the 3−1 victory at Wembley on 1 December 1954. I thought of Nobby Stiles scoring the only goal of the game in the 1−0 victory in the same stadium on 23 February 1966. I thought of a Geoff Hurst hat-trick on 30 July 1966.

Gareth Southgate, the defender who normally wore the same Aston Villa colours as found on the party bobble-hat belonging to Prince William, and who had scored as many competitive penalties as the young royal, stepped forward.

I thought of the last time Germany had missed a penalty in a tournament shoot-out − 20 years before, when Uli Hoeness kicked over the bar in the 1976 European Championship final in Belgrade.

Southgate placed the ball on the spot. He stepped backwards. He hobbled forward. He appeared to trip over. A limp-ankled thump followed. The German goalkeeper saved the shot with the calm, furrow-browed efficiency of a Hans Tilkowski or Thorsten Riedel.

They had done it again.

36 · Final Score

Despite England's defeat, the summer of 1996 was among the best we had experienced for 30 years. The ball's amber glow really did start to shine on every part of national life.

Tony Blair pledged to harness the passion and energy which had characterised the championships to sweep away decades of negativity and failure. His new government, elected a year later, was backed by a nationwide clamour of populist fever. It was not enough that we had a strong economy and a dour, Scottish chancellor slaving laboriously in the background. It was not enough that the House of Commons was full of faceless reserves – 'Blair Babes' and radio pagers with non-thinking, 'on-message' backbenchers attached to them.

The British people were looking for so much more in their lives than safe financial packages and willing plodders with the personalities of Ossie refuse-collectors. The New Labour leader was forced to respond to a new set of demands. Ignoring the dynamic spirit represented by Euro '96 and our World Cup football could only end in relegation and another 18 years in the political wilderness.

There was a promise to bring even greater international football tournaments to England. Our bid for the 2006 World Cup was accompanied by a two-volume, 700-page report promoting the contemporary icons of the new, revitalised Britain. The publication, *We Are Ready. We Are Right*, was not solely about rootless pop groups who provided easy listening for pre-pubescent schoolgirls, or thrusting entrepreneurs wearing thick-rimmed spectacles and combat trousers while producing Internet sites valued by nobody except for withdrawn Net surfers with day jobs in the financial-services industry. It extolled the wonders of our heritage, like William Shakespeare and Charles Dickens. It told of a unique culture which was proud of its historical legacy, not burdened by it.

The heart of the new 'footballing' Britain was to be rejuvenated. Within a few years there was to be a £475 million New Wembley National Stadium. The now-jaded towers erected by the lumpen hands of British squaddies would be replaced by a futuristic masterpiece, designed by the suave and angular Sir Norman Foster. His state-of-the-art vision would preserve the best, and get rid of what was outdated. There would be every chance that the strip of grass upon which almost 80 years of high drama had unfolded would remain the same. Best of all, though, was a pledge that statues of Sir Alf Ramsey and Bobby Moore would take pride of place among the plunging arches and multiplex hotdog stands.

Our relationship with Germany improved considerably, and we started to beat them at a few things too. Despite the smouldering animosity over the safety of British beef and their late equalisers, Tony Blair became one of Gerhard Schroeder's closest allies. The Labour leader and the Social Democrat chancellor saw themselves as a dynamic pair of forwards, leading Europe into the new millennium. They erred towards the left wing but one day hoped to surge through the centre of the continent and thrill the EU's 370 million citizens with a refined interpretation of Helmut Kohl's vision of a single currency. The German people came to love the dynamic British playmaker as much as they had loved Kevin Keegan during his light-perm playing days at Hamburg. Both represented unity, prosperity and a slightly bedraggled but ultimately in-control hairstyle.

'Tony Blair ist ein Genie,' Germans would shout, even in arch-conservative states like Bavaria. As soon as he came to power, Blair set up inter-governmental working parties for Berlin and London to swap advice on the important issues of the day: agricultural policy, currency reform, penalty taking, that kind of thing.

Deutschlish epitomised a cultural triumph over the Germans. Our greatest export – our language – became as commonplace at firms like Mercedes and Bosch as it was in England. There were continual references to 'der Laptop', 'das Marketing' and 'ein Hursty', which means 'hat-trick' in German.

The 1966 World Cup ball also reminded Blair that he had a duty to the new generation who would ensure our successful future in the international game. He pledged that his primary commitments were 'education, education and education'. Most touching of all, he abandoned his summer-holiday football matches in Italy to concentrate on producing a fourth offspring, Leo, who might one day pull on a white England shirt rather than the stripes of Bologna.

We were still trying to beat Germany at our own game, but with the World Cup ball back in the country, we were perfectly poised for victory. After 1996 there were no immediate fixtures with the old enemy, but by the year 2000 a hat-trick had been announced. We would play them at least once in the Euro 2000 championships in the Low Countries and twice in the World Cup qualifiers for the 2002 World Cup. We had spent years hanging around for the greatest fixture in the international game when, just like buses, three had come along at once.

As well as the amber ball, there was success at club level which might act as an omen for international triumphs. Franz Beckenbauer, the president of Bayern Munich, watched his team being beaten 2–1 (poignantly, a late equaliser and last-minute winner) by Manchester United in the 1999 European Champions Cup final in Barcelona. It was a sobering lesson for the Kaiser, whose teams had ground us into desperate defeats over four decades.

Beckenbauer, the biggest opponent of our 2006 World Cup bid, said after the game: 'It's difficult to talk. The full cruelty of football has hit us. We have lost a battle. We won't commit suicide. We have to keep our nerve. We simply lost a game.' English journalists recording the Kaiser's words tried to sound as non-committal as possible as they rolled about the floor with tears of laughter pouring down their faces.

Other old footballing enemies became close allies and friends. Antonio Rattin, the Argentine captain of the 1966 'Animals', said he bore no bitterness towards the English, and wanted us to host the 2006 World Cup. He apologised for his behaviour in the 1966 quarter-final with the proviso: 'Every game was violent. It wasn't just England against Argentina. Pelé was slaughtered by fouls. Eusébio, too'. In the confessional spirit of the 1990s, Rattin added a personal thanks to the people of England for their support and understanding in helping him 'come to terms' with his disgrace. 'I went out in London on the Sunday after the game with my family,' he said, 'and taxis refused to charge me. People who recognised me in the shops came and asked for my autograph.'

By 1999 Rattin was a truly reformed character. He voluntarily contacted the British Embassy in Buenos Aires – the one which had come close to being fire-bombed in 1966 – to endorse our World Cup bid. In a letter, he wrote: 'England is a country where a different type of football is played – a fast, open game with little man-marking. Sincerely, I like English football.'

Carlos Menem, the Argentine leader and predecessor of the corrupt military junta which had presided over Argentina's Dirty War and the invasion of the Falklands Islands, also backed our World Cup bid during a state visit to Britain in 1998.

The return of the 1966 football was followed by a knighthood for Geoff Hurst. In 1998 he visited Buckingham Palace with his wife Judith and two of his daughters, Claire and Charlotte. A third daughter, Joanne, waited outside just as so many patriotic crowds had done on the evening of 30 July 1966 when her father was the most famous footballer in the world.

At the age of 56 Hurst said he had been more nervous of meeting the Queen than he had been as a 24-year-old in the most glorious summer of his youth. Standing before Elizabeth II he again remembered all his team-mates, living and dead. As he finally received the ultimate recognition for his contribution to England's greatest sporting triumph, Sir Geoff felt like punching the air and screaming, 'Yesss!' Then he remembered that he was a senior member of an insurance firm and a knight of the realm in the presence of royalty.

There had been more good news for Hurst. When he turned up at the Royal Spa Hotel in Leamington Spa on 30 April 1996, there had been no sign of a mysterious 'Wolfgang from Düsseldorf' – a German who had pledged to reveal the 'true' World Cup ball to Hurst. The threat did not upset Geoff. 'It would be fair to say that it did not ruin my evening,' he said. 'I'm more than satisfied that the ball I received from Helmut Haller is the right one.' Scotland Yard forensics experts later confirmed his belief.

By the year 2000, Alan Ball, George Cohen, Roger Hunt, Nobby Stiles and Ray Wilson had also turned up at Buckingham Palace to be awarded the MBE. 'It's been a long time coming but it's here now and we are very happy,' said Cohen, whose nephew Ben Cohen – not even born in 1966 – was by now an established rugby international in one of the best England sides in history.

As she awarded the players' honours, the Queen said she would never forget the day she had presented them with the Jules Rimet trophy, even though she had never been much of a football supporter. They had always suspected as much.

For me, the summer of 1996 could not have been better. My formative decade had been the 1970s, and my earliest football memory was of England losing a World Cup qualifier during those grim days. More than anyone, I felt entitled to my place under the warm glow of our amber talisman.

I unexpectedly got tickets for every single one of England's European Championship games. The first was given to me at the last moment by the same reporter who had done all the tedious ground work before I flew to Germany to get the ball back. While I prepared to watch England against Switzerland on television, he phoned to say he had to work on the day of the match. Worse than that, he had been told to write a feature about the overpriced fast-food being sold along Wembley Way. While I watched our victory from his £90 seat behind the royal box, my colleague was dishing out £3 meatless rolls as an undercover hotdog salesman. The only contact he had with the game being played a few hundred yards away was a crackly radio commentary.

Free tickets for the rest of England's campaign followed, as I covered the news side of Euro '96. The only game I came close to missing was the one against Germany. My name went into a hat with hundreds of foreign journalists for the few remaining press seats for the semi-final. A UEFA press officer read out the winners' names as they were pulled out. By the time he got to the last, my name had not been mentioned. Something like 'Monsieur Pierre Cadoret of the *International Brussels Bugle*' was announced instead. There was no answer. The name was put over the tannoy a couple of times but no one came forward. Pierre had missed his Eurostar. It was agreed that another name should be chosen. It was me.

The return of the ball affected my journalism in every way. I realised that there was far more to it than grim courtrooms on a damp Monday morning, celebrity ring-rounds and windswept vigils at the end of smoothly gravelled drives. Instead, it always had to be imbued with vigour and excitement – with determined pursuits across far-off landscapes and seas, and passionate altercations in foreign restaurants.

The World Cup ball made me reach above and beyond. It made me as committed to greatness as the 11 golden heroes who had once propelled the amber icon to ultimate glory. It taught me to look for heroism in the most ordinary of lives, even the nasally vowelled Yorkshiremen in Gannex raincoats whom you see hanging around public playing-fields.

I wanted to try and make life a celebration of human endeavour – to try and find something decent and true above the tragedy, the squalor, the pettiness and the unadulterated tedium of so many aspects of modern life.

Eugene Duffy and Andy Lines presented me with a gold cup of my own. It was inscribed with my name and looked like the kind of trophy an amateur darts player might receive in recognition of the amount of bitter he's drunk over a night of 'arrows' at a Midlands Labour club. The Mirror news editors also bought me a red 1966 non-acrylic England shirt and a white casual sports top emblazoned with the famous photograph of Hurst's third goal. Both were of the same quality as all cheap textile imports from Milan – the kind which disintegrate when they first come into contact with the inside of a washing-machine.

It really was an extraordinary summer for me. The guaranteed England defeats, powercuts and deconstructed Airfix models of the 1970s were all a thing of the past. I had returned our 1966 World Cup ball from Germany. I had received tickets to every important game of our biggest football competition for 30 years. Instead of swearing at me continually and sending me to motor-way service stations, my news editors were presenting me with tacky souvenirs and signing off dry-cleaning bills for sauerkraut-stained suits. I'd met legendary sporting heroes like Geoff Hurst and Helmut Haller, and I had a couple of one-wash T-shirts to prove it all.

Then something even more inspiring happened. I met a girl who liked football and beer. After years of hanging around half-time refreshment stands and club social bars, there she was sitting just five seats away in the Olympic Gallery at Wembley Stadium. It was as if the ball's glow had lifted her out of the shadows of the main stand and showed her off to the entire crowd, just as the Jules Rimet trophy had been when it was lifted up by Bobby Moore almost three decades ago to the day. She was smiling delightfully and was full of passion and energy. Her enthusiasm for life was matched only by her adulation of Tottenham Hotspur striker Jurgen Klinsmann. She was a girl whom it would be impossible to miss, even in a crowd of almost 100,000.

She was German.

Both of us were on duty as journalists at the Euro'96 final. At half-time we shared a bottle of Sprite lemonade and talked about everything and anything – particularly Gazza's last-ditch attempt to score in the semi-final when we had literally been centimetres away from certain victory against the old enemy. Strangely, she appeared more interested in her countrymen's on-going struggle against the Czech Republic.

When the Germans won the match with an extra-time 'Golden Goal', she raised her arms in the air and displayed a smile worthy of the delicately carved wooden angels which line Bavaria's Romantic Road. I watched her interview every one of the German players' wives after Klinsmann had graciously accepted a trophy from a smiling Elizabeth II. The women's celebration to the tune of Queen's 'We Are the Champions' was executed with the rigid discipline associated with all German get-togethers. As the women robotically moved their arms from side to side over their heads to the lyrics 'No time for losing', they reminded me of Heinrich tapping his fingers on his dashboard to 'Boom, boom, boom. Vee like to party'.

We shared glasses of beer in the press bar afterwards before taking the tube to Trafalgar Square. I was stunned by my new girlfriend's composure and dignity. The way she kept her mouth shut when a couple of English hooligans approached her was incredibly moving. As they chanted, swore and asked if there were any Germans worth beating up, she pretended to be any nationality apart from her own.

It was an odd summer's evening in the capital. Most of Trafalgar Square was full of contented, forward-thinking football supporters. They waved the black-red-and-gold tricolours of their federal republic in a non-committal, half-hearted celebration of another conciliatory but ultimately triumphant European campaign.

They might have been Germans, but there was still a sense of universal optimism in the clammy London air. By the following summer, 1997, it would be 31 years since the Germans had pledged to wipe out all those years of

English victories. There would be plenty of other fixtures around the turn of the century, and the symmetry behind so much football legend would surely be in our favour.

We stood next to one of the four wise British lions, the one which stares authoritatively down Northumberland Avenue, tilting its aloof head away from Whitehall and the Mother of Parliaments. The crowds and noise evoked memories of vibrant London street scenes throughout the centuries – outpourings of jubilation celebrating the achievements of men like Horatio Nelson, so eternally British as he surveyed his country in Royal Navy uniformed splendour from the top of his column.

My immediate thoughts, though, were still with historic figures whose greatest feats had lifted the nation just 30 years before. I imagined the faces of Gordon Banks, George Cohen, Ray Wilson, Nobby Stiles, Jack Charlton, Bobby Moore, Alan Ball, Roger Hunt, Geoff Hurst, Bobby Charlton and Martin Peters. I pictured the Englishmen who had enriched our lives with their skill and heroism.

I also contemplated all that we had been through to get their World Cup ball back. I thought of Sir Alf Ramsey, and what he would have made of it all. He would have loved the thrill of the chase, the controlled aggression, the disciplined execution of a difficult job, the occasional bursts of flair and initiative which underpinned the whole operation. What he would have loved most, though, was the feeling of English pride and glory which had been revitalised by the final return of the amber talisman.

On that Wednesday night the ball was on public display less than half a mile from Trafalgar Square, across Hungerford Bridge on the approach to the Eurostar platforms at Waterloo Station.

Anybody who looked at the ball, including thousands of visitors from abroad, would be reminded of a time when Sir Alf's team – England's team – really had been the very best in the world.

Now, though, it was getting late. The 30-year exile of the 1966 World Cup ball was at an end and there were new challenges to think about. It really was all over.

If Sir Alf Ramsey had been staring down at us that night instead of Admiral Lord Nelson, his guidance would have been as wise and prophetic as ever. Something like: 'Thank you, Peter. I think we've probably had enough of all that now.'

He would have been right, of course.

Postscript

It had to happen, and it did happen. England's first tournament victory over Germany since 30 July 1966 took place on 17 June 2000. On a clammy, threatening evening of brutal tackles and unflinching stares, a single goal wiped away more than three decades of despair.

The epic encounter in which the illusion of German invincibility was finally shattered took place in Charleroi, a few miles from the place where British and Prussian forces had united at Waterloo. Wellington's stirring observation – 'Hard pounding, this, gentlemen. Let us see who will pound longest' – was as relevant to the red-shirted footballers who took the field at the Stade Communal as it had been to the Iron Duke's redcoats in the summer of 1815. It was a scrappy game, hard fought and often ugly, but ultimately glorious. As the Germans limped off after the final whistle, their eyes were brimming with tears of shock and recrimination. What had caused a steely-eyed striker to miss an open goal? How had the successors of Weber and Muller failed to poach a last-minute equaliser? Where were the penalties?

Tony Blair, who had watched the game with his young family at Downing Street, made the pithy, managerial admission that he was 'delighted'. The Queen, celebrating her official birthday, was as pleased as she had been when the Coldstream Guards trooped their colours in front of her at Horseguards Parade earlier in the day. Like everyone else, she knew there were still problems, of course. The players' goal celebration was as tired and predictable as their pre-match interview technique. There was no one with the style and individuality to perform a cheeky wink to camera following a darting run through midfield. Many of our supporters, including barristers and accountants, were to be deported from Belgium for throwing chairs. But, for one Saturday night at least, it was the bright, optimistic side of 'Footballing Britain' that was really coming home.

Patriotic tears flowed. 'Rule Britannia' was sung on squares and greens. Strangers embraced. Conga lines snaked down bunting-clad high streets. And Gary Lineker spoke up for the whole of England when, live on BBC1, he grimaced, punched the air like a maniac and yelled: 'Yessss . . . !'